美国总统演讲系列

BUSH SPEECH RADICALISM
UNDER TERRORISM

布什演说
恐怖主义下的激进

任宪宝◎编著

中国言实出版社

图书在版编目（ＣＩＰ）数据

布什演说：恐怖主义下的激进：汉英对照 / 任宪宝编．—北京：中国言实出版社，2014.5

ISBN 978-7-5171-0533-6

Ⅰ．①布… Ⅱ．①任… Ⅲ．①英语－汉语－对照读物 ②布什，G.W．—演讲－汇编 Ⅳ．①H319.4：K

中国版本图书馆CIP数据核字 (2014) 第 077126 号

责任编辑：陈昌财

出版发行　中国言实出版社
　　　　　　地　址：北京市朝阳区北苑路 180 号加利大厦 5 号楼 105 室
　　　　　　邮　编：100101
　　　　　　编辑部：北京市西城区百万庄路甲 16 号五层
　　　　　　邮　编：100037
　　　　　　电　话：64924853（总编室）　　64924716（发行部）
　　　　　　网　址：www.zgyscbs.cn
　　　　　　E-mail：yanshicbs@126.com
经　销　新华书店
印　刷　北京市玖仁伟业印刷有限公司
版　次　2014 年 8 月第 1 版　　2014 年 8 月第 1 次印刷
规　格　787 毫米 ×1092 毫米　　1/16　　印张 18.25
字　数　251 千字
定　价　35.00 元　　　　　ISBN 978-7-5171-0533-6

出版说明

　　自 1776 年《独立宣言》发表至今，美国建国已有两百三十多年。在这一历史阶段中，先后产生了四十四任总统。作为总统共和制国家的美国，其总统兼国家元首和政府首脑双重身份于一身，其在三权分立的国家政治架构中拥有极大的权力和影响力，在国家政治生活中拥有举足轻重的地位。正如美国第二十六任总统西奥多·罗斯福所说，美国总统是"国王和总理大臣的统一体"。

　　在美国，演讲是任何一个准备从政的人士必须具备的基本技能。无论地方议会议员、地方行政首脑还是美国联邦国会议员乃至美国总统，都是通过以演讲为基本形式的竞选活动产生的，这就决定了演讲这种活动在美国政治生活中的重大意义。而作为国家最高领导人的美国总统，他们的演讲往往在表明个人政治见解和基本立场、展露自身意志品质和性格特点的同时，在某种程度上还代表了美国的制度设计与价值观念、反映了美国的文化背景与社会演变。他们的演讲大都是针对当时美国所面临的国内外重大问题，讨论国家内政外交政策的优劣得失，表明解决问题的态度，指出今后的施政方向，激励和动员美国人民克服困难、奋力前行。从美国总统的演讲中，我们可以看到他们对时代潮流的认识、把握和对国家意志的充分表达，可以看到他们的政治才华和不同的人格魅力，还可以看到美国在其国家发展所经历的一个又一个时代转折点上，怎样面对困难、迎接挑战、坚韧不拔，一步步走向成功与成熟。

美国总统的演讲事先大多经过了精心的准备，语言精炼、用词规范、措辞讲究、逻辑严密，不但文采斐然、优美动人，而且有的放矢、言之有物。同时，每个总统的演讲都具有鲜明的个性特色。有的晓之以理，发人深省；有的动之以情，感人肺腑；有的则充满思辨，促使人们对人生、社会乃至世界进行更深层次的思考。

《美国总统演讲系列》丛书，重点选取了美国自成立以来几位重要总统的演讲，其中既有他们的就职演讲、卸任演讲，也有他们在重大事件发生时发表的演讲以及针对一些特定案例向公众发表的演讲等。选取这些演讲，并不代表我们认同其所包含的思想倾向或价值取向，只是想帮助广大读者从这些演讲中，加深对美国国情、美国社会的了解。相信广大读者在对这些演讲进行欣赏的同时，一定会对其反映出的世界观、价值观等做出正确的分析和判断。

编　者

2014 年 5 月

备受争议仍坚定信念

前美国总统乔治·布什的长子、德州州长小布什于 2001 年 1 月 20 日在美国首都华盛顿宣誓就任美国第四十三任总统。小布什是美国有史以来最受争议的总统，在有些人看来小布什毫无才能，讲话屡屡出错，根本不是当总统的材料。但就是这样一个不被一些人看好的人，不仅当上了美国总统，而且还当得风生水起。

亚当斯父子先后当选美国第二任和第六任总统，期间相隔二十八年。小布什当选总统时，仅与其父亲就任总统相隔八年。他创造了神话，使布什家族成为美国第二个"一门两总统"的家族，与美国第二任总统亚当斯家族前后辉映。

小布什作为 21 世纪美国首任总统，翻开了美国历史新的一页。小布什被《时代》杂志列为 2000 年和 2004 年的年度风云人物，认为他是这两年中世界上最具影响力的人物。

小布什是过去百年间入主白宫前公职生涯最短的总统之一。大器晚成的小布什从一个放荡不羁的纨绔子弟，摇身一变成为位高权重的美国总统，其

人生经历了一段奇特的过程。日后的历史学家也许会将小布什的从政经历称为最神奇的通往白宫之途。

小布什入主白宫后，任命大批保守派的成员，其中大部分是其父亲老布什担任总统时期的旧臣，使其内阁成为自里根总统以来最保守的一届政府。因此，有人将小布什上台与其新政府班子的组成称之为"复辟"。此外，他还全面否定克林顿政府实行已达八年的内外政策，把自己一套保守的政纲带进白宫。对内，他全面推销减税政策；对外，他实行以美国为中心的单边主义。他的一系列政策对美国的内政外交产生了深远影响，同时也给他带来正反不一的评价。

从第一个总统任期开始，小布什即以连任为己任，誓必要打破历史上的总统父子兵只在白宫做一任的历史宿命。从小布什当上总统的那天起，美国媒体与政治分析家们就在分析猜测他是否会步其父亲老布什的后尘，或是能够打破历史的宿命。小布什是带着人们的疑问尴尬上台的，美国有近半数的选民，特别是民主党的支持者质疑他当总统的合法性。小布什上台后不到半年，美国媒体与公众对他处理内外事务的不满一直在增长。当佛蒙特州的联邦参议员杰福兹因不满布什政府的内外政策而宣布退出共和党成为独立参议员时，参议院的控制权转到民主党手中，从而使国会与媒体对小布什的批评更加严厉。他的民意支持率下滑到他上任以来的最低点，许多人开始预测他可能像他老爸一样，只有在白宫待四年的命。

就在小布什的内外政策遭到众多批评，他的民意支持率不断下降时，突然发生的"9·11"恐怖袭击事件震撼了美国与世界。"9·11"恐怖袭击事件改变了一切，它不仅改变了美国在21世纪初的政治生态、社会面貌与历史方向，也改变了小布什在美国人民心目中的地位，并由此改变了他个人的政治命运。

"9·11"恐怖袭击事件之后，布什的认可度不断跃升，一度超过85%，并且在攻击后的四个月里一直维持在80%～90%的比例。但自此之后，布什在处理国内和国外政策上的民调认可度持续下跌，到 2006 年已经跌至大约 40%，使他创下历史上美国总统认可度的最低纪录。面对民调的大起大落他坦然应对，尽管他的声望持续下降，但是布什执着地认为，历史对其执政业绩的裁定在其死后多年才会最终揭晓。

以"9·11"为转折点，小布什成为 21 世纪美国的首位战争总统。作为一位战争总统，他的威望与权力在反恐战争中得到空前的提高与膨胀。几乎所有的政治分析家与研究美国总统的历史学者都认为，作为一位战争总统，小布什在历史上的地位将由他在伊拉克的实践与结果来确定。伊拉克战争将是小布什留给他个人以及美国人民最大的一笔历史遗产。

布什执掌白宫八年，对外政策总体上乏善可陈，唯一的亮点是他的对华政策，在他的任期内美国与中国的关系获得重大改善。美国共和与民主两党人士和外交政策智库学者都认为布什的对华政策是成功的。

布什虽然已经下野成为一介平民，但他执政八年对美国及世界的影响是深远的，而且这种影响还会持续相当长的一段时间。不论人们是否喜欢他，他在白宫任内的八年，已成为美国和世界政治历史的一部分。如果没有他执政的八年，也不会有今天奥巴马的执政、变革与新政。当今与后世的政治学家和历史学家还会继续关注研究小布什执政的八年。

回望小布什执政的八年，可谓褒贬不一。有人认为他是美国历史上最倒霉的总统，刚上台就遇到美国有史以来最大的恐怖袭击"9·11"，下台时又赶上美国最严重的金融风暴。可以说他是在灾难中上台，在灾难中离任。还有人认为他是一位糟糕的总统，他在任内发动了两场战争，其中的伊拉克战争让美国深陷战争泥潭。经济上他并没有做出正确的决策，致使美国经济陷入历史上最严重的危机之中。总之，小布什是美国历史上最受争议的一位总统。

小布什政府虽然在决策上存在一定的失误，但把所有犯错的板子都打在小布什的屁股上，未免过于偏颇。小布什是一个具有坚定信念的人，他有自

己的目标，并且渴望在其任内实现内心的目标，发挥一国领导人的作用。他的这种信念促使他做出了一些重大决策，然而这些决策在其他人看来是不协调的。在一个民主国家中，很多政治家为了选票，而最终放弃了自己的信念屈从于民意，这样的例子比比皆是。

每一个具有坚定信念的人都是孤独的，世上很少有人会对一个拥有坚定信念的人表示理解。这正是小布什饱受争议的原因之一。据某民意机构调查，美国有 72% 的民众认为小布什是好人，他不仅是一个好人，而且是一个具有强烈人格魅力的好人，他的这种人格魅力远超其他政治领导人。

相信大家都不会忘记这位总统，在他的任期内发生了太多让人无法忘怀的事，这些事不止影响了美国本土，甚至波及全世界。布什这位 21 世纪之初最受瞩目的美国总统，在一片唏嘘声中上任，在一片争议声中卸任，面对人们的指责与不屑，他毫不退缩依然坚持自己的信念，带领着美国人闯过一个又一个难关。

目 录
Contents

第一章

自由和团结

第一节 背景介绍

  1946 年 7 月 6 日，乔治·沃克·布什生于美国康涅狄格州，在德克萨斯州米德兰市和休斯敦市长大。他的祖父是华尔街一位富有的金融家，曾是国会（共和党）参议院议员。其父亲为美国第五十一届总统乔治·赫伯特·沃克·布什。十八岁的小布什中学毕业后，进入耶鲁大学主修历史学，后成为耶鲁大学著名的骷髅会成员。毕业后小布什进入得克萨斯州国民警卫队空军，成为一名战斗机驾驶员，1973 年离开空军。

  小布什于 1994 年 11 月 8 日当选为得克萨斯州州长，四年后再次当选得州州长。2000 年 11 月，小布什作为共和党总统候选人，在美国历史上竞争最为激烈的总统选举中战胜民主党总统候选人戈尔，当选美国第五十四届四十三任总统。2001 年 1 月 20 日小布什正式宣誓就职入主白宫。他是继美国第六任总统约翰·昆西·亚当斯之后，第二位踏着父亲的足迹走进白宫的总统。因此，人们称他为小布什，称其父亲为老布什。

  小布什一直强调公立学校要对教学成果负起责任。在上任总统后他便开始积极筹措一项名为"不让任何孩子落后"的教育法案，这个法案也得到了民主党参议员泰德·肯尼迪的支持。第一任期里小布什增加了对国家科学基金会和国家卫生研究院的资金援助，并且开办了一些用以增强美国高中学生科学和数学学科能力的活动。不过，对国家卫生研究院的资金援助由于2004年和2005年的通货膨胀而无法维持，不得不扣减了其中一部分预算。在第二届任期里，布什开始了大规模的社会福利改革，当时美国的社会福利制度已经面临空前的预算赤字。国会和媒体都把社会福利改革视为是一项棘手的议题，由于担忧遭致公众的反弹，很少有人会想试图改变之，然而布什仍然展开了改革，并将其作为第一优先处理的议题。社会福利一直被视为是民主党的领域，共和党则被指控曾在过去试图将之解散或民营化。在2005年的总统就职演说中，布什讨论到了社会福利制度即将破产的可能性，并且批评政治的偏见妨碍了改革的进展。他提议应该让人们有机会选择从他们的社会福利税款里挪出一部分来投资其他领域，让那些钱花在更有意义的地方以促进经济成长。尽管布什不断强调改革拥有万全的预防措施和配套计划，依然有些人批评他的提议花费过高。

布什的政府组成人员是美国历史上最多元的政府之一，包括了从没有过的拉丁美洲裔司法部部长和华裔商务部部长，还有康多莉扎·赖斯，她是第一位成为政府部长级的非洲裔。此外，小布什还挽留了遭受了大量批评，同时还被许多国会议员要求下台的国防部部长唐纳德·拉姆斯菲尔德。

布什在2005年8月极具争议性地提名了约翰·博尔顿任美国驻联合国大使，这项提名遭到民主党议员的阻挠。于是布什使用了相当罕见的停会任命手段，使博尔顿得以顺利就职。民主党则批评这是滥用总统权力的作法。

在国际上布什也遭遇了许多批评。全球的反战和反全球化人士将其做为主要的批评对象，他的外交政策尤其饱受批评，布什在各地的外交行程常遭遇大规模的抗议示威。

不过，美国保守派选民还是坚定地支持小布什，同时他还得到了军人和主战派的支持。在2004年的选举中，95%～99%的共和党选民都认可了他。不过，由于布什在控制联邦开销和移民议题上的疏失，共和党人对他的支持

也开始有所下跌。许多共和党人批评布什在伊拉克战争上的政策，以及伊朗和巴勒斯坦领土的议题。

从当选美国总统开始，小布什的智力水平就成为许多媒体和公众津津乐道的话题，有些人甚至质疑布什的智商过低。更有甚者经常引出布什在各种公开演讲中犯下的一些文法错误和语无伦次，布什在发音上的一些错误也常被反布什的媒体和人士做为笑柄。其实，早在2000年的总统选举中，布什的发音错误和语无伦次、自造词汇就成为了电视脱口秀节目嘲笑的话题。不过，小布什并不是第一个遭受此批评的美国总统。

毫无疑问，老布什是一位杰出的政治家，即使是如此高龄，他依然可以在十分钟之内，总结出世界上热点问题的精华部分，令人叹服。而小布什则是"平民""牛仔"的风格，这也是他本性的流露，他从不装腔作势。

第二节 布什于 2001 年在白宫的第一次就职演讲

Chief Justice Rehnquist, President Carter, President Bush, President Clinton, distinguished guests and my fellow citizens:

The peaceful transfer of authority is rare in history, yet common in our country. With a simple oath, we affirm old traditions and make new beginnings.

As I begin, I thank President Clinton for his service to our nation. And I thank Vice President Gore for a contest conducted with spirit and ended with grace.

I am honored and humbled to stand here, where so many of America's leaders have come before me, and so many will follow.

We have a place, all of us, in a long story—a story we continue, but whose end we will not see. It is the story of a new world that became a friend and liberator of the old, a story of a slave-holding society that became a servant of freedom, the story of a power that went into the world to protect but not possess, to defend but not to conquer. It is the American story—a story of flawed and fallible people, united across the generations by grand and enduring ideals.

The grandest of these ideals is an unfolding American promise that everyone belongs, that everyone deserves a chance, that no insignificant person was ever born.

Americans are called to enact this promise in our lives and in our laws. And though our nation has sometimes halted, and sometimes delayed, we must follow no other course.

Through much of the last century, America's faith in freedom and democracy was a rock in a raging sea. Now it is a seed upon the wind, taking root in many nations.

Our democratic faith is more than the creed of our country, it is the inborn hope of our humanity, an ideal we carry but do not own, a trust we bear and pass along. And even after nearly 225 years, we have a long way yet to travel.

While many of our citizens prosper, others doubt the promise, even the justice, of our own country. The ambitions of some Americans are limited by failing schools and hidden prejudice and the circumstances of their birth. And sometimes our differences run so deep, it seems we share a continent, but not a country.

We do not accept this, and we will not allow it. Our unity, our union, is the serious work of leaders and citizens in every generation. And this is my solemn pledge: I will work to build a single nation of justice and opportunity.

I know this is in our reach because we are guided by a power larger than ourselves who creates us equal in His image.

And we are confident in principles that unite and lead us onward.

America has never been united by blood or birth or soil. We are bound by ideals that move us beyond our backgrounds, lift us above our interests and teach us what it means to be citizens. Every child must be taught these principles. Every citizen must uphold them. And every immigrant, by embracing these ideals, makes our country more, not less, American.

Today we affirm a new commitment to live out our nation's promise through civility, courage, compassion, and character.

America, at its best, matches a commitment to principle with a concern for civility. A civil society demands from each of us good will and respect, fair dealing and forgiveness.

Some seem to believe that our politics can afford to be petty, because in a time of peace, the stakes of our debates appear small.

But the stakes for America are never small. If our country does not lead the cause of freedom, it will not be led. If we do not turn the hearts of children toward knowledge and character, we will lose their gifts and undermine their idealism. If we permit our economy to drift and decline, the vulnerable will suffer most.

We must live up to the calling we share. Civility is not a tactic or a sentiment. It is the determined choice of trust over cynicism, of community over chaos. And this commitment, if we keep it, is a way to shared accomplishment.

America, at its best, is also courageous.

Our national courage has been clear in times of depression and war, when defending common dangers defined our common good. Now we must choose if the example of our fathers and mothers will inspire us or condemn us. We must show courage in a time of blessing by confronting problems instead of passing them on to future generations.

Together, we will reclaim America's schools, before ignorance and apathy claim more young lives.

We will reform Social Security and Medicare, sparing our children from

struggles we have the power to prevent. And we will reduce taxes, to recover the momentum of our economy and reward the effort and enterprise of working Americans.

We will build our defenses beyond challenge, lest weakness invite challenge.

We will confront weapons of mass destruction, so that a new century is spared new horrors.

The enemies of liberty and our country should make no mistake: America remains engaged in the world by history and by choice, shaping a balance of power that favors freedom. We will defend our allies and our interests. We will show purpose without arrogance. We will meet aggression and bad faith with resolve and strength. And to all nations, we will speak for the values that gave our nation birth.

America, at its best, is compassionate. In the quiet of American conscience, we know that deep, persistent poverty is unworthy of our nation's promise.

And whatever our views of its cause, we can agree that children at risk are not at fault. Abandonment and abuse are not acts of God, they are failures of love.

And the proliferation of prisons, however necessary, is no substitute for hope and order in our souls.

Where there is suffering, there is duty. Americans in need are not strangers, they are citizens; not problems, but priorities. And all of us are diminished when any are hopeless.

Government has great responsibilities for public safety and public health, for civil rights and common schools. Yet compassion is the work of a nation, not just a government.

And some needs and hurts are so deep they will only respond to a mentor's touch or a pastor's prayer. Church and charity, synagogue and mosque lend our communities their humanity, and they will have an honored place in our plans and in our laws.

Many in our country do not know the pain of poverty, but we can listen to those who do.

And I can pledge our nation to a goal: When we see that wounded traveler on the road to Jericho, we will not pass to the other side.

America, at its best, is a place where personal responsibility is valued and expected.

Encouraging responsibility is not a search for scapegoats, it is a call to conscience. And though it requires sacrifice, it brings a deeper fulfillment.

We find the fullness of life not only in options, but in commitments. And we find that children and community are the commitments that set us free.

Our public interest depends on private character, on civic duty and family bonds and basic fairness, on uncounted, unhonored acts of decency which give direction to our freedom.

Sometimes in life we are called to do great things. But as a saint of our times has said, every day we are called to do small things with great love. The most important tasks of a democracy are done by everyone.

I will live and lead by these principles: to advance my convictions with civility, to pursue the public interest with courage, to speak for greater justice and compassion, to call for responsibility and try to live it as well.

In all these ways, I will bring the values of our history to the care of our times.

What you do is as important as anything government does. I ask you to

seek a common good beyond your comfort; to defend needed reforms against easy attacks; to serve your nation, beginning with your neighbor. I ask you to be citizens: citizens, not spectators; citizens, not subjects; responsible citizens, building communities of service and a nation of character.

Americans are generous and strong and decent, not because we believe in ourselves, but because we hold beliefs beyond ourselves. When this spirit of citizenship is missing, no government program can replace it. When this spirit is present, no wrong can stand against it.

After *the Declaration of Independence* was signed, Virginia statesman John Page wrote to Thomas Jefferson: "We know the race is not to the swift nor the battle to the strong. Do you not think an angel rides in the whirlwind and directs this storm?"

Much time has passed since Jefferson arrived for his inauguration. The years and changes accumulate. But the themes of this day he would know: our nation's grand story of courage and its simple dream of dignity.

We are not this story's author, who fills time and eternity with his purpose. Yet his purpose is achieved in our duty, and our duty is fulfilled in service to one another.

Never tiring, never yielding, never finishing, we renew that purpose today, to make our country more just and generous, to affirm the dignity of our lives and every life.

This work continues. This story goes on. And an angel still rides in the whirlwind and directs this storm.

God bless you all, and God bless America.

尊敬的芮恩奎斯特大法官，卡特总统，布什总统，克林顿总统，尊敬的来宾们，我的同胞们：

这次权利的和平过渡在历史上是罕见的，但在美国是平常的。我们以朴素的宣誓庄严地维护了古老的传统，同时开始了新的历程。

首先，我要感谢克林顿总统为这个国家作出的贡献，也感谢副总统戈尔在竞选过程中的热情与风度。

站在这里我很荣幸，也有点受宠若惊。在我之前，许多美国领导人从这里起步；在我之后，也会有许多领导人从这里继续前进。

在美国悠久的历史中，我们每个人都有自己的位置。我们还在继续推动着历史前进，但是我们不可能看到它的尽头。这是一部新世界的发展史，是一部后浪推前浪的历史。这是一部美国由奴隶制社会发展成为崇尚自由社会的历史。这是一个强国保护而不是占有世界的历史，是捍卫而不是征服世界的历史。这就是美国史。它不是一部十全十美的民族发展史，但它是一部在伟大和永恒的理想指导下几代人团结奋斗的历史。

这些理想中最伟大的是正在慢慢实现的美国的承诺：每个人都有自身的价值，每个人都有成功的机会，每个人天生都会有所作为。

美国人民肩负着一种使命，要竭力将这个诺言变成生活中和法律上的现实。虽然我们的国家过去在追求实现这个承诺的途中停滞不前甚至倒退，但我们仍将坚定不移地完成这一使命。

在上个世纪的大部分时间里，美国自由民主的信念犹如汹涌大海中的岩石。现在它更像风中的种子，把自由带给每个民族。

在我们的国家，民主不仅仅是一种信念，而是全人类的希望。民主，我们不会独占，而会竭力让大家分享。民主，我们将铭记于心，并且不断传播。225 年过去了，我们仍有很长的路要走。

有很多公民取得了成功，但也有人开始怀疑，怀疑我们自己的国家所许下的诺言，甚至怀疑它的公正。失败的教育、潜在的偏见和出身的环境限制

了一些美国人的雄心。有时我们的分歧是如此之深，似乎我们虽身处同一个大陆，但不属于同一个国家。

我们不能接受这种分歧，也无法允许它的存在。我们的团结和统一是每一代领导人和每一个公民严肃的使命。在此我郑重宣誓：我将竭力建设一个公正、充满机会的统一国家。

我知道这是我们的目标，因为上帝平等地按自己的意向创造了我们，上帝高于一切的力量将引导我们前进。

对这些将我们团结起来并指引我们向前的原则，我们充满信心。

血缘、出身或地域从未将美国联合起来。只有理想才能使我们心系一处，超越自我，放弃个人利益，并逐步领会何谓公民。每个孩子都必须学习这些原则。每个公民都必须坚持这些原则。每个移民只有接受这些原则，才能使我们的国家不丧失而更具美国特色。

今天，我们在这里重申一个新的信念，即通过发扬谦恭、勇气、同情心和个性的精神来实现我们国家的理想。

美国在最鼎盛时期也没忘记遵循谦逊有礼的原则。一个文明的社会需要我们每个人品质优良，尊重他人，为人公平和宽宏大量。

有人认为我们的政治制度是如此的微不足道，因为在和平年代，我们所争论的话题都是无关紧要的。

但是，对美国来说，我们所讨论的问题从来都不是小事。如果我们不领导和平事业，那么和平将无人来领导。如果我们不引导我们的孩子们真心地热爱知识、发挥个性，他们的天分将得不到发挥，理想将难以实现。如果我们不采取适当措施，任凭经济衰退，最大的受害者将是平民百姓。

我们应该时刻听取时代的呼唤。谦逊有礼不是战术也不是感情用事。这是我们最坚定的选择——在批评声中赢得信任，在混乱中寻求统一。如果遵循这样的承诺，我们将会享有共同的成就。

美国有强大的国力作后盾，将会勇往直前。

在大萧条和战争时期，我们的人民在困难面前表现得无比英勇，克服我们共同的困难体现了我们共同的优秀品质。现在，我们正面临着选择，如果我们作出正确的选择，祖辈一定会激励我们；如果我们的选择是错误的，祖辈会谴责我们的。上帝正眷顾着这个国家，我们必须显示出我们的勇气，敢于面对问题，而不是将它们遗留给我们的后代。

我们要共同努力，健全美国的学校教育，不能让无知和冷漠吞噬更多年轻的生命。

我们要改革社会医疗和保险制度，在力所能及的范围内拯救我们的孩子。我们要减低税收，恢复经济，酬劳辛勤工作的美国人民。

我们要防患于未然，懈怠会带来麻烦。

我们还要阻止武器泛滥，使新的世纪摆脱恐怖的威胁。

反对自由和反对我们国家的人应该明白：美国仍将积极参与国际事务，力求世界力量的均衡，让自由的力量遍及全球。这是历史的选择。我们会保护我们的盟国，捍卫我们的利益。我们将谦逊地向世界人民展示我们的目标。我们将坚决反击各种侵略和不守信用的行径。我们要向全世界宣传孕育了我们伟大民族的价值观。

正处在鼎盛时期的美国并不缺乏同情心。当我们静心思考，我们就会明白根深蒂固的贫穷根本不值得我国作出承诺。

无论我们如何看待贫穷的原因，我们都必须承认孩子敢于冒险不等于在犯错误。放纵与滥用都为上帝所不容。这些都是缺乏爱的结果。

监狱数量的增长虽然看起来是有必要的，但并不能代替我们心中的希望——人人遵纪守法。

哪里有痛苦，我们的义务就在哪里。对我们来说，需要帮助的美国人不是陌生人，而是我们的公民；不是负担，而是急需救助的对象。当有人陷入绝望时，我们大家都会因此变得渺小。

对公共安全和大众健康，对民权和学校教育，政府都应负有极大的责

任。然而，同情心不只是政府的职责，更是整个国家的义务。

有些需要是如此的迫切，有些伤痕是如此的深刻，只有导师的爱抚、牧师的祈祷才能有所感触。不论是教堂还是慈善机构、犹太会堂还是清真寺，都赋予了我们的社会它们特有的人性，因此它们理应在我们的建设和法律上受到尊重。

我们国家的许多人都不知道贫穷的痛苦。但我们可以听到那些感触颇深的人们的倾诉。

我发誓我们的国家要达到一种境界：当我们看见受伤的行人倒在远行的路上时，我们决不会袖手旁观。

正处于鼎盛期的美国重视并期待每个人担负起自己的责任。

鼓励人们勇于承担责任不是让人们充当替罪羊，而是对人的良知的呼唤。虽然承担责任意味着牺牲个人利益，但是你能从中体会到一种更加深刻的成就感。

我们实现人生的完整不单是通过摆在我们面前的选择，而且是通过我们的实践来实现。我们知道通过对整个社会和我们的孩子们尽我们的义务，我们将得到最终的自由。

我们的公共利益依赖于我们独立的个性；依赖于我们的公民义务、家庭纽带和基本的公正；依赖于我们无数默默无闻正义的行为，正是它们指引我们走向自由。

在生活中，有时我们被召唤着去做一些惊天动地的事情。但是，正如我们时代的一位圣人所言，每一天我们都被召唤带着挚爱去做一些小事情。一个民主制度最重要的任务是由每一个人来完成的。

我为人处事的原则是：坚信自己而不强加于人，为公众的利益勇往直前，追求正义而不乏同情心，勇担责任而决不推卸。

我要通过这一切，用我们历史上的传统价值观来哺育我们的时代。

你们所做的一切和政府的工作同样重要。我希望你们不要仅仅追求个人享受而忽略公众的利益；要捍卫既定的改革措施，使其不会轻易被攻击；要从身边小事做起，为我们的国家效力。我希望你们成为真正的公民，而不是旁观者，更不是臣民。你们应成为有责任心的公民，共同来建设一个互帮互助的社会和有特色的国家。

美国人民慷慨、强大、正义，这并非因为我们信任自己，而是因为我们拥有超越自己的信念。一旦这种公民精神丧失了，无论何种政府计划都无法弥补它。一旦这种精神出现了，无论任何错误都无法抗衡它。

在《独立宣言》签署之后，弗吉尼亚州的政治家约翰·佩齐曾给托马斯·杰弗逊写信说："我们知道身手敏捷不一定就能赢得比赛，力量强大不一定就能赢得战争。难道这一切不都是上帝安排的吗？"

杰斐逊就任总统的那个年代离我们已经很远了，时光飞逝，美国发生了翻天覆地的变化。但是有一点他肯定能够预知，即我们这个时代的主题仍然是：我们国家无畏向前的恢宏故事和它追求尊严的纯朴梦想。

我们不是这个故事的作者，是作者杰斐逊本人的伟大理想穿越时空，并通过我们每天的努力在变为现实。我们大家正在通过自身的努力履行着各自的职责。

带着永不疲惫、永不气馁、永不完竭的信念，今天我们重树这样的目标：使我们的国家变得更加公正、更加慷慨，去验证我们每个人和所有人生命的尊严。

这项工作必须继续下去。这个故事必须延续下去。上帝会驾驭我们航行的。

愿上帝保佑大家！愿上帝保佑美国！

第三节 精彩语录

Everyone belongs, that everyone deserves a chance, that no insignificant person was ever born.

每个人都有自身的价值，每个人都有成功的机会，每个人天生都会有所作为。

A civil society demands from each of us good will and respect, fair dealing and forgiveness.

一个文明的社会需要我们每个人品质优良，尊重他人，为人公平和宽宏大量。

We must live up to the calling we share. Civility is not a tactic or a sentiment. It is the determined choice of trust over cynicism, of community over chaos. And this commitment, if we keep it, is a way to shared accomplishment.

我们应该时刻听取时代的呼唤。谦逊有礼不是战术也不是感情用事。这是我们最坚定的选择——在批评声中赢得信任，在混乱中寻求统一。如果遵循这样的承诺，我们将会享有共同的成就。

Encouraging responsibility is not a search for scapegoats, it is a call to conscience. And though it requires sacrifice, it brings a deeper fulfillment.

鼓励人们勇于承担责任不是让人们充当替罪羊，而是对人的良知的呼唤。虽然承担责任意味着牺牲个人利益，但是你能从中体会到一种更加深刻的成就感。

We find the fullness of life not only in options, but in commitments. And we find that children and community are the commitments that set us free.

我们实现人生的完整不单是通过摆在我们面前的选择，而且是通过我们的实践来实现。我们知道通过对整个社会和我们的孩子们尽我们的义务，我们将得到最终的自由。

第二章

人人都能当总统

第一节 背景介绍

　　美国耶鲁大学建校三百周年时，刚当选总统的小布什应邀担任毕业礼演讲嘉宾。根据耶鲁大学的规定，正式毕业礼是没有演讲嘉宾的，除非校方决定对现任总统授予名誉学位，在小布什以前肯尼迪和老布什都曾如此发过言。

　　小布什对耶鲁的态度和感情是十分复杂的。他的大学生活远不如他的父亲精彩风光，但小布什与人交往大度的天性并没有因此受到影响。他开始结识很多人并与他们建立了亲密的友谊。他凭着对棒球浓厚的兴趣及高超的球技，跟他的父亲老布什一样也当上了棒球队队长。他在大一时就为耶鲁大学棒球队效力，担任投球手。在某些方面小布什也显示出过人的才华。他刚被吸纳为大学生联谊会会员时，老会员给新会员出难题，叫他们背诵联谊会创始会员的名字，其他人只能背出三四个，而小布什竟然一口气说出了全部的人名。毕业时，他已经是联谊会的会长，这个联谊会是校园里最崇拜运动员的一个团体。

　　在耶鲁时，小布什由于受学校反叛文化影响，在生活中他表现出叛逆的一面。他曾两次被抓到警察局，第一次是在一家商店门口偷走了圣诞花环挂在他们联谊会的门上，第二次是在一次足球比赛后和一帮朋友推倒了普林斯顿大学的球门柱。为此，他还被《耶鲁时报》评为公众人物。

虽然小布什在学习方面一直不是很有长进，但他人缘很好极受欢迎。美国人非常看重别人对自己的印象，他们一直非常推崇受大家喜欢的人，因此，他们总是希望能同别人无拘无束地接触，甚至结识更多的朋友。他们在互相交往时，不喜欢服从别人，也不喜欢别人过分客气地恭维自己。他们最担心的是被别人视为不易亲近而受到孤立，这对平民百姓来说，意味着寂寞；对于政客们来说，则代表着竞选的失败。而这一点对于小布什无论从政前还是从政后都不成问题，他极具亲和力，他那乐观开朗的性格成为他后来进入政界广受群众爱戴的资本。

小布什在耶鲁大学的发言，为他赢尽了掌声。他在致辞中回忆了自己的耶鲁岁月，还不断自嘲拿自己的 C 等平均分作笑话，坦言读书时只顾着参加聚会，耽误了学业。小布什还开起了中途退学的副总统切尼的玩笑，说自己因为有耶鲁学位，所以做了总统，切尼没有拿到学位，就只能当副总统。这类美式幽默令场内人士十分受用，除了缓和气氛，也巧妙地显示出自己不是以总统身份讲话，而是以一个成绩糟糕的师兄身份来自白的，他说自己从小就不确定自己要当什么。他在祝福成绩优秀的毕业生之余，更祝福那些以 C 等成绩毕业的学生，因为人人都有可能当总统。他的演讲引来阵阵笑声和掌声，连当天在场的示威者也忍俊不禁。

最后，演讲在出奇和谐的气氛中结束。无论是校方还是小布什，既要做门面功夫，又对这种行为自嘲，对示威学生的态度更是唯恐他们不来，这样可以确保大学里的批判思想能同时得以被尊重。这是毕业前的最后一课，就算四年大学生涯中一节课也没上过，这一节课也值了。

第二节 布什于 2001 年在耶鲁大学毕业典礼上的演讲

President Levin, thank you very much. Dean Brodhead, fellows of the Yale Corporation, fellow Yale parents, families, and graduates:

It's a special privilege to receive this honorary degree. I was proud 33 years ago to receive my first Yale degree. I'm even prouder that in your eyes I've earned this one.

I congratulate my fellow honorees. I'm pleased to share this honor with such a distinguished group. I'm particularly pleased to be here with my friend, the former of Mexico. Senor Presidente, usted es un verdadero lider, y un gran amigo. (Bush addresses former Mexican president Ernesto Zedillo in Spanish)

I congratulate all the parents who are here. It's a glorious day when your child graduates from college. It's a great day for you; it's a great day for your wallet.

Most important, congratulations to the class of 2001. To those of you who received honors, awards, and distinctions, I say, well done. And to the C students—I say, you, too, can be President of the United States. A Yale degree is worth a lot, as I often remind Dick Cheney—who studied here, but left a little early. So now we know—if you graduate from Yale, you become President. If you drop out, you get to be Vice President.

I appreciate so very much the chance to say a few words on this occasion. I know Yale has a tradition of having no commencement speaker. I also know that you've carved out a single exception. Most people think that to speak at Yale's commencement, you have to be President. But over the years, the specifications have become far more demanding. Now you have to be a Yale graduate, you have to be President, and you have had to have lost the Yale vote to Ralph Nader.

This is my first time back here in quite a while. I'm sure that each of you will make your own journey back at least a few times in your life. If you're like me, you won't remember everything you did here. That can be a good thing. But there will be some people, and some moments, you will never forget.

Take, for example, my old classmate, Dick Brodhead, the accomplished dean of this great university. I remember him as a young scholar, a bright lad—a hard worker. We both put a lot of time in at the Sterling Library, in the reading room, where they have those big leather couches. We had a mutual understanding—Dick wouldn't read aloud, and I wouldn't snore.

Our course selections were different, as we followed our own path to academic discovery. Dick was an English major, and loved the classics. I loved history, and pursued a diversified course of study. I like to think of it as the academic road less traveled. For example, I took a class that studied Japanese Haiku. Haiku, for the uninitiated, is a 15th century form of poetry, each poem having 17 syllables. Haiku is fully understood only by the Zen masters. As I recall, one of my academic advisers was worried about my selection of such a specialized course. He said I should focus on English. I still hear that quite

often. But my critics don't realize I don't make verbal gaffes. I'm speaking in the perfect forms and rhythms of ancient Haiku.

I did take English here, and I took a class called "The History and Practice of American Oratory," taught by Rollin G. Osterweis. And, President Levin, I want to give credit where credit is due. I want the entire world to know this—everything I know about the spoken word, I learned right here at Yale.

As a student, I tried to keep a low profile. It worked. Last year the *New York Times* interviewed John Morton Blum because the record showed I had taken one of his courses. Casting his mind's eye over the parade of young faces down through the years, Professor Blum said, and I quote, "I don't have the foggiest recollection of him."

But I remember Professor Blum. And I still recall his dedication and high standards of learning. In my time there were many great professors at Yale. And there still are. They're the ones who keep Yale going after the commencements, after we have all gone our separate ways. I'm not sure I remembered to thank them the last time I was here, but now that I have a second chance, I thank the professors of Yale University.

That's how I've come to feel about the Yale experience—grateful. I studied hard, I played hard, and I made a lot of lifelong friends. What stays with you from college is the part of your education you hardly ever notice at the time. It's the expectations and examples around you, the ideals you believe in, and the friends you make.

In my time, they spoke of the "Yale man". I was really never sure what that was. But I do think that I'm a better man because of Yale. All universities, at their best, teach that degrees and honors are far from the full measure of life. Nor is that measure taken in wealth or in titles. What matters most are the standards you live by, the consideration you show others, and the way you use the gifts you are given.

Now you leave Yale behind, carrying the written proof of your success here, at a college older than America. When I left here, I didn't have much in the way of a life plan. I knew some people who thought they did. But it turned out that we were all in for ups and downs, most of them unexpected. Life takes its own turns, makes its own demands, writes its own story. And along the way, we start to realize we are not the author.

We begin to understand that life is ours to live, but not to waste, and that the greatest rewards are found in the commitments we make with our whole hearts—to the people we love and to the causes that earn our sacrifice. I hope that each of you will know these rewards. I hope you will find them in your own way and your own time.

For some, that might mean some time in public service. And if you hear that calling, I hope you answer. Each of you has unique gifts and you were given them for a reason. Use them and share them. Public service is one way—an honorable way—to mark your life with meaning.

Today I visit not only my alma mater, but the city of my birth. My life began just a few blocks from here, but I was raised in West Texas. From there, Yale always seemed a world away, maybe a part of my future. Now it's part of my past, and Yale for me is a source of great pride.

I hope that there will come a time for you to return to Yale to say that, and feel as I do today. And I hope you won't wait as long.

Congratulations and God bless.

雷文校长，非常感谢。布罗德黑德主任，耶鲁大学的董事们，耶鲁大学学子的家长们、家人们，毕业生们：

能获此荣誉学位，我感到不胜荣幸。三十三年前我骄傲地获得了我的第一个耶鲁学位，这次我更为能在你们面前获此荣誉学位而骄傲。

祝贺你们，与我同获殊荣的人们。我很高兴能和如此杰出的团体共享这份荣誉，尤其是能和墨西哥前总统一起在这里分享。总统先生，您是一位真正的领袖和伟大的朋友。（布什用西班牙语对墨西哥前总统埃内斯托·塞迪略说）

祝贺你们，在场的所有家长们。今天是你们的孩子大学毕业光辉灿烂的日子，对你们来说是难得的日子，对你们的钱袋也是不同寻常的一天。

最重要的是，祝贺2001级。祝贺你们中曾获得过荣誉、奖金和荣衔的人，你们的确非常出色。同时也祝贺成绩C等的同学们，你们也能成为美国总统。耶鲁学位价值不菲。我时常这么提醒切尼，他在早年也短暂就读于此。所以，我想提醒正就读于耶鲁的莘莘学子，如果你们从耶鲁顺利毕业，你们也许可以当上总统；如果你们中途辍学，那么你们只能当副总统了。

能有机会在这个盛会上发言真是荣幸之至，我知道耶鲁的传统是学位颁授典礼上没有演讲者的。我也知道你们开创了一个例外。多数人认为要在耶鲁学位颁授典礼上演讲必须是总统，但是这么多年来规格要求越来越高。现在必须是耶鲁毕业的，必须是总统，必须是曾与拉尔夫·内德竞选时丧失过耶鲁选票的。

许久以来，这是我第一次返回母校，我相信你们每个人一生中都会回来几次。如果你们像我一样，你们在这儿经历的事就不会样样记得。这也许是一件好事，但是有些人和事你们永远不会忘记。

比如，我的老同学迪克·布罗德黑德，这位学识渊博、才华横溢的主任。我记得他那时是一位年轻学者，聪明的年轻人，一位学习很努力的人。我们俩倾注了大量时间在斯特灵图书馆和阅览室，记得那里有张大长皮沙发。我们有个君子协定，迪克不会大声朗读干扰我，我不会打呼噜影响他。

我们选择的课程不同，因为我们各自按照自己的道路进行学术探索。迪克主修英语，他喜欢经典名著。我喜欢历史，寻求多样化的学习课程，并愿意将其视为较少有人涉足的学术道路。比如，当时我选修了日本俳句课。俳句对外行人来说，只是 15 世纪的一种诗歌形式，每首有 17 个音节。俳句只有禅学大师才能完全领会。在我的记忆中，就有一位学术顾问对我选择这么一门专业课感到担忧。他说我应该集中精力学习英语，这个建议现在仍然经常听到。但是我的批评者们没有注意到我并非经常口误失言，我只是在以古老俳句的完美形式和节奏演讲。

我的确是在这里掌握了英语，并选修了由罗林·G.奥斯特维斯执教的被称为"美国演讲的历史与实践"的课程。雷文校长，我认为该赞美的就要赞美。我想让全世界知道，我在演讲方面所掌握的一切都是在耶鲁这里学到的。

做学生时，我尽力保持低姿态，果然有效。去年《纽约时报》采访了约翰·莫顿·布卢姆，因为有记载表明，我曾经选修过他的课。这么多年过去了，布卢姆教授在记忆中搜寻这群年轻人的面孔，但他的回答是："我一点儿也记不起他。"

不过，我记得布卢姆教授，我仍然记得他的奉献精神和高深的学识。在我就读期间，耶鲁大学有许多伟大的教授，当然现在仍然拥有。在学位颁授典礼之后，我们各奔前程，是他们使耶鲁继续充满活力。我记不清上次来这里时是否向他们表达过谢意，但现在既然我又有一次机会，我要说谢谢耶鲁大学的教授们。

这就是我对耶鲁生活经历的感受——感激。我努力学习，尽情玩耍，交了许多终生的朋友。大学生活给予你们并使你们受益终生的，是你们当时几乎不曾注意到的那部分教育，是期望，是你们周围的榜样，是你们信仰的理想和你们所交的朋友。

我们那时人们常说"耶鲁人"，我真的不知道那意味着什么。但我确实认为正是因为耶鲁，我才更加杰出。所有大学最好的教育是使我们懂得学位和荣誉远不是衡量生活的全部标准，财富和头衔也不是标准。至关重要的是你生活的标准，你对他人的关爱和你对天赋才能的使用方式。

现在你们将离耶鲁而去，带着记载你在一所比美国还要悠久的大学里获得成功的证书离去。当我离开这里的时候，对未来生活道路没有太多的计划。我知道有些人自认为是有的，但结果是我们都会遇到坎坷不平，幸运和不幸，其中多数是始料未及的。生活总是变幻莫测，不断提出要求，书写自己的故事。在这条道路上，我们开始认识到我们不是作者。

我们开始懂得生命是让我们用来生活的，而不是用来浪费的，懂得最大的奖赏在于我们全身心的付出——对我们所爱的人和值得我们为之牺牲的事业的付出。我希望你们都能领会这种奖赏。我希望你们能在自己的一生中，以你们的方式获得这种奖赏。

对于有些人也许意味着在公共部门工作一段时日。一旦听到号召，我希望你们能够响应。你们每个人都有独特的才能，而才能赋予你们是有原由的。使用它们并与人分享，公共服务只是一种方式——一种光荣的方式——使你们的生命富有意义。

今天我不仅参观了我的母校，而且参观了我出生的城市。我的生命开始于离这里仅几个街区的地方，但我成长于西得克萨斯。从那里看，耶鲁一直恍若隔世之遥，也许只能成为我的未来。而现在它成为了我的过去，耶鲁对我来说是骄傲的源泉。

我希望有一天你们回到耶鲁时，会和我说同样的话，并且和我今天有同样的感受。我希望这一天你们不会等得太久。

祝贺你们，愿上帝保佑你们。

第三节 精彩语录

A Yale degree is worth a lot, as I often remind Dick Cheney—who studied here, but left a little early. So now we know—if you graduate from Yale, you become President. If you drop out, you get to be Vice President.

耶鲁学位价值不菲。我时常这么提醒切尼，他在早年也短暂就读于此。所以，我想提醒正就读于耶鲁的莘莘学子，如果你们从耶鲁顺利毕业，你们也许可以当上总统；如果你们中途辍学，那么你们只能当副总统了。

What stays with you from college is the part of your education you hardly ever notice at the time. It's the expectations and examples around you, the ideals you believe in, and the friends you make.

大学生活给予你们并使你们受益终生的，是你们当时几乎不曾注意到的那部分教育，是期望，是你们周围的榜样，是你们信仰的理想和你们所交的朋友。

All universities, at their best, teach that degrees and honors are far from the

full measure of life. Nor is that measure taken in wealth or in titles. What matters most are the standards you live by, the consideration you show others, and the way you use the gifts you are given.

所有大学最好的教育是使我们懂得学位和荣誉远不是衡量生活的全部标准，财富和头衔也不是标准。至关重要的是你生活的标准，你对他人的关爱和你对天赋才能的使用方式。

Now you leave Yale behind, carrying the written proof of your success here, at a college older than America. When I left here, I didn't have much in the way of a life plan. I knew some people who thought they did. But it turned out that we were all in for ups and downs, most of them unexpected. Life takes its own turns, makes its own demands, writes its own story. And along the way, we start to realize we are not the author.

现在你们将离耶鲁而去，带着记载你在一所比美国还要悠久的大学里获得成功的证书离去。当我离开这里的时候，对未来生活道路没有太多的计划。我知道有些人自认为是有的，但结果是我们都会遇到坎坷不平，幸运和不幸，其中多数是始料未及的。生活总是变幻莫测，不断提出要求，书写自己的故事。在这条道路上，我们开始认识到我们不是作者。

We begin to understand that life is ours to live, but not to waste, and that the greatest rewards are found in the commitments we make with our whole hearts—to the people we love and to the causes that earn our sacrifice. I hope that each of you will know these rewards. I hope you will find them in your own way and your own time.

我们开始懂得生命是让我们用来生活的，而不是用来浪费的，懂得最大的奖赏在于我们全身心的付出——对我们所爱的人和值得我们为之牺牲的事业的付出。我希望你们都能领会这种奖赏。我希望你们能在自己的一生中，以你们的方式获得这种奖赏。

Each of you has unique gifts and you were given them for a reason. Use them and share them. Public service is one way—an honorable way—to mark your life with meaning.

你们每个人都有独特的才能，而才能赋予你们是有原由的。使用它们并与人分享，公共服务只是一种方式——一种光荣的方式——使你们的生命富有意义。

第三章

你们和我在一起

第一节 背景介绍

　　美国当地时间 2001 年 9 月 11 日上午，十九名恐怖分子劫持了四架美国国内航班，分别对纽约市世贸中心和国防部所在地五角大楼发动了恐怖袭击，造成了举世震惊的 "9·11" 恐怖事件。

　　当地时间 11 日早上 8 时 45 分，被恐怖分子劫持的载有九十二名乘客的美洲航空公司 11 次航班撞向纽约市标志性建筑——世贸中心的其中一座大楼，并随即引发爆炸。就在当地电视台进行现场直播时，另一架载有六十五名乘客的美国联合航空公司的飞机从相反的方向高速而精确地撞向世贸中心的另一座大楼随即也发生了巨大爆炸，两次爆炸仅相隔十八分钟。时隔不久，又一架载着六十四名乘客的美洲航空公司飞机撞向美国国防部所在地——弗吉尼亚州阿灵顿的五角大楼，毁坏了大楼的一角并造成大火。近 10 时遭到撞击的纽约世贸中心正在疏散人群时，其中一座大楼发生巨烈爆炸，并从上向下迅速坍塌。之后，第二座大楼也跟着倒塌，整个纽约市烟尘蔽日，这对伟大的标志性建筑瞬间消失。同日 10 点左右，第四架遭劫持的联合航空公司的客机在宾夕法尼亚州匹兹堡附近坠毁。四架客机上共计 266 名乘客及机组成员全部遇难。事后，美国官方公布，在 "9·11" 事件中死亡总人数达到 3126 人，5000 多人受伤，直接经济损失达上千亿美元。

世界各国人民都认为冷战结束后，人类可能迎来前所未有的和平时代，事实上却并非如此，民族纠纷、地域争斗等变得更加激烈，南北之间的贫富差距也越来越大。

恐怖分子制造 "9·11" 恐怖袭击事件的本质是对美国强权政治的挑战，这也直接导致了布什政府将 "9·11" 事件定义为战争行为。经历了如此沉重的恐怖袭击事件，美国政府面临着一个重要的转折点。

美国政府采取了一系列紧急措施应对此次事件。确立了新的反恐战略和策略，建立了广泛的国际反恐联盟，采取以军事手段为主，辅之以政治、外交、情报、安全、法律、财经、社会、文化、传媒等各种手段，对恐怖主义进行坚决而彻底地打击。

这次恐怖袭击震惊了全世界，这也是美国历史上第一次针对美国本土进行的恐怖袭击。美国政府对此次恐怖袭击事件的谴责和立场也受到了大多数国家的同情和支持，全球各地在事件发生后进行了各种悼念活动。从此之后，超级大国美国的外交政策就发生了巨大的改变，而该事件也导致了此后国际范围内多国合作进行反恐怖活动，包括阿富汗战争和伊拉克战争。同时，"恐怖主义"成为一个全球性的议题。至今，"9·11" 事件带来的一系列影响仍未消散。

第二节 布什于"9·11"事件当晚
在白宫发表电视讲话

Good evening.

Today, our fellow citizens, our way of life, our very freedom came under attack in a series of deliberate and deadly terrorist acts. The victims were in airplanes or in their offices. Secretaries, business men and women, military and federal workers. Moms and dads. Friends and neighbors.

Thousands of lives were suddenly ended by evil, despicable acts of terror.

The pictures of airplanes flying into buildings, fires burning, huge structures collapsing, have filled us with disbelief, terrible sadness and a quiet, unyielding anger.

These acts of mass murder were intended to frighten our nation into chaos and retreat. But they have failed. Our country is strong. A great people has been moved to defend a great nation.

Terrorist attacks can shake the foundations of our biggest buildings, but they cannot touch the foundation of America. These acts shatter steel, but they cannot dent the steel of American resolve.

America was targeted for attack because we're the brightest beacon for freedom and opportunity in the world. And no one will keep that light from shining.

Today, our nation saw evil, the very worst of human nature, and we responded with the best of America, with the daring of our rescue workers, with the caring for strangers and neighbors who came to give blood and help in any way they could.

Immediately following the first attack, I implemented our government's emergency response plans. Our military is powerful, and it's prepared. Our emergency teams are working in New York City and Washington, D.C., to help with local rescue efforts.

Our first priority is to get help to those who have been injured and to take every precaution to protect our citizens at home and around the world from further attacks.

The functions of our government continue without interruption. Federal agencies in Washington, which had to be evacuated today, are reopening for essential personnel tonight and will be open for business tomorrow.

Our financial institutions remain strong, and the American economy will be open for business as well.

The search is under way for those who are behind these evil acts. I've directed the full resources for our intelligence and law enforcement communities to find those responsible and bring them to justice. We will make no distinction between the terrorists who committed these acts and those who harbor them.

I appreciate so very much the members of Congress who have joined me in strongly condemning these attacks. And on behalf of the American people, I thank the many world leaders who have called to offer their condolences and assistance.

America and our friends and allies join with all those who want peace and security in the world and we stand together to win the war against terrorism.

Tonight I ask for your prayers for all those who grieve, for the children whose worlds have been shattered, for all whose sense of safety and security has been threatened. And I pray they will be comforted by a power greater than any of us spoken through the ages in *Psalm 23*: "Even though I walk through the valley of the shadow of death, I fear no evil for you are with me."

This is a day when all Americans from every walk of life unite in our resolve for justice and peace. America has stood down enemies before, and we will do so this time.

None of us will ever forget this day, yet we go forward to defend freedom and all that is good and just in our world.

Thank you. Good night and God bless America.

晚上好。

今天，我们的同胞，我们的生活，我们的自由，遭到了恐怖分子一系列有预谋的惨无人道的袭击。许多人在飞机上或者是在他们的办公室中不幸遇难，他们中有秘书，有商业人士，有军人和政府工作人员；有父亲和母亲，还有朋友和邻居。

数千个生命瞬间被邪恶的恐怖主义袭击吞噬了。

飞机撞到了高楼上，浓烟滚滚，巨大的建筑物坍塌了，我们无法相信这一画面。我们心中充满了极度的悲痛和震惊，以及无法妥协的愤怒。

这次大规模屠杀行为目的是为了恐吓我们的国家，使美国陷入一片混乱之中。但他们失败了。我们的国家非常强大，我们伟大的人民已经行动起来，勇敢地保卫我们伟大的祖国。

恐怖主义袭击能够摧毁我们最高的大楼，却动摇不了美国人民坚定的信念。恐怖活动能够破坏钢铁大厦，却摧毁不了美国人民钢铁般坚强的意志。

美国成为恐怖分子的袭击目标，是因为我们在世界上高举自由和理想的火炬，但是任何人都不可能将这一火炬熄灭。

今天我们的国家遭遇了邪恶，这种邪恶是人性中最恶毒的，美国人民将全力以赴应对这一邪恶。我们的救援人员英勇无畏，无论是陌生人还是我们的朋友，他们纷纷伸出援助之手，向我们提供血液，给予他们力所能及的帮助。

事件发生之后，我立即启动了政府的紧急应对计划，我们的军队是强大的，他们已经做好了充分的准备。我们的紧急救援队伍正在纽约和华盛顿特区紧张地工作着，和当地救援人员并肩作战。

我们的当务之急是帮助那些受伤者，并保持高度警惕，随时保护国内和世界各地的美国公民不再受到袭击。

我们的政府将保持正常运转不会中断。今天，华盛顿的联邦政府机构大多被疏散，一些重要工作人员将于今天晚上恢复工作，而整个政府机构也将于明天全面正常办公。

我们的金融机构依然强大，美国经济也将恢复正常。

搜救受伤人员的工作正在展开。我已经下令所有情报及司法部门全力协作，找出应为此事负责的人，并将他们绳之以法。我们将对恐怖分子和那些庇护他们的人一视同仁，决不姑息。

我对国会议员们能与我一起强烈谴责此次袭击事件的行为表示赞赏。在此，我还代表美国人民，向对此事表示哀悼和伸出援助之手的世界各国的领导人表示诚挚的感谢。

美国和我们的朋友及盟友将与那些企盼和平与安全的国家携手，共同为打赢反抗恐怖主义的战争而奋斗。

今晚，我要求你们一同祈祷，为所有处于灾难之中的人们，为所有美好世界被无情击碎的孩子，为所有安全受到威胁的人们。我祈祷他们能够从《第

23 诗篇》中得到更大的力量和安慰，正如诗篇中所说："就算我走过被死亡阴影笼罩的山谷，我也毫不畏惧，因为有你们和我在一起。"

今天，所有的美国人在公正和和平的信念下团结在一起。美国从前曾经击败过它的敌人，这次我们也能够做到。

没有人会忘记这一天，我们会继续捍卫自由，捍卫我们这个世界上美好和正义的事业。

谢谢各位，晚安，愿上帝保佑美国！

第三节 精彩语录

Terrorist attacks can shake the foundations of our biggest buildings, but they cannot touch the foundation of America. These acts shatter steel, but they cannot dent the steel of American resolve.

恐怖主义袭击能够摧毁我们最高的大楼，却动摇不了美国人民坚定的信念。恐怖活动能够破坏钢铁大厦，却摧毁不了美国人民钢铁般坚强的意志。

Even though I walk through the valley of the shadow of death, I fear no evil for you are with me.

就算我走过被死亡阴影笼罩的山谷，我也毫不畏惧，因为有你们和我在一起。

第四章

悲痛化为愤怒

第一节 背景介绍

"9·11"恐怖袭击事件留下的不只是记忆，在世贸中心双子大厦轰然倒塌后，弥漫在美国上空的，不仅是建筑物的尘土和人们的哀伤，还带来了一些健康问题，其中包括呼吸困难和精神创伤。同时还有华尔街和学者们对经济将陷入长期衰退的极度恐慌。恐怖的气息贯穿人们的生活。

自从发生"9·11"恐怖袭击事件，纽约市的恐怖袭击警报级别始终处于橙色，这座美国最大的城市一直被认为是恐怖袭击的重点目标。

纽约世贸中心大楼遭飞机撞击当天，正在里面工作的辛迪亚拨通了丈夫的电话。在告知自己的情况并询问该怎样自救后，她说："亲爱的，我爱你，等到这一切结束后我们就会见面了。"辛迪亚的丈夫没想到这竟成了他与妻子的诀别，"9·11"恐怖袭击事件彻底改变了他和其他遇难者家属的生活。他在接受记者采访时说："时间可能会渐渐抚平那些失去亲人的创伤，但没有人能说清楚究竟要多久，是十年还是二十年，谁也不敢保证。""9·11"恐怖袭击事件打碎了他美满而平静的生活。他说，最初他还试着依靠自己的努力重新振作起来，但无济于事，于是他开始接受心理治疗。他认为没人能真正理解遇难者家属的感受，失去亲人的痛苦只有那些亲身体验过的人才能体会。

纽约市的市民们已经开始慢慢适应了在恐怖袭击的阴影下生活。乘飞机出行，他们都会提前几个小时到达机场，连鞋子也要脱掉的严格安全检查他们也已习以为常；开车穿过隧道和过桥时，他们也明白要耐心等待警方的仔细盘查和搜寻。对于不断发出的各类警报，纽约的市民们也都以"宁可信其有，不可信其无"的心态对待。于是，天上飞的农用飞机、观光直升机，地上跑的运货卡车，水上开的游艇、轮船，都有可能成为恐怖分子用来袭击的可怕工具；越来越多的标志性建筑、关键公共设施和各类知名机构都有可能成为恐怖分子攻击的目标。看来既要保持高度警惕并忍受各种严密的保安措施带来的不便，又要努力过一种"正常人"的生活，在很长时间内将是纽约人乃至所有美国人面临的一种无奈。

"9·11"对美国人民在生理和心理上的创伤无疑是巨大的，但是美国的经济并没有朝着当初经济学家们预测的轨迹发展，在采取了一系列应对措施之后，美国重上复苏轨道。

在袭击发生的当天，美联储及时表态确认不会引发金融崩溃。美联储发表声明称，已经做好了准备，可以向任何陷于短期危机的金融机构提供充足现金，以保证交易的正常进行。一天之内美联储向金融系统注入超过100亿美元的资金。

在金融市场基本恢复运作之后，美联储开始削减利率。9月17日纽交所恢复运作当日，美联储宣布减息0.5个百分点，从而使利率降到了2.5%，这是美国2001年的第八次减息。美联储的这些举措有效稳定了股市，并将其从2000年科技股泡沫破灭的低谷中带出，同时也促进了房地产市场的繁荣。

在"9·11"恐怖袭击事件发生后，美国国会授权政府拨款近600亿美元以处理善后事宜。

时间可以改变一切，甚至可以改变一个人，但"9·11"给美国和全世界人民留下的心理创伤不会随着时间流逝，不管过去十天还是十年依然存在。

第二节 布什于"9·11"事件后在国会发表电视讲话

Mr. Speaker, Mr. President Pro Tempore, members of Congress, and fellow Americans,

In the normal course of events, Presidents come to this chamber to report on the state of the Union. Tonight, no such report is needed. It has already been delivered by the American people.

We have seen it in the courage of passengers, who rushed terrorists to save others on the ground—passengers like an exceptional man named Todd Beamer. And would you please help me to welcome his wife, Lisa Beamer, here tonight.

We have seen the state of our Union in the endurance of rescuers, working past exhaustion. We have seen the unfurling of flags, the lighting of candles, the giving of blood, the saying of prayers—in English, Hebrew, and Arabic. We have seen the decency of a loving and giving people who have made the grief of strangers their own.

My fellow citizens, for the last nine days, the entire world has seen for itself the state of our Union—and it is strong.

Tonight we are a country awakened to danger and called to defend freedom. Our grief has turned to anger, and anger to resolution. Whether we bring our enemies to justice, or bring justice to our enemies, justice will be done.

I thank the Congress for its leadership at such an important time. All of America was touched on the evening of the tragedy to see Republicans and Democrats joined together on the steps of this Capitol, singing "God Bless America." And you did more than sing; you acted, by delivering $40 billion to rebuild our communities and meet the needs of our military.

Speaker Hastert, Minority Leader Gephardt, Majority Leader Daschle and Senator Lott, I thank you for your friendship, for your leadership and for your service to our country.

And on behalf of the American people, I thank the world for its outpouring of support. America will never forget the sounds of our National Anthem playing at Buckingham Palace, on the streets of Paris, and at Berlin's Brandenburg Gate. We will not forget South Korean children gathering to pray outside our embassy in Seoul, or the prayers of sympathy offered at a mosque in Cairo. We will not forget moments of silence and days of mourning in Australia and Africa and Latin America.

Nor will we forget the citizens of 80 other nations who died with our own: dozens of Pakistanis; more than 130 Israelis; more than 250 citizens of India; men and women from El Salvador, Iran, Mexico and Japan; and hundreds of British citizens. America has no truer friend than Great Britain. Once again, we are joined together in a great cause—so honored the British Prime Minister has crossed an ocean to show his unity of purpose with America. Thank you for coming, friend.

On September the 11th, enemies of freedom committed an act of war

against our country. Americans have known wars—but for the past 136 years, they have been wars on foreign soil, except for one Sunday in 1941. Americans have known the casualties of war—but not at the center of a great city on a peaceful morning. Americans have known surprise attacks—but never before on thousands of civilians. All of this was brought upon us in a single day—and night fell on a different world, a world where freedom itself is under attack.

Americans have many questions tonight. Americans are asking: Who attacked our country?

The evidence we have gathered all points to a collection of loosely affiliated terrorist organizations known as al Qaeda. They are the same murderers indicted for bombing American embassies in Tanzania and Kenya, and responsible for bombing the USS Cole.

Al Qaeda is to terror what the mafia is to crime. But its goal is not making money; its goal is remaking the world—and imposing its radical beliefs on people everywhere.

The terrorists practice a fringe form of Islamic extremism that has been rejected by Muslim scholars and the vast majority of Muslim clerics—a fringe movement that perverts the peaceful teachings of Islam. The terrorists' directive commands them to kill Christians and Jews, to kill all Americans, and make no distinction among military and civilians, including women and children.

This group and its leader—a person named Osama bin Laden—are linked to many other organizations in different countries, including the Egyptian Islamic Jihad and the Islamic Movement of Uzbekistan. There are thousands of these terrorists in more than 60 countries. They are recruited from their own nations and neighborhoods and brought to camps in places like Afghanistan, where they are trained in the tactics of terror. They are sent back to their homes or sent to hide in countries around the world to plot evil and destruction.

The leadership of al Qaeda has great influence in Afghanistan and supports the Taliban regime in controlling most of that country. In Afghanistan, we see al Qaeda's vision for the world.

Afghanistan's people have been brutalized—many are starving and many have fled. Women are not allowed to attend school. You can be jailed for owning a television. Religion can be practiced only as their leaders dictate. A man can be jailed in Afghanistan if his beard is not long enough.

The United States respects the people of Afghanistan—after all, we are currently its largest source of humanitarian aid—but we condemn the Taliban regime. It is not only repressing its own people, it is threatening people everywhere by sponsoring and sheltering and supplying terrorists. By aiding and abetting murder, the Taliban regime is committing murder.

And tonight, the United States of America makes the following demands on the Taliban: Deliver to United States authorities all the leaders of al Qaeda who hide in your land. Release all foreign nationals, including American citizens, you have unjustly imprisoned. Protect foreign journalists, diplomats and aid workers in your country. Close immediately and permanently every terrorist training camp in Afghanistan, and hand over every terrorist, and every person in their support structure, to appropriate authorities. Give the United States full access to terrorist training camps, so we can make sure they are no longer operating.

These demands are not open to negotiation or discussion. The Taliban must act, and act immediately. They will hand over the terrorists, or they will share in their fate.

I also want to speak tonight directly to Muslims throughout the world. We respect your faith. It's practiced freely by many millions of Americans, and by millions more in countries that America counts as friends. Its teachings are good and peaceful, and those who commit evil in the name of Allah blaspheme

the name of Allah. The terrorists are traitors to their own faith, trying, in effect, to hijack Islam itself. The enemy of America is not our many Muslim friends; it is not our many Arab friends. Our enemy is a radical network of terrorists, and every government that supports them.

Our war on terror begins with al Qaeda, but it does not end there. It will not end until every terrorist group of global reach has been found, stopped and defeated.

Americans are asking, why do they hate us?

They hate what we see right here in this chamber—a democratically elected government. Their leaders are self–appointed. They hate our freedoms—our freedom of religion, our freedom of speech, our freedom to vote and assemble and disagree with each other.

They want to overthrow existing governments in many Muslim countries, such as Egypt, Saudi Arabia, and Jordan. They want to drive Israel out of the Middle East. They want to drive Christians and Jews out of vast regions of Asia and Africa.

These terrorists kill not merely to end lives, but to disrupt and end a way of life. With every atrocity, they hope that America grows fearful, retreating from the world and forsaking our friends. They stand against us, because we stand in their way.

We are not deceived by their pretenses to piety. We have seen their kind before. They are the heirs of all the murderous ideologies of the 20th century. By sacrificing human life to serve their radical visions—by abandoning every value except the will to power—they follow in the path of fascism, and Nazism, and totalitarianism. And they will follow that path all the way, to where it ends: in history's unmarked grave of discarded lies.

Americans are asking: How will we fight and win this war?

We will direct every resource at our command—every means of diplomacy, every tool of intelligence, every instrument of law enforcement, every financial influence, and every necessary weapon of war—to the disruption and to the defeat of the global terror network.

This war will not be like the war against Iraq a decade ago, with a decisive liberation of territory and a swift conclusion. It will not look like the air war above Kosovo two years ago, where no ground troops were used and not a single American was lost in combat.

Our response involves far more than instant retaliation and isolated strikes. Americans should not expect one battle, but a lengthy campaign, unlike any other we have ever seen. It may include dramatic strikes, visible on TV, and covert operations, secret even in success. We will starve terrorists of funding, turn them one against another, drive them from place to place, until there is no refuge or no rest. And we will pursue nations that provide aid or safe haven to terrorism. Every nation, in every region, now has a decision to make. Either you are with us, or you are with the terrorists. From this day forward, any nation that continues to harbor or support terrorism will be regarded by the United States as a hostile regime.

Our nation has been put on notice: We are not immune from attack. We will take defensive measures against terrorism to protect Americans.

Today, dozens of federal departments and agencies, as well as state and local governments, have responsibilities affecting homeland security. These efforts must be coordinated at the highest level. So tonight I announce the creation of a Cabinet–level position reporting directly to me—the Office of Homeland Security.

And tonight I also announce a distinguished American to lead this effort, to strengthen American security: a military veteran, an effective governor, a true

patriot, a trusted friend—Pennsylvania's Tom Ridge. He will lead, oversee and coordinate a comprehensive national strategy to safeguard our country against terrorism, and respond to any attacks that may come.

These measures are essential. But the only way to defeat terrorism as a threat to our way of life is to stop it, eliminate it, and destroy it where it grows.

Many will be involved in this effort, from FBI agents to intelligence operatives to the reservists we have called to active duty. All deserve our thanks, and all have our prayers. And tonight, a few miles from the damaged Pentagon, I have a message for our military: Be ready. I've called the Armed Forces to alert, and there is a reason. The hour is coming when America will act, and you will make us proud.

This is not, however, just America's fight. And what is at stake is not just America's freedom. This is the world's fight. This is civilization's fight. This is the fight of all who believe in progress and pluralism, tolerance and freedom.

We ask every nation to join us. We will ask, and we will need, the help of police forces, intelligence services, and banking systems around the world. The United States is grateful that many nations and many international organizations have already responded—with sympathy and with support. Nations from Latin America, to Asia, to Africa, to Europe, to the Islamic world. Perhaps the NATO Charter reflects best the attitude of the world: An attack on one is an attack on all.

The civilized world is rallying to America's side. They understand that if this terror goes unpunished, their own cities, their own citizens may be next. Terror, unanswered, can not only bring down buildings, it can threaten the stability of legitimate governments. And you know what—we're not going to allow it.

Americans are asking: What is expected of us?

I ask you to live your lives, and hug your children. I know many citizens have fears tonight, and I ask you to be calm and resolute, even in the face of a continuing threat.

I ask you to uphold the values of America, and remember why so many have come here. We are in a fight for our principles, and our first responsibility is to live by them. No one should be singled out for unfair treatment or unkind words because of their ethnic background or religious faith.

I ask you to continue to support the victims of this tragedy with your contributions. Those who want to give can go to a central source of information, libertyunites.org, to find the names of groups providing direct help in New York, Pennsylvania, and Virginia.

The thousands of FBI agents who are now at work in this investigation may need your cooperation, and I ask you to give it.

I ask for your patience, with the delays and inconveniences that may accompany tighter security; and for your patience in what will be a long struggle.

I ask your continued participation and confidence in the American economy. Terrorists attacked a symbol of American prosperity. They did not touch its source. America is successful because of the hard work, and creativity, and enterprise of our people. These were the true strengths of our economy before September 11th, and they are our strengths today.

And, finally, please continue praying for the victims of terror and their families, for those in uniform, and for our great country. Prayer has comforted us in sorrow, and will help strengthen us for the journey ahead.

Tonight I thank my fellow Americans for what you have already done and for what you will do. And ladies and gentlemen of the Congress, I thank you, their representatives, for what you have already done and for what we will do together.

Tonight, we face new and sudden national challenges. We will come together to improve air safety, to dramatically expand the number of air marshals on domestic flights, and take new measures to prevent hijacking. We will come together to promote stability and keep our airlines flying, with direct assistance during this emergency.

We will come together to give law enforcement the additional tools it needs to track down terror here at home. We will come together to strengthen our intelligence capabilities to know the plans of terrorists before they act, and find them before they strike.

We will come together to take active steps that strengthen America's economy, and put our people back to work.

Tonight we welcome two leaders who embody the extraordinary spirit of all New Yorkers: Governor George Pataki, and Mayor Rudolph Giuliani. As a symbol of America's resolve, my administration will work with Congress, and these two leaders, to show the world that we will rebuild New York City.

After all that has just passed—all the lives taken, and all the possibilities and hopes that died with them—it is natural to wonder if America's future is one of fear. Some speak of an age of terror. I know there are struggles ahead, and dangers to face. But this country will define our times, not be defined by them. As long as the United States of America is determined and strong, this will not be an age of terror; this will be an age of liberty, here and across the world.

Great harm has been done to us. We have suffered great loss. And in our grief and anger we have found our mission and our moment. Freedom and fear are at war. The advance of human freedom—the great achievement of our time, and the great hope of every time—now depends on us. Our nation—this generation—will lift a dark threat of violence from our people and our future. We will rally the world to this cause by our efforts, by our courage. We will not tire, we will not falter, and we will not fail.

It is my hope that in the months and years ahead, life will return almost to normal. We'll go back to our lives and routines, and that is good. Even grief recedes with time and grace. But our resolve must not pass. Each of us will remember what happened that day, and to whom it happened. We'll remember the moment the news came—where we were and what we were doing. Some will remember an image of a fire, or a story of rescue. Some will carry memories of a face and a voice gone forever.

And I will carry this: It is the police shield of a man named George Howard, who died at the World Trade Center trying to save others. It was given to me by his mom, Arlene, as a proud memorial to her son. This is my reminder of lives that ended, and a task that does not end.

I will not forget this wound to our country or those who inflicted it. I will not yield; I will not rest; I will not relent in waging this struggle for freedom and security for the American people.

The course of this conflict is not known, yet its outcome is certain. Freedom and fear, justice and cruelty, have always been at war, and we know that God is not neutral between them.

Fellow citizens, we'll meet violence with patient justice—assured of the rightness of our cause, and confident of the victories to come. In all that lies before us, may God grant us wisdom, and may He watch over the United States of America.

Thank you.

众议院议长、参议院临时议长、国会全体议员以及美国民众：

在正常情况下，总统来此是为了发表国情咨文，然而这样的国情咨文今晚已经没有必要了，因为美国人民为了美国已经发出了他们的呐喊。

我们在被劫飞机乘客的英勇行动中看到了这一切，他们奋不顾身地与恐怖分子展开搏斗，目的是为了拯救地面上的我们。他们当中有一名叫泰德·毕默的勇士。今晚在这里，请允许我向他的妻子莉莎致意。

我们在救援人员顽强和不知疲倦的工作中看到了美国人民不屈的精神。我们看到了飘扬的旗帜、燃烧的烛光、献血的民众以及祈祷中的人们，无论他们是说英语、希伯来语还是阿拉伯语，他们都在为美国祈祷。我们看到了民众相互关爱，无私捐助，他们把陌生人的悲痛当成自己的痛苦。

我的同胞们，在过去九天的时间里，整个世界都目睹了美国的情况——它依然强大。

今天晚上，我们的国家由于威胁而惊醒，我们的民众被唤起捍卫自由。悲痛已经化为愤怒，愤怒已经变成决心。我们要将敌人绳之以法，正义终将被伸张。

感谢国会在这样一个重要时刻做出的表率作用。所有被这场悲剧震惊的美国人民已经看到共和党人和民主党人共聚国会山，共唱国歌"上帝保佑美利坚"。而你们，我的国会议员们，你们做出了更多。你们在行动，你们让国会通过了 400 亿美元的紧急拨款，以重建我们的家园和满足军队的需要。

（众议院）议长哈斯塔德，（众议院）少数党领袖格普哈特，（参议院）多数党领袖达施勒和（参议院）少数党领袖洛特，感谢你们的鼎立相助，你们的领导和你们对国家的贡献。

我代表美国人民感谢世界各地提供给美国支持。美国人民永远不会忘记，我们的国歌在白金汉宫，在巴黎街道，在柏林勃兰登堡奏响。美国人民永远不会忘记，韩国儿童聚集在汉城的美国大使馆前低声祈祷。美国人民也不会忘记，开罗一座清真寺里传出的同情之声。美国人民当然也不会忘记，几天来澳大利亚、非洲和拉丁美洲人民举行的纪念和默哀活动。

我们同样不会忘记与美国民众一起遇难的来自八十个国家的人民，其中有几十名巴基斯坦人，130 多名以色列人，250 多名印度人，还有来自萨尔瓦多、伊朗、墨西哥和日本的民众，以及来自英国的数百名民众。美国人民再也找不到比英国更好的朋友了。美国和英国又一次团结起来，为了一个伟大的事业而奋斗。英国首相布莱尔从大洋彼岸赶来，以表明他与美国人民的团结一致，我们感谢布莱尔首相的到来。

9 月 11 日，自由的敌人对我们国家发动了一场战争。美国人民早就领教过战争，然而除了 1941 年那个星期天发生的（珍珠港）事件外，过去 136 年间发生的战争都是在外国领土上进行的。美国人民也早已知道战争的伤亡，但那些伤亡都不是在一个和平的早晨，在一个伟大的城市发生的。美国人民也曾经遭受过袭击，但是袭击事件从来没有针对数以千计的平民。所有这一切都在一天之内发生了，接下来就是黑夜，整个自由世界正遭到威胁。

今晚，美国民众有很多疑问。他们都在问："究竟是谁袭击了我们的国家？"

我们现在所搜集到的证据都指向了一个松散的恐怖主义组织——"基地"组织，他们也是袭击美国驻坦桑尼亚和肯尼亚大使馆的罪魁祸首，而且他们也应对美国驱逐舰"科尔"号爆炸案负责。

"基地"组织之于恐怖主义，就像黑手党之于犯罪一样。他们的目标不是为了钱，而是为了重新改造世界，是为了把他们的极端教义散播给世界各地的人们。

这些伊斯兰极端主义学说早就被穆斯林学者和大部分穆斯林所抛弃，然而这些恐怖分子却将其奉为神明，并肆意曲解倡导和平的伊斯兰教义。恐怖分子的理论就是要把所有的基督教徒杀死，要把所有的美国人杀死，不管是军人还是平民，也不管是妇女还是小孩。

这个恐怖组织和他的首领本·拉登同世界许多国家的组织有着千丝万缕的联系，其中包括埃及伊斯兰组织吉哈德和乌兹别克斯坦的伊斯兰运动组织。这样的恐怖分子成百上千，广泛分布在世界六十多个国家。他们从自己的国家和邻国招募成员，带到像阿富汗之类的国家接受恐怖训练，然后被派回自

己的国家或者隐藏在别的国家，策划罪恶的勾当和进行破坏。

"基地"组织在阿富汗有着深厚的影响，他们支持塔利班控制了阿富汗大部分地区。这些恐怖分子在阿富汗的行动让我们窥见了"基地"组织这个恐怖组织的嘴脸。

他们使阿富汗人民遭受了沉重苦难——许多人被饿死，许多人被迫逃离家园；妇女不能上学；拥有一台电视就可能被打入牢狱；所有的宗教信仰只能按照领袖的命令行事；要是一个人的胡子不够长就有可能被逮捕。

美国人民尊重阿富汗人民——毕竟，美国是阿富汗最大的人道主义援助国，但是我们谴责塔利班政权。它不仅没有尊重自己的民众，而且通过支持、庇护和帮助恐怖分子，把自己的人民吓得惊恐不已，四处躲避。通过资助和煽动恐怖分子搞谋杀，塔利班政权自己也在搞谋杀。

今晚，美国向塔利班分子提出以下要求：将所有藏匿在阿富汗境内的"基地组织"领导人交给美国政府。释放所有非法关押的外国人员，其中包括美国人。保护外国记者、外交官员以及救援人员。立即和永远关闭恐怖分子的训练营地，把恐怖分子悉数交给有关方面。让美国自由进入恐怖分子训练营地，确保这些营地不再被使用。

所有这些要求都是不容谈判的，是没有商量余地的。塔利班政权必须执行，而且必须马上执行。他们应该交出恐怖分子，否则恐怖分子的下场就是塔利班的下场。

今天晚上，我还想直接对世界各地的穆斯林讲一句话：我们尊重你们的信仰。在美国有数百万民众自由地信奉伊斯兰教，而美国的友邦中则有更多的人信仰伊斯兰教。伊斯兰教义是好的，是推崇和平的。那些借真主之名犯罪的人亵渎了真主的神圣。我们的穆斯林朋友和阿拉伯朋友不是美国的敌人。我们的敌人是一个恐怖主义极端组织以及任何一个支持这种组织的政府。

我们反恐怖主义的斗争将从打击"基地"组织开始，但不会在"基地"

组织身上结束。我们将继续战斗，直到发现、阻止和彻底击败世界各地的恐怖主义组织，否则我们就不会停止。

美国人民在问："他们为什么要仇恨我们？"

因为他们仇恨我们这间大厦里的一切——我们是一个经过民主选举的政府，而他们的领导人则是指定的。他们还仇恨我们的自由——我们的宗教自由、言论自由、选举自由、集会自由，拥有反对意见的自由等。

这些恐怖分子妄图推翻许多穆斯林国家的现有政府，比如埃及、沙特阿拉伯和约旦。他们要把以色列人赶出中东，要把基督教徒和犹太教徒从亚洲和非洲的广大地区赶出去。

这些恐怖分子肆意屠杀不仅仅是为了毁灭生命，而是想打乱和终止一种生活方式。他们之所以一次次地制造暴行，就是希望使美国成为一个弥漫着恐惧的国家，从世界舞台上退却下来，并抛弃自己的朋友。他们打击美国，只是因为我们挡住了他们的道路。

我们没有被他们虚伪的宗教虔诚欺骗，我们以前也曾看见过他们所谓的善行，他们只不过是 20 世纪一些臭名昭著的理论指导下的残渣余孽。通过牺牲献出生命来实现他们极端的思想，通过抛弃一切价值观念唯独相信权利的欲望，他们所走的道路与法西斯、纳粹主义和极端主义如出一辙。他们会沿着这条道路走下去，直到这条路的终点：被遗弃的谎言筑成的历史无名冢。

美国人民在问："我们怎样去发动这场战争，怎样赢得这场战争呢？"

我们必须动用所有的资源——所有的外交途径、所有的情报机构、所有的执法机关、所有的金融影响以及所有的战争武器——以瓦解和击败全球恐怖主义犯罪组织。

这场战争不像十年前打击伊拉克一样，那时我们的目标就是解放科威特被占领土，迅速结束战争。这场战争也不像两年前在科索沃进行的战争一样，那时我们没有地面部队参战，没有一个美国人丧生。

除了立即报复和单纯的军事打击外，我们要做的事情还有很多。美国人

民不应该期望只进行一次战役，这将是一场长期的战争，一场我们从来没有经历过的战争。它可能包括一些大规模的打击，这一点你们将在电视上看见；它还可能包括一些秘密的行动计划，即便是成功你们也可能不知道。我们要切断恐怖分子的资金来源，使他们反目成仇、互相争斗，把他们赶得四处逃散，没有藏身之地。世界各个地区的每个国家，你们现在处在一个抉择的时刻，你们要么和我们站在一起，要么和恐怖分子同流合污。从今天开始，美国将把任何继续庇护和支持恐怖主义的国家看作是敌对国家。

我们已经向民众做出告诫，我们仍有可能遭到袭击。我们将采取防御性措施打击恐怖主义，保卫美国民众。

今天，联邦政府数十个部门和办事处，与各州以及各地区的政府部门，都有保卫国家安全的义不容辞的义务。这些工作都必须由一个最高机构来协调，所以今天晚上，我宣布成立直接向我负责的内阁级别机构——祖国安全办公室。

今晚，我将宣布一位卓越的美国人来领导此项工作，以强化美国的安全。他是一位具有丰富军事经验卓有成效的领导人，他是一位真正的爱国主义者，一个我们都信任的朋友——宾夕法尼亚州的汤姆·瑞吉。他将领导、监督和调整一个综合的国家战略来捍卫我们的祖国，抵制恐怖主义，应对任何可能出现的攻击。

这些措施都是最基本的。但是防止恐怖主义对我们生命构成威胁的唯一办法是在它滋长起来的地方制止它，消除它，毁灭它。

很多人将会为这些行动而努力，从联邦调查局到情报部门，再到我们后备役军人。我们应当感谢他们，为他们祈祷。今天晚上，就在离遭袭的五角大楼数英里的此地，我要对我们的军队说："做好准备。"我要求军队时刻待命当然是有原因的。当美国行动的那一刻到来时，我们将为你们而自豪！

然而这不仅仅是美国的斗争，危在旦夕的也不仅仅是美国的自由。这是整个世界的斗争；这是整个人类文明的斗争；这是所有相信进步和多元论，相信宽容和自由的人们的斗争。

我们需要每一个国家都加入我们，我们会请求，而且我们也需要全世界的警察、情报机构、银行系统来帮助我们。很多国家和国际机构已经做出了回应——表达同情和支持，这些国家遍布世界各地，从拉美、亚洲、非洲到欧洲，再到伊斯兰世界，美国十分感激。也许北约宪章最准确地反映了国际社会的态度：攻击一个就是攻击我们大家。

文明的社会都站在美国这一边。他们明白如果恐怖主义不受惩罚，那么他们的城市和他们的民众可能就是下一个目标。毫无疑问恐怖主义不仅仅会袭击大楼，还会威胁合法政府的稳定。我们不会允许他们这样做。

美国人民在问："我们应该做些什么呢？"

我要求你们活着，拥抱你们的孩子。我知道很多民众今晚都感到恐怖，我请求你们镇定，意志坚决，即使威胁仍然存在。

我要求你们弘扬美国的价值观念，记住为什么那么多人来到这里。我们是在为原则而战，我们首要的责任是依靠这些原则生存下去，任何人都不能因为他们的种族和宗教信仰而遭受不公平的对待和不友好的指责。

我希望你们用你们的所有继续支持灾难中的受害者。那些想要捐助的人们可以登录 libertyunites.org 网站，查找在纽约、宾夕法尼亚和弗吉尼亚提供直接帮助的机构的名称。

成千上万正在工作的联邦调查局职员们也需要你们的帮助，我希望你们也能够帮助他们。

我也希望你们在由于加强安全而导致的各种延误和诸多不便中保持耐心，在可能会长期进行的斗争中保持耐心。

我还希望你们继续投入国家建设，对经济前景充满信心。恐怖主义只是袭击了美国繁荣的一个小标志而已，他们不会触及到美国繁荣的根源。美国之所以成功就是因为他们人民的勤奋、创造力和进取心。这些都是我们在 9月 11 日以前真正的经济实力，也是我们今天的力量。

最后，请为我们在恐怖中的受害者及其家人祈祷，为消防员、警察、战士们祈祷，为我们伟大的祖国祈祷。祈祷将会抚平我们的伤痛，为我们未来的行程鼓足士气。

今天晚上，我感谢所有的美国人，感谢你们为国家所作的一切和将要做的一切。国会的各位女士和先生们，我也感谢你们，感谢你们为国家所作的一切和将要做的一切。

今天晚上，我们国家面临新的突如其来的挑战。我们要一起加强在航空方面的安全，大规模地增加国内航班安全检查人员的数量，制定新的措施阻止劫机事件的发生。

我们要加强我们的执法力度，授予执法机关所需的一切，彻底打击国内的一切恐怖活动。我们还要强化我们的情报机关，以便及时截获恐怖分子的信息，将他们的恐怖活动扼杀在摇篮中。

我们要团结一致，积极采取有关步骤，增强美国的经济，使人们恢复工作。

今天晚上，我们看到的就是在这次事件当中表现得相当出色的两位领导者：纽约市长鲁道夫·朱利安尼和纽约州州长乔治·保陶基。作为美国决心的象征，我的内阁将与国会和这两位领导人加强合作，向世人展示我们要重建纽约。

在这一切发生之后，在所有损失发生之后，大家也许会问，美国的前途究竟会怎么样？是不是会生活在恐惧当中？我知道前面依然有挑战，未来依然有危险。但是我们的国家将书写我们的时代，而不是时代来书写国家。只要美国及其民众有坚定的信念，我们将不会受到恐怖主义的打击，因为这不是恐怖主义活动的年代，这是一个自由的年代，无论是这里还是在世界任何地方。

我们在这次事件当中受到了严重的损害和损失。在悲痛和愤怒当中，我们找到了自己的使命，意识到所处的时刻。自由将和恐惧交战。人类自由事业的前进是我们这个时代的伟大成就，同时也是任何时代人们的伟大追求，现在就指望我们了。我们的国家，我们这代人，为了我们的人民和我们光明的未来，一定要将暴力恐怖的黑暗和威胁驱散。我们不会累，我们不会泄气，我们更不会失败。

在接下来的几个月和几年内，人们的生活能够恢复正常是我的希望。我们将重新恢复我们的正常生活，这是人人都渴望以求的。随着时间的推移悲伤会渐渐过去，但是我们打击恐怖主义的决心必将持续下去。我们每个人都会记得那一天、那一时刻发生的事情，以及谁在那一时刻永远地离我们而去。我们会记得那个恐怖消息来临的时刻，我们在哪里，我们又在做什么。我们中的一些人会记得那个着火的场面，或者一则营救的消息。而某个永远离我们而去的面孔和声音将永远凝固在一些人的脑海中。

而我将会永远保留这个纪念品，它是一位名叫乔治·霍华德的曼哈顿警察留下的警徽，而霍华德却在抢救世贸大厦遇难人员时永远离我们而去。他的母亲阿琳娜将它作为对儿子骄傲的纪念给了我。这个警徽时刻提醒我，一个生命就这样结束了，而我们的事业将继续下去。

我不会忘记这次袭击给我们国家造成的创伤，也不会忘记是谁造成的创伤。我将不会屈服，也不会停滞，更不会在这场关系到美国人民自由和安全的斗争中有一念之仁。

这场斗争的道路还不明朗，但是它的结局是肯定的。自由和恐惧，公正和残酷，自古以来就针锋相对，并且我们知道上帝在两者中是会有所取舍的。

同胞们，我们必须要以忍耐、公正来对付恐怖活动，我们对我们事业的正义性和将要取得的胜利充满信心。展望未来，愿上帝赐予我们智慧，保佑美利坚合众国。

谢谢！

第三节 精彩语录

We have seen the unfurling of flags, the lighting of candles, the giving of blood, the saying of prayers—in English, Hebrew, and Arabic. We have seen the decency of a loving and giving people who have made the grief of strangers their own.

我们看到了飘扬的旗帜、燃烧的烛光、献血的民众以及祈祷中的人们，无论他们是说英语、希伯来语还是阿拉伯语，他们都在为美国祈祷。我们看到了民众相互关爱，无私捐助，他们把陌生人的悲痛当成自己的痛苦。

Our grief has turned to anger, and anger to resolution. Whether we bring our enemies to justice, or bring justice to our enemies, justice will be done.

悲痛已经化为愤怒，愤怒已经变成决心。我们要将敌人绳之以法，正义终将被伸张。

They will follow that path all the way, to where it ends: in history's unmarked grave of discarded lies.

他们会沿着这条道路走下去，直到这条路的终点：被遗弃的谎言筑成的历史无名冢。

These measures are essential. But the only way to defeat terrorism as a threat to our way of life is to stop it, eliminate it, and destroy it where it grows.

这些措施都是最基本的。但是防止恐怖主义对我们生命构成威胁的唯一办法是在它滋长起来的地方制止它，消除它，毁灭它。

This is not, however, just America's fight. And what is at stake is not just America's freedom. This is the world's fight. This is civilization's fight. This is the fight of all who believe in progress and pluralism, tolerance and freedom.

然而这不仅仅是美国的斗争，危在旦夕的也不仅仅是美国的自由。这是整个世界的斗争；这是整个人类文明的斗争；这是所有相信进步和多元论，相信宽容和自由的人们的斗争。

I ask you to live your lives, and hug your children. I know many citizens have fears tonight, and I ask you to be calm and resolute, even in the face of a continuing threat.

我要求你们活着，拥抱你们的孩子。我知道很多民众今晚都感到恐怖，我请求你们镇定，意志坚决，即使威胁仍然存在。

I know there are struggles ahead, and dangers to face. But this country will define our times, not be defined by them. As long as the United States of America is determined and strong, this will not be an age of terror; this will be an

age of liberty, here and across the world.

我知道前面依然有挑战，未来依然有危险。但是我们的国家将书写我们的时代，而不是时代来书写国家。只要美国及其民众有坚定的信念，我们将不会受到恐怖主义的打击，因为这不是恐怖主义活动的年代，这是一个自由的年代，无论是这里还是在世界任何地方。

In our grief and anger we have found our mission and our moment. Freedom and fear are at war. The advance of human freedom—the great achievement of our time, and the great hope of every time—now depends on us. Our nation—this generation—will lift a dark threat of violence from our people and our future. We will rally the world to this cause by our efforts, by our courage. We will not tire, we will not falter, and we will not fail.

在悲痛和愤怒当中，我们找到了自己的使命，意识到所处的时刻。自由将和恐惧交战。人类自由事业的前进是我们这个时代的伟大成就，同时也是任何时代人们的伟大追求，现在就指望我们了。我们的国家，我们这代人，为了我们的人民和我们光明的未来，一定要将暴力恐怖的黑暗和威胁驱散。我们不会累，我们不会泄气，我们更不会失败。

The course of this conflict is not known, yet its outcome is certain. Freedom and fear, justice and cruelty, have always been at war, and we know that God is not neutral between them.

这场斗争的道路还不明朗，但是它的结局是肯定的。自由和恐惧，公正和残酷，自古以来就针锋相对，并且我们知道上帝在两者中是会有所取舍的。

第五章

美国的价值观与中国政府的自信

第一节 背景介绍

北京时间 2002 年 2 月 21 日至 22 日，美国总统布什对中国进行了为期两天的工作访问。布什此次访问受到了热情的接待，而且还应邀到著名学府清华大学进行演讲和接受学生们的提问。

来访次日，美国总统布什在中国国家副主席胡锦涛的陪同下来到清华大学举行演讲。清华大学校长王大中先生主持演讲会，胡锦涛副主席首先致词，之后布什总统发表演讲并回答清华学子的提问。

清华大学是一所享誉中外、历史悠久的高等学府，"行胜于言"的校风、"严谨、勤奋、求实、创新"的学风和"自强不息、厚德载物"的校训构成了清华精神的核心内涵，激励着一代又一代清华学子为中华民族的振兴和人类的进步奋斗不止。

清华大学的建立与美国有着深厚的渊源。清华大学始于 1911 年，是由庚子赔款建立的留美预备学校。一位在津鲁最贫穷地区从事传教、医疗、慈善及教育事业达三十多年的美国传教士，在 1906 年回国募捐时，向当时的美国总统西奥多·罗斯福建议：把两千万的庚子赔款用于中国有益的事业，特别是供给中国的学生到美国来留学，并尽力动员国会。罗斯福致函表示赞同，退款议案顺利获得国会通过。清华学堂的建立使用的就是这笔退款的一部分。

自清华大学建立以来，一批批毕业生成为中国社会的中坚，甚至成为中国的领导者。

王大中校长在欢迎辞里强调了"自强不息，厚德载物"的清华校训之后，国家副主席胡锦涛以清华校友的身份再次对布什来访清华表示欢迎，随后便坐在发言席侧同清华的学子们共同倾听演讲。美国总统布什以浅显清晰的英语向听众表达美国的价值理念。

四年前，克林顿也曾到北大演讲，在演讲中他直言不讳地将北大的学生称做"下一代的中国领袖"。因此，清华大学国际传播研究中心主任李希光教授认为，布什此次来清华演讲，也是希望同中国"未来的或潜在的领导人"对话，通过对话与中国未来的栋梁建立一种信任关系。

中美友好符合两国人民的心愿，中美两国有责任维护亚太地区乃至世界的和平与稳定，促进地区经济和全球经济的增长和繁荣，打击恐怖主义和其他跨国犯罪，以及解决环境恶化等全球性问题，也都拥有广泛的共同利益。这是国际形势发展的要求，也是顺应历史发展的潮流。小布什的此次来访，恰逢尼克松访华和中美上海公报发表三十周年。三十年的时间，在人类的历史上只是短暂的一瞬，但却给中美关系带来了巨大的变化，人们将永远不会忘记，它也势必会被永远载入史册。

第二节 布什于 2002 年在清华大学的演讲

Vice President Hu, thank you very much for your kind and generous remarks. Thank you for welcoming me and my wife, Laura, here. I see she's keeping pretty good company, with the Secretary of State, Colin Powell. It's good to see you, Mr. Secretary. And I see my National Security Advisor, Ms. Condoleezza Rice, who at one time was the provost at Stanford University. So she's comfortable on university campuses such as this. Thank you for being here, Condi.

I'm so grateful for the hospitality, and honored for the reception at one of China's, and the world's, great universities.

This university was founded, interestingly enough, with the support of my country, to further ties between our two nations. I know how important this place is to your Vice President. He not only received his degree here, but more importantly, he met his gracious wife here.

I want to thank the students for giving me the chance to meet with you, the chance to talk a little bit about my country and answer some of your questions.

The standards and reputation of this university are known around the world, and I know what an achievement it is to be here. So, congratulations. I don't know if you know this or not, but my wife and I have two daughters who are in college, just like you. One goes to the University of Texas. One goes to Yale. They're twins. And we are proud of our daughters, just like I'm sure your parents are proud of you.

My visit to China comes on an important anniversary, as the Vice President mentioned. Thirty years ago this week, an American President arrived in China on a trip designed to end decades of estrangement and confront centuries of suspicion. President Richard Nixon showed the world that two vastly different governments could meet on the grounds of common interest, in the spirit of mutual respect. As they left the airport that day, Premier Zhou Enlai said this to President Nixon: "Your handshake came over the vastest ocean in the world—25 years of no communication." During the 30 years since, America and China have exchanged many handshakes of friendship and commerce.

And as we have had more contact with each other, the citizens of both countries have gradually learned more about each other. And that's important. Once America knew China only by its history as a great and enduring civilization. Today, we see a China that is still defined by noble traditions of family, scholarship, and honor. And we see a China that is becoming one of the most dynamic and creative societies in the world—as demonstrated by the knowledge and potential right here in this room. China is on a rising path, and America welcomes the emergence of a strong and peaceful and prosperous China.

As America learns more about China, I am concerned that the Chinese people do not always see a clear picture of my country. This happens for many reasons, and some of them of our own making. Our movies and television shows often do not portray the values of the real America I know. Our successful

businesses show a strength of American commerce, but our spirit, community spirit, and contributions to each other are not always visible as monetary success.

Some of the erroneous pictures of America are painted by others. My friend, the Ambassador to China, tells me some Chinese textbooks talk of Americans of "bullying the weak and repressing the poor." Another Chinese textbook, published just last year, teaches that special agents of the FBI are used to "repress the working people." Now, neither of these is true—and while the words may be leftovers from a previous era, they are misleading and they're harmful.

In fact, Americans feel a special responsibility for the weak and the poor. Our government spends billions of dollars to provide health care and food and housing for those who cannot help themselves—and even more important, many of our citizens contribute their own money and time to help those in need. American compassion also stretches way beyond our borders. We're the number one provider of humanitarian aid to people in need throughout the world. And as for the men and women of the FBI and law enforcement, they're working people; they, themselves, are working people who devote their lives to fighting crime and corruption.

My country certainly has its share of problems, no question about that. And we have our faults. Like most nations we're on a long journey toward achieving our own ideals of equality and justice. Yet there's a reason our nation shines as a beacon of hope and opportunity, a reason many throughout the world dream of coming to America. It's because we're a free nation, where men and women have the opportunity to achieve their dreams. No matter your background or your circumstance of birth, in America you can get a good education, you can start your own business, you can raise a family, you can worship freely, and help elect the leaders of your community and your country. You can support the policies of our government, or you're free to openly disagree with them.

Those who fear freedom sometimes argue it could lead to chaos, but it does not, because freedom means more than every man for himself. Liberty gives our citizens many rights, yet expects them to exercise important responsibilities. Our liberty is given direction and purpose by moral character, shaped in strong families, strong communities, and strong religious institutions, and overseen by a strong and fair legal system.

My country's greatest symbol to the world is the Statue of Liberty, and it was designed by special care. I don't know if you've ever seen the Statue of Liberty, but if you look closely, she's holding not one object, but two. In one hand is the familiar torch we call the "light of liberty". And in the other hand is a book of law.

We're a nation of laws. Our courts are honest and they are independent. The President—me—I can't tell the courts how to rule, and neither can any other member of the executive or legislative branch of government. Under our law, everyone stands equal. No one is above the law, and no one is beneath it.

All political power in America is limited and it is temporary, and only given by the free vote of the people. We have a Constitution, now two centuries old, which limits and balances the power of the three branches of our government, the judicial branch, the legislative branch, and the executive branch, of which I'm a part.

Many of the values that guide our life in America are first shaped in our families, just as they are in your country. American moms and dads love their children and work hard and sacrifice for them, because we believe life can always be better for the next generation. In our families, we find love and learn responsibility and character.

And many Americans voluntarily devote part of their lives to serving other

people. An amazing number—nearly half of all adults in America—volunteer time every week to make their communities better by mentoring children, or by visiting the sick, or caring for the elderly, or helping with thousands of other needs and causes.

This is one of the great strengths of my country. People take responsibility for helping others, without being told, motivated by their good hearts and often by their faith.

America is a nation guided by faith. Someone once called us "a nation with the soul of a church" . This may interest you—95 percent of Americans say they believe in God, and I'm one of them.

When I met President Jiang Zemin in Shanghai a few months ago, I had the honor of sharing with him how faith changed my life and how faith contributes to the life of my country.

Faith points to a moral law beyond man's law, and calls us to duties higher than material gain. Freedom of religion is not something to be feared, it's to be welcomed, because faith gives us a moral core and teaches us to hold ourselves to high standards, to love and to serve others, and to live responsible lives.

If you travel across America—and I hope you do some day if you haven't been there—you will find people of many different ethic backgrounds and many different faiths. We're a varied nation. We're home to 2.3 million Americans of Chinese ancestry, who can be found working in the offices of our corporations, or in the Cabinet of the President of the United States, or skating for the America Olympic team. Every immigrant, by taking an oath of allegiance to our country, becomes just as just as American as the President. America shows that a society can be vast and it can be varied, yet still one country, commanding the allegiance and love of its people.

And all these qualities of America were widely on display on a single day, September the 11th, the day when terrorists, murderers, attacked my nation. American policemen and firefighters, by the hundreds, ran into burning towers in desperation to save their fellow citizens. Volunteers came from everywhere to help with rescue efforts. Americans donated blood and gave money to help the families of victims. America had prayer services all over our country, and people raised flags to show their pride and unity. And you need to know, none of this was ordered by the government; it happened spontaneously, by the initiative of free people.

Life in America shows that liberty, paired with law is not to be feared. In a free society, diversity is not disorder. Debate is not strife. And dissent is not revolution. A free society trusts its citizens to seek greatness in themselves and their country.

It was my honor to visit China in 1975—some of you weren't even born then. It shows how old I am. And a lot has changed in your country since then. China has made amazing progress—in openness and enterprise and economic freedom. And this progress previews China's great potential.

China has joined the World Trade Organization, and as you live up to its obligations, they inevitably will bring changes to China's legal system. A modern China will have a consistent rule of law to govern commerce and secure the rights of its people. The new China your generation is building will need the profound wisdom of your traditions. The lure of materialism challenges our society—challenges society in our country, and in many successful countries. Your ancient ethic of personal and family responsibility will serve you well.

Behind China's economic success today are talented, brilliant and energetic people. In the near future, those same men and women will play a full and active role in your government. This university is not simply turning out specialists, it is preparing citizens. And citizens are not spectators in the affairs

of their country. They are participants in its future.

Change is coming. China is already having secret ballot and competitive elections at the local level. Nearly 20 years ago, a great Chinese leader, Deng Xiaoping, said this—I want you to hear his words. He said that China would eventually expand democratic elections all the way to the national level. I look forward to that day.

Tens of millions of Chinese today are relearning Buddhist, Taoist, and local religious traditions, or practicing Christianity, Islam, and other faiths. Regardless of where or how these believers worship, they're no threat to public order; in fact, they make good citizens. For centuries, this country has had a tradition of religious tolerance. My prayer is that all persecution will end, so that all in China are free to gather and worship as they wish.

All these changes will lead to a stronger, more confident China—a China that can astonish and enrich the world, a China that your generation will help create. This is one of the most exciting times in the history of your country, a time when even the grandest hopes seem within your reach.

My nation offers you our respect and our friendship. Six years from now, athletes from America and around the world will come to your country for the Olympic games. And I'm confident they will find a China that is becoming a da guo, a leading nation, at peace with its people and at peace with the world.

Thank you for letting me come.

胡副主席，非常感谢您的欢迎致辞，非常感谢您在这里接待我和我的夫人劳拉。我发现她与鲍威尔先生相处得很好。今天很高兴看到你，国务卿先生。同时我也看到我的助理赖斯女士，她曾经是斯德莫大学的校长，因此她回到校园是最适合不过的了。谢谢你此时能在这儿，赖斯。

非常感谢各位对我的热情接待，很荣幸能够来到这所中国甚至是世界最伟大的学府之一。

这所大学恰好是在美国的支持下成立的，成立的目的是为了推动我们两国间的关系。我也知道清华这所大学对于副主席先生有着十分重要的意义，他不仅在这里获得了学位，而且还在这里与他优雅的夫人相识。

我想同时也感谢在座的各位学生给我这个机会跟大家见面，谈一谈我自己的国家，并且回答大家的一些问题。

清华大学的治学标准和名声闻名于世，我也知道能考入这所大学本身是一个很大的成就，祝贺你们。我不知道大家是不是知道，我和我的太太有两个女儿，像你们一样正在上大学，一个女儿上的是德州大学，一个女儿上的是耶鲁大学，她们是双胞胎。我们对我们的两个女儿备感骄傲，我想你们的父母对你们的成就也是同样的引以为荣。

我这次访华恰逢一个重要的周年纪念日，副主席刚才也谈到了，三十年前的这一周，一个美国总统来到了中国，他的访华之旅是为了结束长达数十年的隔阂，和长达数百年的相互猜疑。理查德·尼克松总统向世界展示了两个迥然不同的政府能够本着相互利益，本着相互尊重的精神站在一起。那天他们离开机场的时候，周恩来总理对尼克松总统说："你与我的握手越过了世界上最为辽阔的海洋，这个海洋就是互不交往的二十五年。"自从那时以来，美国和中国已经握过多次的友谊之手和商业之手。

随着我们两国间接触的日益频繁，我们两国的国民也逐渐地加深了对彼此的了解，这是非常非常重要的。曾经一度，美国人只知道中国是一个历史悠久的伟大国家，有伟大的文明。今天，我们仍然看到中国奉行着重视家庭、学业和荣誉的优良传统，同时，我们所看到的中国正日益成为世界上最富活力和最富创造力的国家之一，这一点最佳的验证便是在座诸位所具备的知识和潜力。中国正走在一个发展的道路上，而美国欢迎一个强大、和平与繁荣的中国出现。

正当美国人在更进一步了解中国的同时，我却担心中国人不一定总是能够很清楚地看到我的国家的真实面貌，这里面有多种原因，其中有一些是我们自己造成的。我们的电影，还有电视节目，往往并没有全面反映出我所认识的美国的真正的价值观。我们成功的企业显示了美国商业的力量，但是我们的精神、我们的社区精神，还有我们相互对彼此的贡献往往并不像我们在金钱方面的成功那样显而易见。

有些关于美国错误的描述则是他人做出的。我的朋友美国驻华大使告诉我，有些中国的教科书里面讲到美国人欺负弱者，压制穷人；另外，有一本去年刚出版的中国教科书，书里面说联邦调查局的特工们被用来压制劳动人民。这两种说法都是不真实的，这种措词很可能是过去时代遗留的产物，不过它确实是误人子弟，而且是有害的。

事实上，美国人民能感受到对弱者和贫者的一种特殊责任感。政府花费数亿美元来向那些无助的人提供卫生保健、食物、房屋。更重要的是，许多公民捐献出自己的时间和金钱来帮助那些需要帮助的人。美国人民甚至将其同情延伸到他国，我们是世界上向需要帮助的人提供人道主义援助的首善。至于联邦调查局和执法机关的人们，他们是劳动人民，是致力于打击犯罪和腐败的劳动人民。

毫无疑问，美国也有自己的问题，我们也有我们的过失。像大多数国家一样，我们在实现平等和公正方面还有很长的路要走。美国成为希望和机会的灯塔，成为全世界的梦想之地是有其原因的。那就是我们是一个自由的国度，无论男性还是女性都有机会实现他们的梦想。无论你的背景如何，无论你的出生环境如何，在美国你都有机会接受良好的教育，可以做自己的生意，可以养家糊口，可以信仰自由，也可以自主选择你所在社区和国家的管理者。你可以支持我们政府的政策，同时你也可以公开地毫不掩饰地表述不同的观点。

有些人害怕自由，他们说自由可能导致混乱，但是实际上并不会这样。

因为自由的含义远远超越了人人为己，自由赋予了我们国民许多的权利，同时也邀请他们履行重大的责任。我们的自由因为有道德，所以是一种有方向，有目的的自由。我们的自由在强健的家庭中，在强健的社区中，在强健的宗教团体生活中得到了熏陶，同时也为一个强大而公平的法律制度所监督。

我的国家显示给世界最伟大的象征是自由女神像，她是经过精心设计而成的。我不知道大家是否见过自由女神像，如果仔细观察会发现她手里拿着两件东西，其中一只手拿的是大家比较熟悉的火炬，那是自由之光，另一只手拿的是一部法典。

我们美国是一个法制的国家，我们的法院是清廉、独立的。即使是总统，哪怕是我，也无法告诉法院要如何来判案，行政部门、立法部门任何一个成员都不可以。根据我们的法律每个人都是平等的，没有任何一个人是凌驾于法律之上的，也没有任何一个人是为法律所不耻的。

在美国，所有的政治权利都是有限的、暂时的，只有通过人民的自由投票才能得到。我们拥有一部宪法，现在已经有两百年的历史，它限制并且平衡三个部门之间的权力，这三个部门就是司法、立法和行政机构。我是行政机构中的一员。

我们美国生活中的很多价值观，首先都是在家庭中陶冶形成的，就像在中国一样，美国的妈妈、爸爸们疼爱他们的孩子，为他们的健康成长作出牺牲，因为我们相信下一代的生活总会更好。在我们的家庭中，我们可以找到关爱，可以学习如何负起责任，如何陶冶人格。

很多美国人都主动抽出时间为其他人提供服务，这是一个惊人的数字，几乎一半的成年人每周都拿出时间使他们的社区办得更好，他们辅导儿童、探访病人、照顾老人，并且帮助许许多多其他的人，这种事情数不胜数。

这就是我的国家的一大优点。人们主动地承担起责任帮助他人，他们的原动力就是善良的心，还有他们的信仰。

美国是一个受信仰指导的国度，曾经有人称呼我们为教会之魂的国度，美国有95%的人称他们信仰上帝，我便是其中之一。

我几个月之前在上海见到江泽民主席时，我非常荣幸和他分享了我个人的经历，信仰如何影响了我的一生，信仰如何充实了我们国家的生活。

信仰为我们指出一种道德的规范，这超越人们的法律，也号召我们承担比物质利益更为崇高的使命。宗教自由不仅不可怕，而且应当受到欢迎，因为信仰给我们一种道德的支柱，它教授我们如何用高标准来要求自己，如何爱护他人，为他人提供服务，并且如何有责任地过我们的生活。

如果你到美国旅行的话，我希望诸位有机会到美国去旅行，你会见到来自不同背景有着不同信仰的人。我们是一个多元文化多姿多彩的国家，在那里有230万华人在繁衍生息，在我们大公司的办公室里有华人工作，在美国政府的内阁里有华人工作，在奥林匹克运动会中也有华人代表美国参加滑冰比赛，每个移民只要宣誓效忠美国，就可以成为不折不扣的美国公民，毫不亚于美国总统。美国表明一个社会可以是多姿多彩的，但仍然是一个国家，它得到其人民的效忠和热爱。

美国的所有这些特征都在一天之中生动而有力地显示出来，这就是9月11日。那天恐怖分子的凶手们攻击了我的国家，美国的警察和救火队员们带着拯救同胞的一线希望，成百上千地冲进了燃烧的大楼，来自各地的志愿者，帮助救援工作的进行。美国人中有的献血，有的捐钱来帮助那些受难者的家庭。美国各地的民众举行祈祷会，人们升起国旗，表明他们作为美国人的荣誉和团结。这些都不是政府下令让他们做的，这些都是自由的人民自发和主动做出来的。

美国的生活表明，自由在法律的辅佐下不一定令人生畏。在一个自由的社会中，多样化不是混乱，辩论不是争斗，不同政见不是革命。一个自由的社会，信任其公民，会在其自身和国家的身上寻找到一种伟大的境界。

我在1975年有幸访问过中国，在座的有些人也许还没有出生，这也表明现在我有多老了。从那时以来，贵国发生了深刻的变化，中国取得了举世闻名的进步，在开放方面，在企业方面，在经济自由方面都是如此。而这样的进步预示着中国具有巨大的潜力。

中国已经加入了世界贸易组织，在诸位履行新义务的同时，这些新义务将为贵国的法律制度带来变化。一个现代化的中国将有一个统一的法制，规范其商业活动，保障其人民的权力。诸位这一代所建设的新中国将需要贵国传统中博大精深的智慧，而物质主义的诱惑在我们的国家给我们的社会造成挑战，在很多成功的国家也造成挑战。重视个人和家庭责任的古老道德传统将使诸位受益匪浅。

在中国如今经济成功的背后是有活力的人才。在不久将来，这些人将在政府中发挥积极和全面的作用。清华大学不仅在培养专家，也是在培育公民。公民在其国家的事务中不是袖手旁观者，而是建设未来的参与者。

变化正在到来，中国已经在地方一级进行不计名投票和差额选举。将近二十年前，中国伟大的领导人邓小平说，中国最终将把这种民主选举推广到中央一级。我期待这一天的到来。

如今，上千万中国人都在重温佛教、道教和各地的传统信仰，还有信仰基督教、伊斯兰教和其他宗教的。不管这些信徒在哪里，从事何种宗教活动，他们都不会对公共秩序造成威胁，实际上他们是很好的公民。多个世纪以来，中国在包容各种宗教方面有着古老的传统，我为一切迫害的终结祈祷，让所有的中国人都有集会和从事宗教活动的自由。

所有这些变化将导致中国更加强大，更加自信，这样的中国将使世界瞩目，也使世界更加丰富。这样的中国就是诸位这一代人所共同创建的中国。现在是中国的历史上非常令人振奋的时刻，此时此刻就连最宏伟的梦想也似乎唾手可得。

我的国度与中国相互尊重，友好相处。再过六年来自美国和世界的运动员将到贵国参加奥林匹克比赛。我坚信他们见到的中国，将是一个正在变成

大国的中国，一个走在世界前沿的国家，一个与其人民无争，与世界和平相
处的中国。

　　谢谢诸位让我来此发言。

第三节 精彩语录

Faith points to a moral law beyond man's law, and calls us to duties higher than material gain. Freedom of religion is not something to be feared, it's to be welcomed, because faith gives us a moral core and teaches us to hold ourselves to high standards, to love and to serve others, and to live responsible lives.

信仰为我们指出一种道德的规范，这超越人们的法律，也号召我们承担比物质利益更为崇高的使命。宗教自由不仅不可怕，而且应当受到欢迎，因为信仰给我们一种道德的支柱，它教授我们如何用高标准来要求自己，如何爱护其他人，并且为其他人提供服务，并且如何有责任地过我们的生活。

A society can be vast and it can be varied, yet still one country, commanding the allegiance and love of its people.

一个社会可以是多姿多彩的，但仍然是一个国家，它得到其人民的效忠和热爱。

Paired with law is not to be feared. In a free society, diversity is not disorder. Debate is not strife. And dissent is not revolution. A free society trusts its citizens to seek greatness in themselves and their country.

自由在法律的辅佐下不一定令人生畏。在一个自由的社会中，多样化不是混乱，辩论不是争斗，不同政件不是革命。一个自由的社会，信任其公民，会在其自身和国家的身上寻找到一种伟大的境界。

I'm confident they will find a China that is becoming a da guo, a leading nation, at peace with its people and at peace with the world.

我坚信他们见到的中国将是一个正在变成大国的中国，一个走在世界前沿的国家，一个与其人民无争，与世界和平相处的中国。

第六章

最后决定的时刻

第一节 背景介绍

1937 年 4 月 28 日，萨达姆·侯赛因出生于伊拉克萨拉赫丁省提克里特的一个农民家庭。他自幼丧父由叔父抚养成人。1960 年，他前往埃及开罗大学攻读法律专业。二十岁时，萨达姆加入阿拉伯复兴社会党，并很快成为该党的主要领导人之一。他曾长期担任该党的地区领导机构副总书记职务。1969 年，萨达姆当选为伊拉克革命指挥委员会副主席。1979 年，出任伊拉克总统，并兼任伊拉克革命指挥委员会主席、总理和阿拉伯复兴社会党地区领导机构总书记。

萨达姆出任伊拉克总统第二年就引发了同邻国伊朗的两伊战争，这场战争耗时八年之久。之后，又入侵科威特，并引发海湾战争，严重威胁到世界的和平与安全。布什曾在发表讲话时提到："萨达姆政权是一个与日俱增的严重威胁，任何其他设想都是不顾事实的一厢情愿。如果认为这个政权会有诚意，就等于拿着亿万人民的生命与世界和平进行一场轻率的赌博。我们绝不能冒这个风险。"

2002 年 11 月 8 日，联合国安理会以 15 票对 0 票一致通过的第 1441 号决议确定，伊拉克已经而且仍在严重违背其义务，这将导致严重后果。此外，国际社会已经对伊拉克的威胁采取了进一步重要的行动，即通过联合国一致要求伊拉克立即和无条件地公开并销毁其大规模毁灭性武器。布什认为第1441号决议是对伊拉克政权的最后一次考验。伊拉克必须立即无条件地完全消除武器，接受全面核查，并彻底改变它坚持了十多年的立场。

自从1991年萨达姆在海湾战争中失败后，他一直表现出对国际社会的蔑视，多次无视联合国强令他销毁核武器的要求。更是从未执行联合国提出的停止迫害伊拉克人民、释放外国囚徒、归还窃取的财物、停止非法利用石油换食品计划的要求。此外，伊拉克在萨达姆的统治下深陷灾难，数以千计的公民常常被任意逮捕，遭受酷刑和被处决。言论自由、宗教活动、政治团体、隐私和合法程序，所有这一切根本都不存在。伊拉克政权用对待任何反对其统治或试图主张某种独立的团体的无情手段来迫害和利用伊拉克的宗教社团。

巴格达更是残酷运动的主战场，他们对什叶派穆斯林领袖和信徒长期施行无故逮捕和草率处决的残酷暴行。而且还利用伊拉克军事和安全机构，对整片伊拉克地区实行民族清洗，使全国约100万人流离失所，并残酷迫害少数民族和那些被认为是异议人士的人。在对他们发动的攻击中，伊拉克部队越来越疯狂地对手无寸铁的伊拉克平民使用化学武器。萨达姆不顾国际核查人员的检查和全面制裁规定，不惜以伊拉克人民的苦难为代价，大肆谋取化学、生物和核武器。

伊拉克政权长期以来一直大力进行恐怖主义训练和组织活动，而且还推行在政治上给各种恐怖主义组织撑腰和为它们提供长期庇护的政策，这充分体现了伊拉克是一个支持恐怖主义的国家。

萨达姆将偷运石油作为其非法收入的主要来源，暗中对石油买卖附加收费并以种种手段操纵利用联合国的石油换食品计划。然而，这些非法收入不是用于改善伊拉克人民的福利上，而是被他的家族和支持者所瓜分。整个国家如同归萨达姆及其家族所有，腐败在伊拉克四处蔓延。

自 1979 年萨达姆全面掌权以来，他曾两次把伊拉克推入灾难性的冲突中——两伊战争和入侵科威特。两次战争给伊拉克人民带来的都是苦难、死亡、失败和民族耻辱。

我们希望看到一个没有萨达姆及其家族、同伙和支持者的新伊拉克政府。渴望伊拉克成为一个民主、统一的国家，与邻国和平共处，并成为国际社会中受尊重的一员。只有这样，国际社会才有机会和伊拉克一起愈合过去十年来的创伤，帮助伊拉克公民重新建设他们的国家和生活。因此，布什发布最后通牒：限令伊拉克总统萨达姆·侯赛因在 48 小时内离开伊拉克。

第二节 布什限萨达姆四十八小时内
离开伊拉克的电视讲话

My fellow citizens, events in Iraq have now reached the final days of decision. For more than a decade, the United States and other nations have pursued patient and honorable efforts to disarm the Iraqi regime without war. That regime pledged to reveal and destroy all its weapons of mass destruction as a condition for ending the Persian Gulf War in 1991.

Since then, the world has engaged in 12 years of diplomacy. We have passed more than a dozen resolutions in the United Nations Security Council. We have sent hundreds of weapons inspectors to oversee the disarmament of Iraq. Our good faith has not been returned.

The Iraqi regime has used diplomacy as a ploy to gain time and advantage. It has uniformly defied Security Council resolutions demanding full disarmament. Over the years, U.N. weapon inspectors have been threatened by Iraqi officials, electronically bugged, and systematically deceived. Peaceful efforts to disarm the Iraqi regime have failed again and again—because we are not dealing with peaceful men.

Intelligence gathered by this and other governments leaves no doubt that the Iraq regime continues to possess and conceal some of the most lethal weapons ever devised. This regime has already used weapons of mass destruction against Iraq's neighbors and against Iraq's people.

The regime has a history of reckless aggression in the Middle East. It has a deep hatred of America and our friends. And it has aided, trained and harbored terrorists, including operatives of al Qaeda.

The danger is clear: using chemical, biological or, one day, nuclear weapons, obtained with the help of Iraq, the terrorists could fulfill their stated ambitions and kill thousands or hundreds of thousands of innocent people in our country, or any other.

The United States and other nations did nothing to deserve or invite this threat. But we will do everything to defeat it. Instead of drifting along toward tragedy, we will set a course toward safety. Before the day of horror can come, before it is too late to act, this danger will be removed.

The United States of America has the sovereign authority to use force in assuring its own national security. That duty falls to me, as Commander-in-Chief, by the oath I have sworn, by the oath I will keep.

Recognizing the threat to our country, the United States Congress voted overwhelmingly last year to support the use of force against Iraq. America tried to work with the United Nations to address this threat because we wanted to resolve the issue peacefully. We believe in the mission of the United Nations. One reason the U.N. was founded after the second world war was to confront aggressive dictators, actively and early, before they can attack the innocent and destroy the peace.

In the case of Iraq, the Security Council did act, in the early 1990s. Under Resolutions 678 and 687—both still in effect—the United States and our allies are authorized to use force in ridding Iraq of weapons of mass destruction. This is not a question of authority, it is a question of will.

Last September, I went to the U.N. General Assembly and urged the nations of the world to unite and bring an end to this danger. On November 8th, the Security Council unanimously passed Resolution 1441, finding Iraq in material breach of its obligations, and vowing serious consequences if Iraq did not fully and immediately disarm.

Today, no nation can possibly claim that Iraq has disarmed. And it will not disarm so long as Saddam Hussein holds power. For the last four and a half months, the United States and our allies have worked within the Security Council to enforce that Council's long-standing demands. Yet, some permanent members of the Security Council have publicly announced they will veto any resolution that compels the disarmament of Iraq. These governments share our assessment of the danger, but not our resolve to meet it. Many nations, however, do have the resolve and fortitude to act against this threat to peace, and a broad coalition is now gathering to enforce the just demands of the world. The United Nations Security Council has not lived up to its responsibilities, so we will rise to ours.

In recent days, some governments in the Middle East have been doing their part. They have delivered public and private messages urging the dictator to leave Iraq, so that disarmament can proceed peacefully. He has thus far refused. All the decades of deceit and cruelty have now reached an end. Saddam Hussein and his sons must leave Iraq within 48 hours. Their refusal to do so will result in military conflict, commenced at a time of our choosing. For their own safety, all foreign nationals—including journalists and inspectors— should leave Iraq immediately.

Many Iraqis can hear me tonight in a translated radio broadcast, and I have a message for them. If we must begin a military campaign, it will be directed

against the lawless men who rule your country and not against you. As our coalition takes away their power, we will deliver the food and medicine you need. We will tear down the apparatus of terror and we will help you to build a new Iraq that is prosperous and free. In a free Iraq, there will be no more wars of aggression against your neighbors, no more poison factories, no more executions of dissidents, no more torture chambers and rape rooms. The tyrant will soon be gone. The day of your liberation is near.

It is too late for Saddam Hussein to remain in power. It is not too late for the Iraqi military to act with honor and protect your country by permitting the peaceful entry of coalition forces to eliminate weapons of mass destruction. Our forces will give Iraqi military units clear instructions on actions they can take to avoid being attacked and destroyed. I urge every member of the Iraqi military and intelligence services, if war comes, do not fight for a dying regime that is not worth your own life.

And all Iraqi military and civilian personnel should listen carefully to this warning. In any conflict, your fate will depend on your action. Do not destroy oil wells, a source of wealth that belongs to the Iraqi people. Do not obey any command to use weapons of mass destruction against anyone, including the Iraqi people. War crimes will be prosecuted. War criminals will be punished. And it will be no defense to say, "I was just following orders."

Should Saddam Hussein choose confrontation, the American people can know that every measure has been taken to avoid war, and every measure will be taken to win it. Americans understand the costs of conflict because we have paid them in the past. War has no certainty, except the certainty of sacrifice.

Yet, the only way to reduce the harm and duration of war is to apply the full force and might of our military, and we are prepared to do so. If Saddam Hussein attempts to cling to power, he will remain a deadly foe until the end. In desperation, he and terrorists groups might try to conduct terrorist operations against the American people and our friends. These attacks are not inevitable. They are, however, possible. And this very fact underscores the reason we cannot live under the threat of blackmail. The terrorist threat to America and the world will be diminished the moment that Saddam Hussein is disarmed.

Our government is on heightened watch against these dangers. Just as we are preparing to ensure victory in Iraq, we are taking further actions to protect our homeland. In recent days, American authorities have expelled from the country certain individuals with ties to Iraqi intelligence services. Among other measures, I have directed additional security of our airports, and increased Coast Guard patrols of major seaports. The Department of Homeland Security is working closely with the nation's governors to increase armed security at critical facilities across America.

Should enemies strike our country, they would be attempting to shift our attention with panic and weaken our morale with fear. In this, they would fail. No act of theirs can alter the course or shake the resolve of this country. We are a peaceful people—yet we're not a fragile people, and we will not be intimidated by thugs and killers. If our enemies dare to strike us, they and all who have aided them, will face fearful consequences.

We are now acting because the risks of inaction would be far greater. In one year, or five years, the power of Iraq to inflict harm on all free nations would be multiplied many times over. With these capabilities, Saddam Hussein and his terrorist allies could choose the moment of deadly conflict when they are strongest. We choose to meet that threat now, where it arises, before it can appear suddenly in our skies and cities.

The cause of peace requires all free nations to recognize new and undeniable realities. In the 20th century, some chose to appease murderous dictators, whose threats were allowed to grow into genocide and global war. In this century, when evil men plot chemical, biological and nuclear terror, a policy

of appeasement could bring destruction of a kind never before seen on this earth.

Terrorists and terror states do not reveal these threats with fair notice, in formal declarations—and responding to such enemies only after they have struck first is not self-defense, it is suicide. The security of the world requires disarming Saddam Hussein now.

As we enforce the just demands of the world, we will also honor the deepest commitments of our country. Unlike Saddam Hussein, we believe the Iraqi people are deserving and capable of human liberty. And when the dictator has departed, they can set an example to all the Middle East of a vital and peaceful and self-governing nation.

The United States, with other countries, will work to advance liberty and peace in that region. Our goal will not be achieved overnight, but it can come over time. The power and appeal of human liberty is felt in every life and every land. And the greatest power of freedom is to overcome hatred and violence, and turn the creative gifts of men and women to the pursuits of peace.

That is the future we choose. Free nations have a duty to defend our people by uniting against the violent. And tonight, as we have done before, America and our allies accept that responsibility.

Good night, and may God continue to bless America.

同胞们，伊拉克事态现已进入最后决定的时刻。十多年来，美国和其他国家进行了耐心和真诚的努力，以便不用战争方式解除伊拉克政权的武器。作为1991年海湾战争的停战条件，伊拉克政权保证公布并销毁其所有大规模毁灭性武器。

自那时起，全世界进行了十二年的外交努力。我们在联合国安理会通过了十多项决议。我们派出了数百名武器核查人员，监督伊拉克消除武器。我们的良好用心没有得到回报。

伊拉克政权一直把外交作为争取时间和优势的策略。它一贯违抗安理会要求其全面消除武器的各项决议。多年来，联合国武器核查人员遭到伊拉克官员的威胁，他们受到电子窃听和蓄意欺骗。和平解除伊拉克政权武器的努力一次次失败——因为我们面对的不是和平之士。

我国和其他政府收集的情报毫无疑问地说明，伊拉克政权继续拥有并隐藏某些有史以来最具杀伤力的武器。该政权已经对伊拉克的邻国和伊拉克人民使用过大规模毁灭性武器。

该政权有在中东地区肆意侵犯的历史。它对美国和美国的盟友怀着刻骨仇恨。它帮助、训练并庇护恐怖主义分子，其中包括"基地"组织成员。

危险是明显的：利用在伊拉克的帮助下获得的化学和生物武器，也许终有一天还会有核武器，恐怖主义分子可能实现他们昭彰的野心，在我国或其他任何国家，杀害成千上万无辜的民众。

美国和其他国家不应受到也没有招致这种威胁。但我们将竭尽全力击败它。我们不会随波逐流滑向悲剧的深渊，而是要开辟通往安全之路。在恐怖来临之前，在采取行动尚未太晚之时，必须铲除这一危险。

美国有使用武力确保自己国家安全的最高权力，作为总司令这一职责落在我的肩上。这既是我发过的誓言，也将是我信守的誓言。

美国国会认识到我国所面临的威胁，于去年以压倒多数的投票支持对伊拉克使用武力。美国同联合国一道努力对付这一威胁，因为我们希望和平解决这个问题。我们相信联合国的使命。在第二次世界大战之后成立联合国的原因之一，就是为了主动、及早地遏制侵略成性的独裁者，不让他们有可能对无辜者发动攻击和破坏和平。

在伊拉克问题上，安理会在 20 世纪 90 年代初确实采取过行动。仍然有效的第 678 和 687 号决议授权美国和美国的盟友用武力解除伊拉克的大规模

毁灭性武器。这不是一个是否有授权的问题，而是一个是否有意愿的问题。

2002年9月，我在联合国大会上敦促世界各国团结起来结束这种危险。2002年11月8日，安理会一致通过第1441号决议，确定伊拉克实质性地违反了其义务，并郑重警告伊拉克，若不立即全面消除武器就将承担严重后果。

今天，没有一个国家能说伊拉克消除了武器。只要萨达姆还在掌权，伊拉克政权就不会消除武器。在过去的四个半月里，美国和美国的盟友一直在安理会内部为落实安理会的长期要求而努力。但某些安理会常任理事国却公开表示，他们将否决任何迫使伊拉克解除武器的决议。这些政府认同我们对危险的评估，但却不认同我们解除这种危险的决心。不过，很多国家确实有决心、有意志对和平的威胁予以反击，一个广泛的联盟目前正在形成，以落实全世界的正义要求。由于联合国安理会未能履行它的职责，我们将站出来承担我们的责任。

最近几天，一些中东国家一直在尽他们的努力。他们公开和不公开地传递信息，敦促这个独裁者离开伊拉克，以便使解除武器的工作和平地进行下去。到目前为止他拒不接受。几十年的欺骗和暴行行将告终，萨达姆和他的儿子们必须在48小时之内离开伊拉克。如果他们拒绝这么做将会导致军事冲突，开始时间由我们选择。所有外国人，包括新闻记者和核查人员，都应为自身安全起见立即离开伊拉克。

今晚，许多伊拉克人通过收音机广播翻译可以听到我的讲话，我在此向他们发出一个信息。如果我们必须开始军事行动，所针对的是那些统治你们国家的不法之徒而不是你们。在我们的联军解除他们权力的同时，我们将提供给你们所需要的食物和药品。我们将摧毁恐怖的机器，帮助你们建立一个繁荣而自由的新伊拉克。在自由的伊拉克，将不再有侵略你们邻国的战争，不再有毒气工厂，不再对持不同政见人士进行杀害，不再有酷刑室和强暴间。这个独裁者很快将一去不复返，你们获得解放的日子即将来临。

现在，萨达姆·侯赛因想要继续掌权已为时过晚。但是对伊拉克军队而言，采取正义的行动，通过让联军和平进入，销毁大规模毁灭性武器保护你们的国家，尚为时不晚。我们的军队将向伊拉克部队提供明确的指示，告诉他们可以采取何种行动来避免遭到攻击和被摧毁。我敦促伊拉克军队和情报部门的每位成员，一旦战争发生，不要为一个行将灭亡的政权而战，它不值得你们牺牲生命。

所有伊拉克军事和非军事人员必须仔细听取这一警告。在任何冲突中，你们的行为将决定你们的命运。不得摧毁油井，这一财富资源属于伊拉克人民。不得服从对包括伊拉克人民在内的任何人动用大规模毁灭性武器的命令。战争罪将受到起诉，战犯将受到惩罚。"我只是执行命令"将不能成为理由。

如果萨达姆·侯赛因选择对抗，美国人民将看到，我们已经为避免战争采取了一切措施，我们也将为赢得战争采取一切措施。美国人民懂得冲突的代价，因为我们过去已为此付出过代价。战争是无常的，而牺牲是必然的。

然而，减少战争伤害，缩短战争时间的唯一途经便是运用我军全部的力量和实力。我们已严阵以待，如果萨达姆·侯赛因妄图握权不放，他至死都将是我们的死敌。他和恐怖主义组织可能孤注一掷，对美国人民和我们的友邦发动恐怖袭击。这些袭击并非不可避免，但却是可能发生的。这一点更加突出说明我们为什么不能在讹诈的威胁中生活。萨达姆·侯赛因一旦被解除武器，恐怖主义对美国和世界的威胁就将减少。

我国政府提高了对这些危险的警戒。我们为确保在伊拉克获胜而进行准备的同时，也在采取进一步行动保护我国国土。近日美国有关当局将某些同伊拉克情报机构有关联的人驱逐出境。其他措施还包括我指示对我国机场加强保安，并且增加了海岸警卫队在重要海港的巡逻。国土安全部同全国各州州长密切合作，增加对全美各地重要设施的武装安全保卫。

敌人想通过对我国发动袭击，妄图制造惊慌来转移我们的注意力，制造恐惧来削弱我们的斗志。他们的企图不会得逞，他们的任何行动都不能改变我们的行动方向，也动摇不了我们国家的决心。我们是爱好和平的民族，然

而我们不是脆弱的民族，我们不会被暴徒和杀人凶手所吓倒。如果敌人胆敢向我们发动攻击，他们及其所有支持者都将面临可怕的后果。

我们现在之所以采取行动是因为不行动的危险还要大得多。再过一年或者五年，伊拉克危害所有自由国家的力量将会成倍增加。有了这些能力，萨达姆·侯赛因及其恐怖主义同伙就可能选择在他们最有力量的时刻，挑起致命的冲突。我们选择现在这个时刻，在它刚刚产生，还未能突然出现在我们的天空和城市之前迎战这一威胁。

和平的事业要求所有自由国家认识到当前无可否认的现实。在 20 世纪，有些国家对杀人不眨眼的独裁者采取了绥靖政策，使其威胁得以发展成灭绝种族的大屠杀和全球大战。在 21 世纪，在邪恶之徒策划化学、生物和核恐怖之时，绥靖政策可能给地球带来的巨大破坏，将会是前所未见的。

恐怖主义分子和恐怖国家不会以开诚布公、正式宣布的方式来预示这样的威胁。面对这样的敌人，待他们出击之后再做回应，不是自卫而是自杀。世界安全要求现在就解除萨达姆·侯赛因的武器。

我们在执行世界的正义要求之际，还将信守我们国家深深的承诺。不同于萨达姆·侯赛因，我们认为伊拉克人民有权利并且有能力享有人类自由。在独裁者垮台后，他们能为整个中东树立一个极其重要的和平和自治国家的榜样。

美国将同其他国家一道努力推进那个地区的自由与和平。我们的目标不会在一夜之间实现，但是假以时日必将实现。每一个生命、每一片土地都能够感受到人类自由的力量和美好。自由的最大力量就是战胜仇恨和暴力，将人们的创造力转化为对和平的追求。

这就是我们选择的未来。自由国家有责任联合起来打击暴力之徒，保卫我们的人民。今晚，如同我们过去所做的一样，美国及盟国将承担这一责任。

晚安，愿上帝继续保佑美国。

第三节 精彩语录

Instead of drifting along toward tragedy, we will set a course toward safety. Before the day of horror can come, before it is too late to act, this danger will be removed.

我们不会随波逐流滑向悲剧的深渊，而是要开辟通往安全之路。在恐怖来临之前，在采取行动尚未太晚之时，必须铲除这一危险。

In any conflict, your fate will depend on your action.

在任何冲突中，你们的行为将决定你们的命运。

We are a peaceful people—yet we're not a fragile people, and we will not be intimidated by thugs and killers. If our enemies dare to strike us, they and all who have aided them, will face fearful consequences.

我们是爱好和平的民族，然而我们不是脆弱的民族，我们不会被暴徒和杀人凶手所吓倒。如果敌人胆敢向我们发动攻击，他们及其所有支持者都将面临可怕的后果。

We choose to meet that threat now, where it arises, before it can appear suddenly in our skies and cities.

我们选择现在这个时刻，在它刚刚产生，还未能突然出现在我们的天空和城市之前迎战这一威胁。

Our goal will not be achieved overnight, but it can come over time. The power and appeal of human liberty is felt in every life and every land. And the greatest power of freedom is to overcome hatred and violence, and turn the creative gifts of men and women to the pursuits of peace.

我们的目标不会在一夜之间实现，但是假以时日必将实现。每一个生命、每一片土地都能够感受到人类自由的力量和美好。自由的最大力量就是战胜仇恨和暴力，将人们的创造力转化为对和平的追求。

第七章

抬起眼帘，望向天空

第一节 背景介绍

1981 年 4 月 12 日，"哥伦比亚"号航天飞机首次发射，这是美国第一架正式服役的航天飞机。"哥伦比亚"号航天飞机是为了纪念 18 世纪第一艘环绕世界航行的美国籍帆船"哥伦比亚"号而命名的。"哥伦比亚"号机舱长 18 米，能装运 36 吨货物，外形像一架大型三角翼飞机，整个组合装置重约 2,000 吨，在滑行中还能向两侧方向作 2,000 公里的机动飞行，以选择合适的着陆场地。美国东部时间 2003 年 2 月 1 日上午 9 时，美国"哥伦比亚"号航天飞机在得克萨斯州北部上空解体坠毁，七名宇航员全部遇难。

2003 年 1 月 16 日，"哥伦比亚"号航天飞机发射升空。1 月 24 日航天飞机项目承包商美国波音公司技术人员撰写了事故报告，并于 1 月 27 日提交给宇航局飞行控制部门。报告称，在"哥伦比亚"号发射 82 秒后，有三个泡沫材料碎块从连接外部燃料箱和航天飞机的支架区域脱落，每个碎块长约 50 厘米，它们击中航天飞机后"似乎出现了瓦解"，化为大量更小的碎片。美国宇航局在公布这份报告时强调说，根据报告得出的结论，泡沫碎块撞击不会影响航天飞机飞行的安全性。宇航局飞行控制部门也"同意这一结论"。

　　尽管宇航局飞行控制部门同意这一结论，但是新报告公布之后，泡沫材料撞击在"哥伦比亚"号失事中所起的作用，再次引起了人们的关注。2月1日，"哥伦比亚"号解体坠毁后不久，泡沫碎块问题就浮出水面。虽然美国宇航局一直坚持认为，泡沫碎块撞击不会产生严重后果，但负责对"哥伦比亚"号事故进行调查的独立委员会，仍对泡沫碎块产生的影响进行了深入分析。这一独立调查委员会得出的最主要结论是，"哥伦比亚"号机壳上可能出现孔洞，导致超高温气体进入航天飞机，最终酿成事故。而根据美国宇航局1月21日公布的文件，宇航局一位工程师1月29日就曾在电子邮件中警告，航天飞机外部隔热瓦受损，有可能导致轮舱或起落架舱门出现裂孔。

　　2004年8月13日，美国宇航局进一步确认，美国"哥伦比亚"号航天飞机外部燃料箱表面泡沫材料安装过程中存在的缺陷，是造成整起事故的祸首。"哥伦比亚"号航天飞机事故调查委员会公布的调查报告称，外部燃料箱表面脱落的一块泡沫材料，击中航天飞机左翼前缘名为"增强碳碳"的材料。当航天飞机返回时，经过大气层产生剧烈摩擦，使温度高达1400℃的空气冲入左机翼后融化了内部结构，致使机翼和机体融化，导致悲剧的发生。事故发生后，由于无法迅速找回事发时的泡沫材料和燃料箱进行检验，宇航局和事故调查委员会一直没对事故原因做出最终定论。

　　目前，"哥伦比亚"号外部燃料箱约50万块碎片已被找到并重新拼接。宇航局负责"哥伦比亚"号外部燃料箱工程的首席工程师尼尔·奥特说，宇航局经多次试验确定，泡沫材料安装过程有缺陷是造成事故的主要原因。奥特说，泡沫材料本身的化学成分没有问题，问题出在用喷枪在燃料箱外敷设泡沫材料的过程。试验表明敷设时会在各块泡沫材料之间留下缝隙，使液态氢能够渗入其间。航天飞机起飞后，氢气受热膨胀，最终导致大块泡沫材料脱落。撞击"哥伦比亚"号的泡沫材料有手提箱大小，重约0.75公斤。几乎是被整块"撕下"后，高速撞击到航天飞机左翼前缘"增强碳碳"的材料上并形成裂隙。航天飞机重返大气层时，超高温气体从裂隙处进入"哥伦比亚"

号机体，造成航天飞机解体。

奥特说，根据新标准对燃料箱进行检测是摆在美国宇航局面前的最大障碍。新标准要求，不允许有 0.5 盎司（14.17 克）以上的燃料箱外泡沫材料脱落。美国宇航局需要对航天飞机上的 11 个燃料箱进行检测，而检查每个燃料箱需要 4000 万美元。

美国"哥伦比亚"号航天飞机事故委员会专家指出，起飞时遭遇强风，发射前临时更换火箭助推器，以及"年龄太大"，都可能是造成这艘"功勋宇航器"解体的根本原因。在"哥伦比亚"号起飞 62 秒钟后，突然遭遇异常猛烈的大风，可能导致其左侧机身发生"内伤"，为日后坠毁埋下了隐患，此后仅仅 20 秒钟，从机身下部主燃料箱上脱落的泡沫绝缘材料击中了左侧机翼前端，造成直接"外伤"。专家认为这些损伤对其他航天飞机来说可能不算什么，但是对"哥伦比亚"号这样二十一岁高龄的"老飞机"则是致命的。

调查委员会指出，有关方面认为美国航空航天局是否在"机体老化"问题上重视不够，以致最终酿成本次悲剧。目前，有关"哥伦比亚"号失事的直接原因基本确定：超高温空气从机体表面缝隙入侵隔热瓦，最终造成航天飞机在返航途中解体坠毁。据介绍飞机起飞一分钟后，遭遇的风力强度已经接近美国航空航天局允许的极限。因此专家认为，原本已老化的机翼因遭受强风吹袭，才在外界异物的撞击下出现破损，为返航途中的超高温空气入侵留下了隐患。

此外，2002 年 8 月，原本和"哥伦比亚"号主燃料箱配套的助推火箭被拆卸下来，安装到另外一艘航天飞机上。直到当年 11 月，美国航空航天局才重新为"哥伦比亚"号安装了新的助推火箭，可能在拆装过程中，有关人员的操作对燃料箱表面材料形成了伤害，从而造成绝缘材料脱落击中航天飞机左翼。

此外，由于"年事已高"，"哥伦比亚"号左翼前端的超强碳纤维隔热板下面可能发生"缺损现象"。过去十年中，其他航天飞机的类似部位也曾遭受过不同的损伤，其中包括外力（小陨石）撞击、刮伤、密封不严等。调查委员会指出，必须搞清楚的是，美国航空航天局是否对包括"哥伦比亚"号在内的美国航天飞机上述容易受损部位及时进行了检查和更换。据介绍，"哥伦比亚"号首次升空是在1981年，为美国使用时间最长的航天飞机。在事故发生后进行的地面风洞试验发现，"哥伦比亚"号在最后时刻发生的翻滚飞行现象，就是由于左翼前端保护层丢失造成的。专家估计，当时至少有5块U形隔热板脱落才会产生如此强大的拉力。搜索人员已经发现了超过2.8万块"哥伦比亚"号残骸，并将其送到肯尼迪航天中心接受分析调查。据悉，这些残骸不过是"哥伦比亚"号庞大机身的19%。

美国航空航天局在2009年12月30日，公布了"哥伦比亚"号航天飞机失事的最终调查报告，细述了"哥伦比亚"号解体前舱内的最后情况。这份长400页的最终报告还原了更多"哥伦比亚"号解体前舱内宇航员的活动细节。航天飞机翻滚着失去控制，宇航员威廉·麦库尔按下数个按键，试图控制航天飞机。其他大多数宇航员也按美国航空航天局既定程序操作。报告还重点针对宇航员安全问题，提出多项改进意见。

"哥伦比亚"号坠毁了，七条鲜活的生命瞬间消逝。失事前乘员舱里到底发生了什么，宇航员们想了些什么，又做了些什么，人们都无从知晓。痛惜、遗憾、伤心……都不足以表达人们的悲痛之情，人们能做的就是在悼念他们的同时，记住他们伟大的贡献。

第二节 布什于 2003 年 "哥伦比亚" 号失事后的演讲

My fellow Americans, this day has brought terrible news and at sadness to our country. At 9:00 a.m. this morning, Mission Control in Houston lost contact with our Space Shuttle Columbia. A short time later, debris was seen falling from the skies above Texas. The Columbia is lost; there are no survivors.

On board was a crew of seven: Colonel Rick Husband; Lt. Colonel Michael Anderson; Commander Laurel Clark; Captain David Brown; Commander William McCool; Dr. Kalpana Chawla; and Ilan Ramon, a Colonel in the Israeli Air Force. These men and women assumed at risk in the service to all humanity.

In an age when space flight has come to seem almost routine, it is easy to overlook the dangers of travel by rocket, and the difficulties of navigating the fierce outer atmosphere of the Earth. These astronauts knew the dangers, and they faced them willingly, knowing they had a high and noble purpose in life. Because of their courage and daring and idealism, we will miss them all the more.

All Americans today are thinking, as well, of the families of these men and women who have been given this sudden shock and grief. You're not alone. Our entire nation grieves with you. And those you loved will always have the respect and gratitude of this country. The cause in which they died will continue. Mankind is led into the darkness beyond our world by the inspiration of discovery and the longing to understand. Our journey into space will go on.

In the skies today we saw destruction and tragedy. Yet farther than we can see there is comfort and hope. In the words of the prophet Isaiah, "Lift your eyes and look to the heavens. Who created all these? He who brings out the starry hosts one by one and calls them each by name. ause of His at power and mighty strength, not one of them is missing."

The same Creator who names the stars also knows the names of the seven souls we mourn today. The crew of the shuttle Columbia did not return safely to Earth; yet we can pray that all are safely home.

May God bless the grieving families, and may God continue to bless America.

我的美国同胞们，今天传来噩耗，巨大的悲痛降临我们的国家。今早 9 点钟，位于休斯敦的航天地面指挥中心同我们的"哥伦比亚"号航天飞机失去了联系。此后不久，便发现得克萨斯州的上空有残骸飘落。"哥伦比亚"号失事，无一人生还。

机上的七名机组成员分别是：里克·赫斯本德空军上校、迈克尔·安德森空军中校、劳蕾尔·克拉克海军中校、戴维·布朗海军上校和威廉·麦库尔海军中校、卡尔帕娜·乔娜博士和以色列空军上校伊兰·拉蒙。这些宇航员为造福全人类承担了巨大的风险。

在一个太空飞行似乎已成为常规作业的时代，人们很容易忽视乘坐火箭飞行的危险性和在恶劣的地球外层空间遨游的难度。虽然宇航员们知道这些危险，但他们甘愿面对，因为他们知道自己拥有远大而崇高的人生目标。正

是因为他们的勇气、胆量和崇高的理想，我们才更加缅怀他们。

今天所有的美国人都在牵挂着遭受这种突如其来打击和悲伤的宇航员家人。你们并不孤单，我们全体国民同你们一起哀悼他们。你们所爱的人将永远受到这个国家的尊重和感激。他们为之献身的事业仍将继续。人类正是在探索精神和求知欲望的引导下，超越我们的世界进入到黑暗的外层空间。我们的太空之旅仍将继续。

今天，我们在空中目睹了毁灭和悲剧。然而，在我们看不到的远方有着慰藉与希望。预言家以赛亚说："抬起眼帘，望向天空。是谁创造了这一切？是造物主创造了点点繁星，并将其逐个命名。由于他的伟大才智与神奇力量才无一遗漏。"

给群星命名的造物主也知道我们今天缅怀的七位亡灵的名字。"哥伦比亚"号航天飞机的机组人员虽未平安返回地球，但我们祈祷他们均已安息。

愿上帝保佑宇航员们悲伤的家属，愿上帝继续保佑美国。

第三节　精彩语录

These astronauts knew the dangers, and they faced them willingly, knowing they had a high and noble purpose in life. Because of their courage and daring and idealism, we will miss them all the more.

虽然宇航员们知道这些危险，但他们甘愿面对，因为他们知道自己拥有远大而崇高的人生目标。正是因为他们的勇气、胆量和崇高的理想，我们才更加缅怀他们。

Mankind is led into the darkness beyond our world by the inspiration of discovery and the longing to understand. Our journey into space will go on.

人类正是在探索精神和求知欲望的引导下，超越我们的世界进入到黑暗的外层空间。我们的太空之旅仍将继续。

In the skies today we saw destruction and tragedy. Yet farther than we can see there is comfort and hope. In the words of the prophet Isaiah, "Lift your eyes and look to the heavens. Who created all these? He who brings out the

starry hosts one by one and calls them each by name. ause of His at power and mighty strength, not one of them is missing."

今天，我们在空中目睹了毁灭和悲剧。然而，在我们看不到的远方有着慰藉与希望。预言家以赛亚说："抬起眼帘，望向天空。是谁创造了这一切？是造物主创造了点点繁星，并将其逐个命名。由于他的伟大才智与神奇力量才无一遗漏。"

第八章
自由所到之处，仇恨无不让道

第一节 背景介绍

　　2003 年 3 月 20 日，伊拉克战争爆发。伊拉克战争又称美伊战争，是以英美军队为主的联合部队对伊拉克发动的军事行动。在"9·11"恐怖袭击事件发生后，美国总统布什将伊拉克等多个国家列入"邪恶轴心国"，并宣布向恐怖主义作战。布什在下令进攻伊拉克之前，曾发布最后通牒：限令伊拉克总统萨达姆·侯赛因在 48 小时内离开伊拉克。萨达姆拒绝了最后的一线生机，于是引发了伊拉克战争。美国以伊拉克藏有大规模杀伤性武器并暗中支持恐怖分子为由，绕开联合国安理会单方面对伊拉克实施军事打击。到 2010 年 8 月美国战斗部队撤出伊拉克为止，历时七年多美方最终没有找到所谓的大规模杀伤性武器，反而找到萨达姆政权早已将其销毁的文件和人证。2011 年 12 月 18 日，美军全部撤出。

　　以美国和英国为主的联合部队于 2003 年 3 月 20 日正式宣布对伊拉克开战。澳大利亚和波兰的军队也参与了此次联合军事行动。军事行动是在美国总统乔治·W.布什对伊拉克总统萨达姆·侯赛因所发出的，要求他和他的儿子在 48 小时内离开伊拉克的最后通牒到期后开始的。联合部队是由 12 万人的美军部队、4.5 万人的英军部队、2 千多人的澳大利亚军队和 200 人的波兰军队所组成的，除此之外还有大约 5 万人的伊拉克反叛军。他们是通过驻扎在科威特的美军基地正式对伊拉克发动军事打击的，并得到了海湾地区大量的空基和海基航空兵的支援。

美国第三步兵师从科威特西北方向的沙漠向巴格达挺进，伴随他们作战的还有美国第 101 空中突击师和第 82 空降师的若干部队。另外，在伊拉克东南部，美国海军陆战队第一远征部队和英国远征军则发动了钳形攻势以打开伊拉克的海运通道。在战争进行两周后，美军又在伊拉克北部山区投入了173 空降旅以及特种部队，并和当地的库尔德武装力量结成同盟。美国预期在北方投入的第 4 步兵师，则由于土耳其议会的反对而未能在该地参加战斗。经过两个星期的激战，英军首先控制了伊拉克南部的石油重镇，伊拉克的第二大城市巴士拉。在伊拉克全境都出现了断水和停电等人道主义危机。国际多个人道组织向伊拉克运输救援物资。这些援助物资大多都从联军所控制的乌姆盖茨尔港进入伊拉克，还有部分则从科威特进入伊拉克。

战争爆发大约三个星期之后，美军顺利进入巴格达市区，途中并没有遇到任何顽强抵抗。伊拉克官员则突然消失去向不明，大批伊拉克军队向美军投降。之后巴格达和巴斯拉等伊拉克城市纷纷陷入无政府状态，巴格达市内频繁发生抢掠事件，城市秩序陷入混乱之中。巴格达博物馆遭到洗劫，上万件珍贵文物失踪。各地大量的古遗迹在战争中遭到破坏，伊拉克民众批评美军并没有努力维持巴格达的市内安全。

伊拉克战争是一场具有争议的战争，遭到世界大多数国家和民众质疑和反对。这场战争在整个世界引起了强烈的震动，产生了广泛而深远的影响，也带给我们多方面的启示和思考，包括政治、军事、经济、外交和文化等许多方面。

美国总统布什于美国东部时间 2003 年 5 月 1 日晚上 8 时 48 分，在美国海军"林肯"号航母的飞行甲板上发表了专门讲话，宣布伊拉克境内的主要战斗已经结束。伊拉克的主要战斗已经结束，推翻萨达姆政权是反恐战争

的一次重大胜利，但反恐战争并没有结束。布什在"林肯"号航母上的讲话并没有宣布伊拉克战争结束，而只是宣称"伊拉克的主要战斗结束"。布什还警告说，美国将在敌人发动袭击前打击他们，暗示美国将坚持推行"先发制人"的反恐政策。

　　演讲持续了二十分钟，演讲结束后，布什还在航母上过了一夜。据悉，布什是第三位在军舰上过夜的美国总统。1994年美国前总统克林顿曾在"华盛顿"号航母上慰问官兵并过夜，以纪念诺曼底登陆五十周年；老布什则在美军"的黎波里"号两栖登陆舰上住了两夜，然后访问索马里。

第二节 布什于 2003 年在"林肯"号航母上的演讲

Thank you all very much. Admiral Kelly, Captain Card, officers and sailors of the USS Abraham Lincoln, my fellow Americans,

Major combat operations in Iraq have ended. In the battle of Iraq, the United States and our allies have prevailed.

And now our coalition is engaged in securing and reconstructing that country.

In this battle, we have fought for the cause of liberty, and for the peace of the world. Our nation and our coalition are proud of this accomplishment—yet, it is you, the members of the United States military, who achieved it. Your courage, your willingness to face danger for your country and for each other, made this day possible. Because of you, our nation is more secure. Because of you, the tyrant has fallen, and Iraq is free.

Operation Iraqi Freedom was carried out with a combination of precision and speed and boldness the enemy did not expect, and the world had not seen before.

From distant bases or ships at sea, we sent planes and missiles that could destroy an enemy division, or strike a single bunker. Marines and soldiers charged to Baghdad across 350 miles of hostile ground, in one of the swiftest advances of heavy arms in history. You have shown the world the skill and the might of the American Armed Forces.

This nation thanks all the members of our coalition who joined in a noble cause. We thank the Armed Forces of the United Kingdom, Australia, and Poland, who shared in the hardships of war. We thank all the citizens of Iraq who welcomed our troops and joined in the liberation of their own country.

And tonight, I have a special word for Secretary Rumsfeld, for General Franks, and for all the men and women who wear the uniform of the United States: America is grateful for a job well done.

The character of our military through history—the daring of Normandy, the fierce courage of Iwo Jima, the decency and idealism that turned enemies into allies—is fully present in this generation.

When Iraqi civilians looked into the faces of our servicemen and women, they saw strength and kindness and goodwill. When I look at the members of the United States military, I see the best of our country, and I'm honored to be your Commander-in-Chief.

In the images of falling statues, we have witnessed the arrival of a new era. For a hundred of years of war, culminating in the nuclear age, military technology was designed and deployed to inflict casualties on an ever-growing scale.

In defeating Nazi Germany and Imperial Japan, Allied forces destroyed entire cities, while enemy leaders who started the conflict were safe until tthe final days. Military power was used to end a regime by breaking a nation.

Today, we have the greater power to free a nation by breaking a dangerous and aggressive regime. With new tactics and precision weapons, we can achieve military objectives without directing violence against civilians.

No device of man can remove the tragedy from war; yet it is a great moral advance when the guilty have far more to fear from war than the innocent.

In the images of celebrating Iraqis, we have also seen the ageless appeal of human freedom. Decades of lies and intimidation could not make the Iraqi people love their oppressors or desire their own enslavement.

Men and women in every culture need liberty like they need food and water and air. Everywhere that freedom arrives, humanity rejoices; and everywhere that freedom stirs, let tyrants fear.

We have difficult work to do in Iraq. We're bringing order to parts of that country that remain dangerous. We're pursuing and finding leaders of the old regime, who will be held to account for their crimes.

We've begun the search for hidden chemical and biological weapons and already know of hundreds of sites that will be investigated.

We're helping to rebuild Iraq, where the dictator built palaces for himself, instead of hospitals and schools. And we will stand with the new leaders of Iraq as they establish a government of, by, and for the Iraqi people.

The transition from dictatorship to democracy will take time, but it is worth every effort. Our coalition will stay until our work is done. Then we will leave, and we will leave behind a free Iraq.

The battle of Iraq is one victory in a war on terror that began on September the 11th, 2001—and still goes on. That terrible morning, 19 evil men—the shock troops of a hateful ideology—gave America and the civilized world a glimpse of their ambitions. They imagined, in the words of one terrorist, that September the 11th would be the "beginning of the end of America."

By seeking to turn our cities into killing fields, terrorists and their allies believed that they could destroy this nation's resolve, and force our retreat from the world. They have failed.

In the battle of Afghanistan, we destroyed the Taliban, many terrorists, and the camps where they trained. We continue to help the Afghan people lay roads, restore hospitals, and educate all of their children.

Yet we also have dangerous work to complete. As I speak, a Special Operations task force, led by the 82nd Airborne, is on the trail of the terrorists and those who seek to undermine the free government of Afghanistan. America and our coalition will finish what we have begun.

From Pakistan to the Philippines to the Horn of Africa, we are hunting down al Qaeda killers. Nineteen months ago, I pledged that the terrorists would not escape the patient justice of the United States. And as of tonight, nearly one-half of al Qaeda's senior operatives have been captured or killed.

The liberation of Iraq is a crucial advance in the campaign against terror. We've removed an ally of al Qaeda, and cut off a source of terrorist funding. And this much is certain: No terrorist network will gain weapons of mass destruction from the Iraqi regime, because the regime is no more.

In these 19 months that changed the world, our actions have been focused and deliberate and proportionate to the offense. We have not forgotten the victims of September the 11th—the last phone calls, the cold murder of children, the searches in the rubble. With those attacks, the terrorists and their supporters declared war on the United States. And war is what they got.

Our war against terror is proceeding according to principles that I have made clear to all: Any person involved in committing or planning terrorist attacks against the American people becomes an enemy of this country, and a target of American justice.

Any person, organization, or government that supports, protects, or harbors terrorists is complicit in the murder of the innocent, and equally guilty of terrorist crimes.Any outlaw regime that has ties to terrorist groups and seeks or possesses weapons of mass destruction is a grave danger to the civilized world—and will be confronted.

And anyone in the world, including the Arab world, who works and sacrifices for freedom has a loyal friend in the United States of America. Click here for a USS Abraham Lincoln photo essay. Our commitment to liberty is America's tradition—declared at our founding; affirmed in Franklin Roosevelt's Four Freedoms; asserted in the Truman Doctrine and in Ronald Reagan's challenge to an evil empire.

We are committed to freedom in Afghanistan, in Iraq, and in a peaceful Palestine. The advance of freedom is the surest strategy to undermine the appeal of terror in the world. Where freedom takes hold, hatred gives way to hope. When freedom takes hold, men and women turn to the peaceful pursuit of a better life.

American values and American interests lead in the same direction: We stand for human liberty. The United States upholds these principles of security and freedom in many ways—with all the tools of diplomacy, law enforcement, intelligence, and finance.

We're working with a broad coalition of nations that understand the threat and our shared responsibility to meet it. The use of force has been—and remains—our last resort. Yet all can know, friend and foe alike, that our nation has a mission: We will answer threats to our security, and we will defend the peace.

Our mission continues. Al Qaeda is wounded, not destroyed. The scattered cells of the terrorist network still operate in many nations, and we know from

daily intelligence that they continue to plot against free people. The proliferation of deadly weapons remains a serious danger.

The enemies of freedom are not idle, and neither are we. Our government has taken unprecedented measures to defend the homeland. And we will continue to hunt down the enemy before he can strike.The war on terror is not over; yet it is not endless. We do not know the day of final victory, but we have seen the turning of the tide.

No act of the terrorists will change our purpose, or weaken our resolve, or alter their fate. Their cause is lost. Free nations will press on to victory.

Other nations in history have fought in foreign lands and remained to occupy andexploit. Americans, following a battle, want nothing more than to return home. And that is your direction tonight.

After service in the Afghan—and Iraqi theaters of war—after 100,000 miles, on the longest carrier deployment in recent history, you are homeward bound. Some of you will see new family members for the first time—150 babies were born while their fathers were on the Lincoln. Your families are proud of you, and your nation will welcome you.

We are mindful, as well, that some good men and women are not making the journey home. One of those who fell, Corporal Jason Mileo, spoke to his parents five days before his death. Jason's father said, "He called us from the center of Baghdad, not to brag, but to tell us he loved us. Our son was a soldier."

Every name, every life is a loss to our military, to our nation, and to the loved ones who grieve. There's no homecoming for these families. Yet we pray, in God's time, their reunion will come.Those we lost were last seen on duty. Their final act on this Earth was to fight a great evil and bring liberty to others.

All of you—all in this generation of our military—have taken up the highest calling of history. You're defending your country, and protecting the innocent from harm.

And wherever you go, you carry a message of hope—a message that is ancient and ever new. In the words of the prophet Isaiah, "To the captives, 'come out,'—and to those in darkness, 'be free.'"

Thank you for serving our country and our cause.

May God bless you all, and may God continue to bless America.

非常感谢大家！凯利将军、卡德上校、"林肯"号航母上的所有官兵、美国同胞们：

伊拉克境内的主要战斗已经结束，美国和美国的盟国在伊拉克战争中已经取得了胜利。

现在，我们的联军部队正在维护伊拉克国内的稳定，并帮助伊拉克人民重建家园。

这次战争我们是为自由事业以及世界和平而战的。我们的国家和联军为这次战争所取得的胜利而感到自豪，是你们——美国的军人们经过浴血奋斗才取得了今天的胜利。正是有了你们的勇气，有了你们为祖国、为自己的战友敢于直面危险的积极态度，才会有今天的胜利。正是由于你们，我们的国家才变得更加安全。正是由于你们，暴君才终于倒台，伊拉克终于获得了自由。

"自由伊拉克"行动集中了精确打击、行动快速和士兵们勇往直前等优势。这是敌人事先没有预料到的，世界各国以前也从来没有领略过。

我们的飞机从远距离的军事基地或是海上的军舰上起飞，我们的导弹从很远的海上向敌人发射，打击了一个又一个敌人的作战单位，摧毁了一个又一个敌方掩体。负责向巴格达推进的海军陆战队员和陆军士兵们，在长达350英里的敌方土地上快速穿插，而且他们还携带着相当多的重型武器，他

们的这一举动在历史上是少有的。你们向世人展示了美国武装部队出众的作战技巧和强大力量！

我们的国家感谢所有参与这一高尚事业的美国士兵及联军士兵们！感谢英国、澳大利亚和波兰的士兵们，他们与我们共同经历了这场战争的苦难。我们还要感谢欢迎我们的军队，参加解放自己国家的所有伊拉克公民！

今晚，我还要向拉姆斯菲尔德部长、弗兰克斯将军和所有身穿美国军装的军人们特别致敬：美国非常感激你们，你们干得非常棒！

我们的军队从历史上保留下来的作战传统，比如我们在诺曼底登陆战役、硫磺岛战役中表现出来的战斗精神，我们最终化敌为友的风格，在我们这一代人身上全部体现出来了。

伊拉克平民凝视我们军人的面孔时，他们看到的是力量、善意和慷慨。我看到美国军人时，我看到的是我们国家最优秀的国民，我为自己是你们的总司令而感到无比光荣。

随着一座座萨达姆雕像的倒塌，我们看到了一个新时代的到来。几百年的战争史历经演变，最终走到了今天的核时代。军事技术日益高度发达，军事手段所能够造成的伤亡规模也迅猛扩大。

在战胜纳粹德国和日本帝国的战争中，盟军部队摧毁了整座整座的城市，然而直到战争行将结束，发动战争的敌国领导人仍旧安然无恙。在那时，要想结束一个政权的统治，就必须给整个民族造成大规模的破坏。

而如今，我们已经具备了摧毁一个富于侵略性的危险政权的更为强大的能力。依靠新的战术和精确制导武器，我们可以在不会对平民造成较大规模伤害的情况下，实现我们的军事目标。

没有哪一样人类的发明可以避免战争所带来的悲剧，然而像今天这样，我们因为担心战争造成更多无辜平民伤亡而内心备感愧疚，也已经是一个了不起的进步了。

从庆祝战争胜利的伊拉克人的脸上，我们还看到了人类自由的永恒魅力。几十年的谎言和压迫并不能使伊拉克人民热爱压迫他们的暴君，他们也不希望再继续受自己同胞的压迫。

每种文化背景的人们都需要自由，就像他们都需要食物、水和空气一样。自由所能够到达的每一个地方，人类的喜悦之情所能够到达的每一个地方，暴君们都会感到恐惧。

我们在伊拉克还有许多艰苦的工作要做。我们正在恢复伊拉克国内一些仍然十分危险地区的正常社会秩序。我们正在继续寻找旧政权里的部分国家领导人，他们将被送上法庭接受审判。

我们已经开始在伊拉克搜寻被隐藏起来的生化武器，已经查明了几百处可疑地点，并将进一步对这些地点展开调查。

我们正在帮助伊拉克人民重建家园，过去的暴君只知道为自己建造一座又一座的宫殿，而没有为平民建造医院和学校。我们将与伊拉克的新领导人站在一起，帮助他们建立一个伊拉克人民民有、民治和民享的政府。

从独裁到民主将要花费一些时日，但为此而付出的每一项努力都是值得的。我们的联军将一直留在这里，直到我们应该做的工作完成。到那时，我们就会离开这里，留下一个自由的伊拉克。

伊拉克战争是自2001年9月11日开始的反恐战争中的一次胜利，反恐战争仍然会继续进行下去。那天上午十九名心怀邪念的人组成了一支突击队，向美国及其文明世界展示了他们的恐怖野心。其中一名恐怖分子说，他们希望"9·11"事件只是美国终结的开始。

恐怖分子和他们的盟友认为，只要把我们的城市变成他们的杀人战场，他们就可以摧毁整个美利坚民族的意志和决心，迫使我们从世界舞台上撤出。但是他们失败了。

在阿富汗战争中，我们摧毁了塔利班政权，同时杀死了大量恐怖分子，还摧毁了他们用来训练恐怖分子的营地。战争结束后，我们继续帮助阿富汗人铺设道路，重建医院和学校，为他们的孩子提供教育条件。

然而，我们面前仍然有许多危险任务必须去完成。正如我所说的，第82空降师派遣的特种作战部队仍然在对恐怖分子进行追捕，他们将把那些敢于破坏阿富汗自由政府的危险分子捉拿归案。美国包括美国的盟国必将完成我们已经开始的事业。

从巴基斯坦到菲律宾，再到非洲之角，我们正在四处搜索"基地"组织杀手。一年半之前，我曾经保证，在我们坚持不懈地努力之下，恐怖分子逃脱不了我们的法律制裁。到今晚为止，将近一半的"基地"组织高级特工已经落网或被击毙。

解放伊拉克是反恐斗争的关键一步。我们已根除了"基地"组织的同盟，同时切断了恐怖分子的资金来源。我们可以十分肯定地说：恐怖主义网络不会从伊拉克政权获得大规模杀伤性武器，因为该政权已不复存在。

这一年半的时间改变了世界。我们的行动是有针对性的，是深思熟虑的，是对我们所受到的攻击做出的恰如其分的反应。我们不会忘记"9·11"事件中无辜死去的人们，不会忘记那最后的电话，不会忘记恐怖分子对孩子们的残酷杀戮，我们也不会忘记废墟中所进行的遗体搜寻工作。恐怖主义分子以这种攻击向我国进行了宣战，而这场战争也是他们罪有应得。

我们的反恐战争正在按照我已向大家讲解清楚的反恐战争的原则向前进行着。任何策划或参与对美国人民实施恐怖袭击的人，都将成为我们国家的敌人，也将成为美国正义事业的打击目标。

任何支持、保护或包庇恐怖分子的个人、组织和政府，他们在残杀无辜生命的活动中与恐怖分子串通一气，也应该被视为犯有恐怖活动罪。任何与恐怖组织有关联的不法政府，任何寻求拥有或已经拥有大规模杀伤性武器的国家，对于文明世界来说都是非常严重的威胁，都将受到打击。

世界上的所有人，包括阿拉伯世界为自由而战，为自由而牺牲的人们在内，都可以在美国找到忠实的朋友。承担对自由的义务是美国的传统，我们建国之初就宣布了这一点。后来，富兰克林·罗斯福的"四项自由"对此进行了进一步证实，"杜鲁门"主义进行了确认，罗纳德·里根对邪恶帝国的挑战声明更进一步进行了强调。

我们致力于阿富汗、伊拉克的自由事业，并致力于建设一个和平的巴勒斯坦。自由的进步是完全肯定的事情，为了追求这一进步，我们就必须摧毁世界上所有胆敢采取恐怖行动的组织。自由所到之处，仇恨无不让道。只要有了自由，人类就会以和平方式寻求更加美好的生活。

美国人的价值和美国人的利益也都是朝着这个方向迈进的。我们是为了人类的解放而斗争。美国以各种方式来保证这些安全与自由的原则得到实施，包括外交、法律、情报和经济等有效手段。

我们一直都与那些能够意识到威胁和担负共同责任的国家一道建立起广泛的联盟，一起在努力着面对目前的这种局势。动用武力将是我们最后的选择。然而无论是我们的朋友，还是我们的敌人，大家都知道我们的国家具有这样一个使命：我们要面对威胁，对我们的安全负责，而且我们将捍卫和平。

我们的使命还将继续。"基地"组织已经遭到了破坏，但是还没有被彻底消灭。分散在世界各地的恐怖网络仍然在许多国家运行着。从我们日常搜集到的情报当中，我们知道它们还在制定针对自由人民的阴谋、计划。致命武器的扩散仍然是一个重大危险。

自由的敌人不是白痴，我们也不是。我们的政府已经采取了前所未有的措施保卫本土，而且我们还将继续跟踪追击，在敌人发起进攻之前将其消灭。反恐战争还没有结束，但是它并不是无止境的。我们不知道最终胜利的时日，但是我们已经看到了这场决战的转折点。

恐怖分子的任何行动都不会改变我们的目的，或者削弱我们坚强的意志，或者改变他们的命运。他们的道路是一条失败的道路，自由国家将获得胜利。

在历史上，有许多国家在他国的土地上曾经战斗过，并占领了那里，对

那些国家进行剥削。而美国在战争结束之后，并不希望得到什么，只是返回自己的国家。这就是今夜"林肯"号航母上美国军人的目标。

在阿富汗和伊拉克战区服役之后，在近代史上航母最远程 10 万英里部署之后，你们现在正在回归家园的途中。你们当中的一些人将第一次见到自己家庭的新成员，在"林肯"号航母为期九个月的海外部署期间，有 150 名婴儿在他们的父亲在这艘航母上服役时诞生。你们的家庭为你们感到自豪，你们的祖国欢迎你们归来。

我们永远都不能忘记，我们的一些人不能做这次回乡之旅。海军下士詹森·梅雷奥就是其中之一，他在牺牲的前五天曾经与家人通过电话。詹森的父亲说："他从巴格达市中心给我们打来电话，并未自夸，而是告诉我们他爱我们。我们的儿子是一名真正的士兵。"

每一个名字、每一个生命对于我们的军队、对于我们的国家、对于那些爱他们并为他们的牺牲而悲痛的人来说都是巨大的损失。对于这些家庭意味着，亲人再也不能回归。因此，我们祈求上帝，让他们与家人心灵团聚的时刻即将到来。那些逝去的人们都是牺牲在他们的岗位上。他们在这个星球上最后的壮举是与一个巨大的恶魔作战，是为了他人的自由而战。

你们之中所有的人，我们军队之中这一代所有的人，响应了最崇高历史使命的呼唤。你们在捍卫你们的国家，使那些无辜的人免受伤害。

无论你们走到哪里，你们都发出了希望的信息——这是一个古老而又常新的信息。先知以赛亚说："那些被迷惑的人，清醒过来吧！那些处于黑暗的人，寻求自由吧！"

谢谢你们为我们的国家和我们的事业所做的一切！

愿上帝保佑你们！愿上帝继续保佑美国！

第三节 精彩语录

No device of man can remove the tragedy from war.

没有哪一样人类的发明可以避免战争所带来的悲剧。

Men and women in every culture need liberty like they need food and water and air. Everywhere that freedom arrives, humanity rejoices; and everywhere that freedom stirs, let tyrants fear.

每种文化背景的人们都需要自由，就像他们都需要食物、水和空气一样。自由所能够到达的每一个地方，人类的喜悦之情所能够到达的每一个地方，暴君们都会感到恐惧。

Where freedom takes hold, hatred gives way to hope. When freedom takes hold, men and women turn to the peaceful pursuit of a better life.

自由所到之处，仇恨无不让道。只要有了自由，人类就会以和平方式寻求更加美好的生活。

And wherever you go, you carry a message of hope—a message that is ancient and ever new. In the words of the prophet Isaiah, "To the captives, 'come out,' —and to those in darkness, 'be free.' "

无论你们走到哪里，你们都发出了希望的信息——这是一个古老而又常新的信息。先知以赛亚说："那些被迷惑的人，清醒过来吧！那些处于黑暗的人，寻求自由吧！"

第九章
宣布连任

第一节 背景介绍

　　2004 年的美国总统大选，是美国历史上竞争最激烈的一次总统选举，得到了全球范围内前所未有的关注。它是自"9·11"后的第一次总统大选，更是美国有史以来最昂贵的选举。大选中的两党差异，以及大选结果对美国和世界未来局势的影响，超过近代所有美国大选而被称为是"最重要的选举"。

　　2004 年的美国总统大选布什成功连任。布什及其竞选班子获得了选举的胜利，这种胜利从本质上说是传播的胜利。本来布什似乎具备了败选的所有因素：国内经济持续走低，四年来失业人数增加了 300 万，财政从盈余变成了亏空；拉登仍逍遥法外；伊拉克乱局愈演愈烈，绑架和恐怖袭击依然风行；虐囚丑闻沸沸扬扬；布什的行事风格备受争议，他本人的越战服役记录充满疑点……即使是选举后，民调显示，仍然有 56% 的美国人认为国家是在错误的方向上，51% 的人认为根本不应该去伊拉克打仗，52% 的人不赞成布什的工作表现。然而，由于竞选的实质是竞选双方在传播领域的竞争，因此选战就是传播战、新闻战。在这场争斗中，很大程度上比拼的是竞选者及其团队对传播语境的分析把握，对传播策略的选择运用，以及对自身形象的有力塑造和对对手形象的成功破坏。

尽管美国总统大选具有多方面的性质，但不可否认，美国的总统大选的根本性质之一是一项庞大复杂的传播活动。选战的传播战性质贯穿于这一活动的整个过程，竞选双方的竞争很大程度上是传播方面的竞争，并且竞选的成功与否也取决于传播与劝服的成功与否。参与竞选的任何一方在竞选过程中都需要做大量的传播工作，如通过报纸、电视、广播、互联网进行大规模的宣传；就竞选策略、方针及施政纲领进行广泛的民意测验、调查和模拟投票；印制各种宣传品和纪念品，寄送邮件……选民们决定自己的投票意向，就是根据参选者针对他们关心的问题所传播的信息来做出的。

决定一场选举胜利与否的关键在于传播。除此之外，根本因素往往还要看候选人能否敏锐地意识到国民的情绪，能否尽可能平和而亲切地触摸到选民的内心感受，让他们感到候选人是值得信赖的，至少相对于其对手而言。在此前提下候选人及其选举团队制定相应的传播方案，选择有效的传播策略，运用各种传播手段进行有针对性的传播，劝服选民将选票投给自己，才能战胜对手获得胜利。

任何一次美国总统竞选都是在当时特定的政治、经济、社会、文化、心理、宗教价值观等条件下进行的，所有这些因素构成了选举传播的传播语境。在不同的历史时期，不同的问题，不同的因素凸现出来，成为决定如何传播和传播如何成功的关键因素。在 2004 年美国总统选举中，最重要的语境因素是国家安全问题、国民保守心态和宗教价值观。

布什在第一个任期内，美国的国家安全环境发生了"历史性的变化"。2001 年的"9·11"恐怖袭击，打破了长期以来美国民众自恃国力强大而产生的安全感，他们认识到恐怖威胁从此将成为生活的一部分。美联社在选举前进行的民意调查显示，事隔三年以后，仍有大约 70% 的选民担心美国本土会再次遭到袭击。由此可以看出，对普通美国人来说，国土安全和反恐仍是第一关切，安全高于一切。谁能给美国带来安全，就能成为本次选举的赢家。

美联社在选举前进行的民意调查显示，多数人都认为美国比几年前更安全，其中大部分认为布什能更好地保护美国。

大选投票前四天的 10 月 29 日，还出现了戏剧性的一幕。卡塔尔半岛电视台播放了一段录像带，"基地"组织一号头目本·拉登在录像中对美国人发表演说。他在录像中首次承认"9·11"袭击由其一手导演，还谈及他在 2001 年对美国发动"9·11"袭击的原因和结果。美国维吉尼亚大学政治研究中心主任拉里·萨博托说："这肯定有利于布什，但我不知道力度会有多大。"

布什在种种不利条件下仍能连任成功，很大程度上得益于这次大选是在这种非常独特的背景下进行的。美国选民的焦虑心态和危机意识，希望在纷乱中求稳定，在恐惧中求安全的心理，以及布什在竞选中对这种心理的巧妙利用，最终使超过 51% 的选民将选票投给了布什。

美国国民心态总体上走向保守。尤其是"9·11"事件后，保守主义在社会和政治议题上占据了优势地位，新保守主义一度主宰了布什政府的外交政策。《爱国者法案》在 2001 年 10 月 24 日得以通过表明，美国社会中对个人自由的推崇正让位于对安全的关注。

本次大选中最能体现国民保守心态对大选结果影响的是，选举中以同性恋婚姻为议题的辩论。在同性恋是否具有合法婚姻权的问题上，美国的保守主义与自由主义的争论由来已久。保守主义的观点站在维护宗教信仰和传统家庭价值的基础上，明确反对同性婚姻；而自由主义者站在人权与个人意志应得到尊重的立场上，不反对同性婚姻。布什总统与民主党候选人克里恰恰是美国保守主义与自由主义两大思潮的代表性人物。

在选举时，共和党利用同性恋婚姻作为大选日公决议题，动员了属于"圣经地带"但传统投票率很低的俄亥俄州南部乡村的大量保守选民，以不到 14 万票之差险胜过去四年美国制造业工作流失最严重的关键一州。另外，美国有十一个州把同性恋婚姻问题和大选捆绑公投。大选日这十一个州以绝对多数通过禁止同性恋婚姻。而相对的，大选年里克里的家乡马萨诸塞州成为同性恋婚姻合法化的先驱。这对克里的选情也有一定影响。所以可以说，美国社会的日趋保守化为布什赢得本次大选创造了良好的客观环境。《纽约时报》大牌专栏作家弗里德曼总结，这次美国总统大选，与其说是奖惩四年政绩的选举，不如说是按照宗教信仰和道德价值的政治站队。

宗教在此次大选中也发挥了不可估量的作用，甚至影响到了选情。"9·11"以后，伊斯兰原教旨主义进一步激发了基督教原教旨主义，右派的宗教团体在美国的影响进一步扩大，并在大选中表现出来成为影响选情的因素之一。NBC的一项民意调查，选民投票时考虑的最重要因素是什么，在国家安全（恐怖主义）、经济、伊战、道德价值观四项选择中，得票最多的是"道德价值观"。远远超过关心战争、反恐怖甚至经济和工作问题的选民数量。所谓道德价值观，在选民心中也就是"宗教价值观"。在把"道德价值观"作为投票最重要因素的人群中70%的人选了布什。

美国四年一度的总统大选，与其说是一场政治抉择，不如说是一场政治游戏。毫无疑问，美国的这次总统大选是历史上竞争最激烈的一次总统选举。双方旗鼓相当，势均力敌，选战十分激烈。民主党誓言要夺回白宫宝座，为报四年前因佛罗里达州500多票之差使本党候选人与白宫失之交臂的一箭之仇；而共和党候选人布什更誓死要拼尽全力力保连任，摆脱布什家族只能干一届的历史宿命。选战空前激烈，最终，布什击败民主党参选人约翰·克里，以至少286张选举人票的绝对优势获胜当选连任。这在美国是史无前例的。

第二节 布什于 2004 年竞选获胜后的演讲

Thank you all. Thank you all for coming.

We had a long night—and a great night. The voters turned out in record numbers and delivered an historic victory.

Earlier today, Senator Kerry called with his congratulations. We had a really good phone call. He was very gracious. Senator Kerry waged a spirited campaign, and he and his supporters can be proud of their efforts. Laura and I wish Senator Kerry and Teresa and their whole family all our best wishes.

America has spoken, and I'm humbled by the trust and the confidence of my fellow citizens. With that trust comes a duty to serve all Americans, and I will do my best to fulfill that duty every day as your president.

There are many people to thank, and my family comes first. Laura is the love of my life. I'm glad you love her, too.

I want to thank our daughters, who joined their dad for his last campaign. I appreciate the hard work of my sister and my brothers. I especially want to thank my parents for their loving support.

I'm grateful to the vice president and Lynne and their daughters, who have worked so hard and been such a vital part of our team.The vice president serves America with wisdom and honor, and I'm proud to serve beside him.

I want to thank my superb campaign team. I want to thank you all for your hard work. I was impressed every day by how hard and how skillful our team was.

I want to thank Chairman Mark Racicot and—the campaign manager Ken Mehlman—the architect, Karl Rove. I want to thank Ed Gillespie for leading our party so well.

I want to thank the thousands of our supporters across our country. I want to thank you for your hugs on the rope lines. I want to thank you for your prayers on the rope lines. I want to thank you for your kind words on the rope lines. I want to thank you for everything you did to make the calls and to put up the signs, to talk to your neighbors, and to get out the vote.

And because you did the incredible work, we are celebrating today.

There's an old saying, "Do not pray for tasks equal to your powers, pray for powers equal to your tasks." In four historic years, America has been given great tasks and faced them with strength and courage. Our people have restored the vigor of this economy and shown resolve and patience in a new kind of war. Our military has brought justice to the enemy and honor to America. Our nation—our nation has defended itself and served the freedom of all mankind. I'm proud to lead such an amazing country, and I am proud to lead it forward.

Because we have done the hard work, we are entering a season of hope. We will continue our economic progress. We will reform our outdated tax code. We will strengthen the Social Security for the next generation. We will make public schools all they can be, and we will uphold our deepest values of family

and faith.

We will help the emerging democracies of Iraq and Afghanistan—so they can—so they can grow in strength and defend their freedom, and then our servicemen and –women will come home with the honor they have earned.

With good allies at our side, we will fight this war on terror with every resource of our national power so our children can live in freedom and in peace.

Reaching these goals will require the broad support of Americans, so today I want to speak to every person who voted for my opponent. To make this nation stronger and better, I will need your support and I will work to earn it. I will do all I can do to deserve your trust.

A new term is a new opportunity to reach out to the whole nation. We have one country, one Constitution, and one future that binds us. And when we come together and work together, there is no limit to the greatness of America.

Let me close with a word to the people of the state of Texas. We have known each other the longest, and you started me on this journey. On the open plains of Texas, I first learned the character of our country; sturdy and honest, and as hopeful as the break of day. I will always be grateful to the good people of my state. And whatever the road that lies ahead, that road will take me home.

A campaign has ended, and the United States of America goes forward with confidence and faith. I see a great day coming for our country, and I am eager for the work ahead.

God bless you. And may God bless America.

谢谢大家，谢谢你们的到来。

我们有一个漫长和伟大的夜晚。此次选民的投票率创下了历史新高，带来了历史性的胜利。

今天早些时候，克里参议员打电话祝贺我竞选成功。我们在电话中谈得很好，他非常亲切。克里参议员发起了猛烈的竞选攻势，他和他的支持者可以为此感到自豪。劳拉和我向克里、特里萨以及他们全家表示最衷心的祝愿。

美国做出了选择。对于同胞们的信任，我很感激。这种信任意味着我将承担为所有美国公民服务的义务。作为你们的总统，我每天都将竭尽全力。

我需要感谢许多人，首先是我的家人。劳拉是我一生的挚爱，我对你们也爱她感到高兴。

我还要感谢在竞选后期加入竞选团的女儿，感谢兄弟姐妹们付出的努力，特别感谢严父慈母的支持。

我感谢副总统、莱尼和他们的女儿。他们付出了努力，是竞选团的重要成员。副总统聪明睿智、正直高贵，我为跟他共事感到自豪。

我感谢优秀的竞选团，感谢你们所有人付出的努力。你们的勤奋和智慧每天都给我留下了深刻的印象。

我感谢前蒙大拿州州长马克·拉西科特，竞选总部主管肯·梅尔曼，总统顾问卡尔·罗孚。我感谢格莱斯比将我们的政党领导得如此之好。

我感谢全国上下成千上万名支持者，感谢你们在竞选集会上的拥抱、祈祷和亲切言语，感谢你们想方设法打出标语，呼吁邻居前去投票。

正是由于你们付出了惊人的努力，我们今天才能庆祝胜利。

俗话说，不要祈求能力所能胜任的任务，要祈求能胜任任务的能力。在四年历史性时期，美国被赋予了伟大的任务，并以实力和勇气面对这些任务。我国人民使经济活力复苏，并在新型战争中显示出决心和耐心。我军已经将敌人绳之以法，给美国带来了荣誉。我国保卫了自己，维护了全人类的自由。领导这样出色的国家，我感到自豪；带领这个国家前进，我感到自豪。

我们已经完成了艰难的任务，进入了充满希望的时期。我们将继续推动经济增长，改革落后的税法，为下一代加强社会保障。我们将尽量改善公立

学校，维护在家庭和信仰方面的核心价值观。

我们将帮助伊拉克和阿富汗建立民主制度，以便他们增强实力和维护自由。然后，我军官兵将带着他们获得的荣誉回国。

在优秀盟国的支持下，我们将动用美国的一切力量打赢这场反恐战争，确保我们孩子们的自由与和平。

要实现这些目标，美国公民的广泛支持是必不可缺的。因此，今天我要对支持对手的所有人说，为了让美国变得更强大更美好，我需要你们的支持，我也将努力获得你们的支持，并将竭尽所能担当得起你们的支持。

新一届任期使我有机会影响整个国家。正是同一个国家、同一部宪法和同一个未来把我们联系到了一起。当我们一起努力的时候，美国的前途无可限量。

作为结束语，请允许我向得克萨斯州人民讲几句话。我们彼此认识的时间最长，你们是我旅程的起点。在得州广阔无垠的平原上，我初次学到了美国的特点：强壮有力、真诚坦率，充满了黎明般的希望。我将永远感谢这个州优秀的人民。不管前方的路怎么样，这条路都将带我回家。

选举已经结束，美利坚合众国将充满自信地前进。我看到我们的国家正迎来伟大的日子，很期待下一周的开始。

愿上帝保佑你们，愿上帝保佑美国！

第三节 精彩语录

There's an old saying, "Do not pray for tasks equal to your powers, pray for powers equal to your tasks."

俗话说，不要祈求能力所能胜任的任务，要祈求能胜任任务的能力。

Because we have done the hard work, we are entering a season of hope. We will continue our economic progress. We will reform our outdated tax code. We will strengthen the Social Security for the next generation. We will make public schools all they can be, and we will uphold our deepest values of family and faith.

我们已经完成了艰难的任务，进入了充满希望的时期。我们将继续推动经济增长，改革落后的税法，为下一代加强社会保障。我们将尽量改善公立学校，维护在家庭和信仰方面的核心价值观。

A new term is a new opportunity to reach out to the whole nation. We have one country, one Constitution, and one future that binds us. And when we come

together and work together, there is no limit to the greatness of America.

新一届任期使我有机会影响整个国家。正是同一个国家、同一部宪法和同一个未来把我们联系到了一起。当我们一起努力的时候，美国的前途无可限量。

We have known each other the longest, and you started me on this journey. On the open plains of Texas, I first learned the character of our country; sturdy and honest, and as hopeful as the break of day. I will always be grateful to the good people of my state. And whatever the road that lies ahead, that road will take me home.

我们彼此认识的时间最长，你们是我旅程的起点。在得州广阔无垠的平原上，我初次学到了美国的特点：强壮有力、真诚坦率，充满了黎明般的希望。我将永远感谢这个州优秀的人民。不管前方的路怎么样，这条路都将带我回家。

第十章

学会感恩

第一节 背景介绍

感恩节的由来要一直追溯到美国历史的发端。感恩节由美国人民独创，是美国和加拿大共有的节日，原意是为了感谢上天赐予的好收成，感谢印第安人的帮助。1620 年，著名的"五月花"号船满载不堪忍受英国国内宗教迫害的 102 名清教徒到达美洲，在那里他们遇到了难以想象的困难，在经历了 1620 年和 1621 年之交饥寒交迫的冬天，他们当中只有 50 几名移民活了下来。心地善良的印第安人给幸存的移民送来了生活必需品，还特地派人教他们狩猎、捕鱼和种植玉米、南瓜。在印第安人的帮助下，移民们终于获得了丰收。在欢庆丰收的日子，移民们按照传统宗教习俗规定了感谢上帝的日子，并决定为了感谢印第安人的真诚帮助，邀请他们一同庆祝节日。

在第一个感恩节，印第安人和移民们欢聚一堂，他们在黎明时鸣放礼炮，列队走进一间用作教堂的屋子，虔诚地向上帝表达谢意，然后点起篝火举行盛大宴会。第二天和第三天又举行了摔跤、赛跑、唱歌、跳舞等活动。第一个感恩节非常成功，其中许多庆祝方式流传了三百多年，一直保留到今天。

每逢感恩节这一天，美国举国上下热闹非凡，人们按照习俗前往教堂做感恩祈祷，城乡市镇到处都有化装游行、戏剧表演或体育比赛等。孩子们还模仿当年印第安人的模样画上脸谱或戴上面具到街上唱歌、吹喇叭。分开了一年的亲人们也从天南海北归来，一家人团团圆圆品尝美味的感恩节火鸡。同时，好客的美国人还会在这一天邀请好友、单身汉或远离家乡的人共度佳节。从18世纪起，美国开始出现在感恩节给贫穷人家送一篮子食物的风俗。当时有一群年轻妇女想在一年中选一天专门做善事，认为选定感恩节是最恰当不过的。所以感恩节一到，她们就装上满满一篮食物亲自送到穷人家。不久就有许多人学着她们的样子做起来。不管遇到谁，他们都会说："THANK YOU！"

最初感恩节没有固定日期，由各州临时决定，直到美国独立后，感恩节才成为全国性的节日。1863年，林肯总统把感恩节定为法定假日。1941年，美国国会通过一项法令，把感恩节定在每年十一月的第四个星期四。加拿大和美国的感恩节不在同一天，加拿大议会将感恩节列为法定假日稍晚于美国。但加拿大的第一个感恩节要比美国早四十年，加拿大感恩节的庆祝活动是在十月的第二个星期一。与美国人缅怀清教徒先辈定居新大陆的传统不同，加拿大人主要感谢上天给予的成功的收获。加拿大的感恩节早于美国的感恩节是因为加拿大更靠近北部，加拿大的收获季节相对于美国早一些。

加拿大的感恩节通常被认为受三个传统习惯的影响。

其一是来自欧洲传统的影响。从大约两千年以前最早的一次收获开始，人们就已经庆祝丰收，感谢富饶的大自然给予他们的恩施和好运。当欧洲人来到加拿大后，也将这一传统带入加拿大，并对后来加拿大的感恩节产生影响。

其二是英国探险家庆祝生存的影响。在清教徒登陆美国马萨诸塞州的前四十年，加拿大就举行了第一个正式的感恩节。1578年，一位英国探险家马丁·法贝瑟试图发现一个连接东方的通道，但是他没有成功。于是他在现今的加拿大纽芬兰省建立了定居点，并举行了一个庆祝生存和收获的宴餐。其

他后来的移居者继续这种"感恩"仪式。此次的庆祝活动被认为是加拿大的第一个感恩节。

其三的影响来自于后来的美国。1621年的秋天，远涉重洋来到美洲新大陆的英国移民，为了感谢上帝赐予的丰收，举行了三天的狂欢活动。从此，这一习俗沿续下来，并逐渐风行各地。在美国革命其间，美国一批忠于英皇室的保皇党迁移到加拿大，并将美国感恩节的习俗和方式带到了加拿大。1750年庆祝丰收的活动被来自美国南部的移居者带到了新斯科舍，同时，法国移居者到达并且举行"感恩"宴餐。这些庆祝活动均对加拿大的感恩节产生了深远的影响。

1879年加拿大议会宣称11月6日是感恩节和全国性的假日。在随后的年代，感恩节的日期多次改变。直到1957年1月31日，加拿大议会宣布每年十月的第二个星期一为感恩节，在这一天感谢万能的上帝保佑加拿大并给予丰富的收获。

在美国，感恩节还有一项特殊的习俗，就是总统放生火鸡仪式。每年一度的总统放生火鸡仪式始于1947年杜鲁门总统当政时期，但实际上这个传统仪式可以追溯到美国内战林肯总统当政的时期。1863年的一天，林肯的儿子泰德突然闯入内阁会议，请求赦免一只名叫杰克的宠物火鸡，因为这只被送进白宫的火鸡，即将成为人们的圣诞节大餐。布什在白宫玫瑰花园举行的感恩节放生仪式上，曾特赦了一只名叫"飞鸟"的火鸡。

第二节 布什于 2004 年感恩节的演讲

Good morning. As Americans gather to celebrate this week, we show our gratitude for the many blessings in our lives. We are grateful for our friends and families who fill our lives with purpose and love. We're grateful for our beautiful country, and for the prosperity we enjoy. We're grateful for the chance to live, work and worship in freedom. And in this Thanksgiving week, we offer thanks and praise to the provider of all these gifts, Almighty God. We also recognize our duty to share our blessings with the least among us. Throughout the holiday season, schools, churches, synagogues and other generous organizations gather food and clothing for their neighbors in need. Many young people give part of their holiday to volunteer at homeless shelters or food pantries. On Thanksgiving, and on every day of the year, America is a more hopeful nation because of the volunteers who serve the weak and the vulnerable.

The Thanksgiving tradition of compassion and humility dates back to the earliest days of our society. And through the years, our deepest gratitude has often been inspired by the most difficult times. Almost four centuries ago, the pilgrims set aside time to thank God after suffering through a bitter winter.

George Washington held Thanksgiving during a trying stay at Valley Forge. And President Lincoln revived the Thanksgiving tradition in the midst of a civil war.

The past year has brought many challenges to our nation, and Americans have met every one with energy, optimism and faith. After lifting our economy from a recession, manufacturers and entrepreneurs are creating jobs again. Volunteers from across the country came together to help hurricane victims rebuild. And when the children of Beslan, Russia suffered a brutal terrorist attack, the world saw America's generous heart in an outpouring of compassion and relief.

The greatest challenges of our time have come to the men and women who protect our nation. We're fortunate to have dedicated firefighters and police officers to keep our streets safe. We're grateful for the homeland security and intelligence personnel who spend long hours on faithful watch. And we give thanks to the men and women of our military who are serving with courage and skill, and making our entire nation proud.

Like generations before them, today's armed forces have liberated captive peoples and shown compassion for the suffering and delivered hope to the oppressed. In the past year, they have fought the terrorists abroad so that we do not have to face those enemies here at home. They've captured a brutal dictator, aided last month's historic election in Afghanistan, and help set Iraq on the path to democracy.

Our progress in the war on terror has made our country safer, yet it has also brought new burdens to our military families. Many servicemen and women have endured long deployments and painful separations from home. Families have faced the challenge of raising children while praying for a loved one's safe return. America is grateful to all our military families, and the families mourning a terrible loss this Thanksgiving can know that America will honor their sacrifices forever.

As Commander-in-Chief, I've been honored to thank our troops at bases around the world, and I've been inspired by the efforts of private citizens to express their own gratitude. This month, I met Shauna Fleming, a 15-year-old from California who coordinated the mailing of a million thank you letters to military personnel. In October, I met Ken Porwoll, a World War II veteran who has devoted years of his retirement to volunteering at a VA medical center in Minneapolis. And we've seen the generosity of so many organizations, like Give2theTroops, a group started in a basement by a mother and son that has sent thousands of care packages to troops in the field.

Thanksgiving reminds us that America's true strength is the compassion and decency of our people. I thank all those who volunteer this season, and Laura and I wish every American a happy and safe Thanksgiving weekend.

Thank you for listening.

早上好。这周美国人民聚集在一起，感谢生活带给我们的诸多祝福，感谢带给我们希望和爱的家人和朋友，感谢我们美丽的祖国，感谢我们享有的繁荣和成功。我们也感谢这些自由生活、自由工作和自由信仰的机会。在这感恩节到来之际，我们要感谢和颂扬赐予我们这一切的全能的上帝。我们也得承认我们有分享我们的幸福的责任。整个节日期间，学校、教堂、犹太教会堂和其他慷慨的机构收集食物和衣服来帮助附近有需要的朋友。许多年轻人将一部分假期时间用于在收容所或食品储藏室中当志愿者。在感恩节期间，乃至在这一年的每一天，美国因这些服务弱势群体的志愿者，将越发成为一个充满希望的国度。

充满同情和谦逊的感恩节传统可以追溯到很久以前的历史。这些年来，我们最真切的感恩往往出自我们最困难的时候。大约四百年前，先辈们在度过一个严酷的冬天之后举行了丰收庆典，感谢上帝的恩赐。乔治·华盛顿总统在艰难度日的福吉谷宣布了第一个举国欢庆的感恩节。林肯总统在内战期

间恢复了这个传统节日。

在过去一年里，美国面对了许许多多的挑战，美国人民在应对每一次挑战时都充满活力、乐观和信心。经济衰退减缓之后，制造商和企业家再次创造就业的机会。来自全国各地的志愿者联合起来帮助遭受飓风的灾民重建家园。当比兰事件发生，俄罗斯遭受残酷的恐怖袭击时，世界从美国人民流露的同情和给予的救济中看到了我们的慷慨。

那些保护祖国安全的人们面临了最大的挑战。在今年的感恩节，我们向恪尽职守维护国土安全的消防队员和警务人员表示感谢。我们向不辞辛劳、坚守岗位的国土安全人员和情报人员表示感谢。我们向为保护我们的国家和促进自由事业正在世界各地服务的美国武装部队人员表示感谢。这些英勇无畏的军人让我们整个国家感到自豪。

和前几代军人一样，今天的军队解放了被俘虏的人民，同情遭受苦难的人们，并将希望带给备受压迫的人。在过去的一年中，他们纷纷转战国外的恐怖分子，让我们不必在祖国的土地上面对敌人。他们已经抓获了一名恐怖组织的领导者，于上月帮助阿富汗举行了一次具有历史性的选举，并在建立民主的道路上帮助了伊拉克一把。

反恐战争的进展使我们的国家更加安全，但它也给我们的军人家庭带来更重的负担。许多军人都要忍受长时间的军事部署和与家人分离的痛苦。军人家属一方面要抚养孩子，另一方面又要祈祷亲人的平安返乡。美国感谢我们所有的军人家属，为每一个失去亲人的家庭默哀，美国人民将永远尊敬他们的牺牲。

作为总指挥，我很荣幸地在此感谢我们驻扎在世界各地基地的军队，我深有所感，所有的普通公民都通过自己的努力来表达各自的感激之情。这个月我会见了绍纳·弗莱明，一个来自加州的 15 岁的少年，他组织写了一百万封感谢信给我们的军事人员。十月，我会见了肯·鲍沃尔，一个二战老兵，退休后一直在维吉尼亚州明尼阿波利斯的医疗中心当志愿者。我们还可以看到许多爱心机构，比如已经看到了这么多的组织，如 Give2theTroops，一个在地下室开始，由一个母亲和一个儿子将数以千计的护具送到前线而形成的组织。

感恩节提醒我们，美国真正的力量是来自我们的同情和尊重。我感谢所有志愿者在这个季节的所有努力，劳拉和我祝愿每一个美国人都能度过一个平安快乐的感恩节周末。

感谢你们的倾听。

第三节 精彩语录

We are grateful for our friends and families who fill our lives with purpose and love. We're grateful for our beautiful country, and for the prosperity we enjoy. We're grateful for the chance to live, work and worship in freedom. And in this Thanksgiving week, we offer thanks and praise to the provider of all these gifts, Almighty God.

感谢带给我们希望和爱的家人和朋友，感谢我们美丽的祖国，感谢我们享有的繁荣和成功。我们也感谢这些自由生活、自由工作和自由信仰的机会。在这感恩节到来之际，我们要感谢和颂扬赐予我们这一切的全能的上帝。

On Thanksgiving, and on every day of the year, America is a more hopeful nation because of the volunteers who serve the weak and the vulnerable.

在感恩节期间，乃至在这一年的每一天，美国因这些服务弱势群体的志愿者，将越发成为一个充满希望的国度。

Thanksgiving reminds us that America's true strength is the compassion and decency of our people.

感恩节提醒我们，美国真正的力量是来自我们的同情和正直。

第十一章

将自由带到全世界

第一节 背景介绍

　　在 2004 年大选中成功连任的美国候任总统布什，于 2005 年 1 月 20 日中午 12 点在美国国会大厦西侧室外正式宣誓就任美国总统。这是他的第二任期。出席就职典礼的除了布什的家族成员，还有美国前总统克林顿、内阁成员、美国国会参众两院议员、最高法院大法官等来宾。在第一夫人劳拉和两个女儿的陪伴下，布什站在最高法院首席法官伦奎斯特面前，庄严地举起右手，模仿美国开国元勋华盛顿的做法，把左手按在一本《圣经》上，面对宪法宣读誓词："我承诺将忠诚地履行美国总统的职务，竭尽所能保护、遵守和捍卫美国宪法。"当布什说完美国总统宣誓就职的最后一句话："愿上帝帮助我。"宣誓就职仪式随着"主佑美国"的乐曲结束。之后，仪仗队鸣放 21 响礼炮，美国陆军铜管乐队演奏前奏曲《鼓号齐鸣》，美国海军陆战队乐队演奏《向统帅致敬》。

　　随后在一片欢呼喝彩声中，布什开始发表他第二任期的就职演说。布什就职演说的主题，除了阐述他在未来四年的治国方略和奋斗目标，还宣扬了自由，呼吁，团结，期待和平。在内政问题上，他谈到要对美国的社会保障、医疗保险和税收制度进行改革。在国外，布什鼓吹传播美国的民主自由。由于布什将于 2 月 2 日到国会发表国情咨文演讲，因此，他的就职演讲只持续了 17 分钟。当天，美国首都华盛顿刚刚迎来了一场大雪，国会山前银装素裹，身为这场盛大庆典的主角，布什春风得意，踌躇满志地迎来了自己的第二个任期。雪花纷飞的华盛顿，大约 25 万人齐集总统就职仪式的国会山前。就在布什欢庆二度入主白宫的胜利之际，美国国内出现了不少对他第一个任期的批评之声。有人指出，布什在四年前首次入主白宫时许下的那些诺言，许多都成为了空话。

当时，布什做出的一个最受关注的承诺就是将正视大规模杀伤性武器，使新世纪不会有新的恐怖主义。据说，布什的父亲美国前总统老布什给儿子四年前就职演说打的分数是"A"。在随后的四年任期内，布什打着"反恐"的旗号，牺牲数以千计的美国士兵的生命，花掉数百亿美元，先后发动了阿富汗战争和伊拉克战争。但是，全球多地发生恐怖袭击的频率较"9·11"前反而明显增加。"9·11"事件加上两场大规模战争，尤其是备受批评的伊拉克战争，使布什的第一个四年任期，似乎一直处于风雨飘摇之中，也使来自美国国内外的非议之声空前增多。

美国多家媒体不约而同地指出身为"战时总统"，布什在第二个任期内将面临巨大挑战。虽然布什最主要的选战幕僚罗夫声称，布什对自己的第二任期专注而乐观。但政治分析家欧汉伦在接受采访时说："布什在第一任期内所犯下最严重的错误，莫过于在缺乏缜密计划的情况下入侵伊拉克，而这场战争将成为他第二任期内深重的阴影。"民主党参议员泰德·肯尼迪干脆直言，伊拉克战争就是布什的"越战"，其后果将会直接作用于布什的第二任期。

从美国历史上看，布什并非唯一被战争地雷"灼伤"的美国总统。从杜鲁门的朝鲜"战后倦怠症"到克林顿的被弹劾，美国历史上不少总统连任之后，反而备受战争和丑闻困扰，尤其是在战后，连任总统的第二任期总是特别艰难。历史学家也指出，一场不受大众支持时间又拖延得太长的战争，往

往会给总统的第二任期带来更为严重的后遗症。

《华盛顿观察》19日刊出长篇分析文章，多名美政治学家对布什的第二任期做出了预测。乔治敦大学著名的美国总统史研究学者维恩教授指出，布什第二任期的首要外交挑战，将是重新修补美国与旧日盟友间因伊拉克战争所造成的嫌隙，其次则是改进美国在中东的形象。但维恩同时指出，对于布什面临的这两大挑战，可以看到希望但不会有太高期待，因为布什政府推行的单边主义很可能会持续下去，不久前美国媒体披露布什可能在第二任期内攻打伊朗就是一个隐患。

在正式宣誓就职的前一天，布什特意偕夫人劳拉到美国国家档案馆参观，阅览了一些珍贵的美国历史资料，包括首任总统华盛顿手写版的就职演说、《独立宣言》和《美国宪法》等。有记者问他是否感到了历史的分量，布什回答："当然。"不久之前，布什的高级助手罗夫接受媒体采访时说的一句话，似乎代表了布什的心迹："他（布什）将在今后四年埋头做自己的事，至于是对是错历史会做出评判。"无论如何，随着布什正式宣誓就职，他的第二任期履历也将呈现在人们面前。

布什在第一个任期的四年间，充分显示出自己是个性情中人。爱说乏味段子，总是坐卧不宁活像老顽童；辞去得州州长一职时曾失声痛哭，在教堂祈祷时坐立不安，受到挑战时向对方横眉怒对，和助手在一起时经常大开玩笑……布什天性爱笑爱闹，即便在"9·11"事发后仍然如此。"9·11"后一个月，布什前往扬基队棒球馆参加开球仪式，在"空军一号"上，布什练起了投球，其间不时开玩笑地将球掷向同僚，还不停地扮鬼脸。

第二节 布什于 2005 年在白宫的第二次就职演讲

Vice President Cheney, Mr. Chief Justice, President Carter, President Bush, President Clinton, members of United States' Congress, reverend clergy, distinguished guests, fellow citizens,

On this day, prescribed by law and marked by ceremony, we celebrate the durable wisdom of our Constitution, and recall the deep commitments that unite our country. I am grateful for the honor of this hour, mindful of the consequential times in which we live, and determined to fulfill the oath that I have sworn and you have witnessed.

At this second gathering, our duties are defined not by the words I use, but by the history we have seen together. For a half century, America defended our own freedom by standing watch on distant borders. After the shipwreck of communism came years of relative quiet, years of repose, years of sabbatical— and then there came a day of fire.

We have seen our vulnerability—and we have seen its deepest source. For as long as whole regions of the world simmer in resentment and tyranny—prone to ideologies that feed hatred and excuse murder—violence will gather, and

multiply in destructive power, and cross the most defended borders, and raise a mortal threat. There is only one force of history that can break the reign of hatred and resentment, and expose the pretensions of tyrants, and reward the hopes of the decent and tolerant, and that is the force of human freedom.

We are led, by events and common sense, to one conclusion: The survival of liberty in our land increasingly depends on the success of liberty in other lands. The best hope for peace in our world is the expansion of freedom in all the world.

America's vital interests and our deepest beliefs are now one. From the day of our Founding, we have proclaimed that every man and woman on this earth has rights, and dignity, and matchless value, because they bear the image of the Maker of Heaven and earth. Across the generations we have proclaimed the imperative of self-government, because no one is fit to be a master, and no one deserves to be a slave. Advancing these ideals is the mission that created our Nation. It is the honorable achievement of our fathers. Now it is the urgent requirement of our nation's security, and the calling of our time.

So it is the policy of the United States to seek and support the growth of democratic movements and institutions in every nation and culture, with the ultimate goal of ending tyranny in our world.

This is not primarily the task of arms, though we will defend ourselves and our friends by force of arms when necessary. Freedom, by its nature, must be chosen, and defended by citizens, and sustained by the rule of law and the protection of minorities. And when the soul of a nation finally speaks, the institutions that arise may reflect customs and traditions very different from our own. America will not impose our own **style** of government on the unwilling. Our goal instead is to help others find their own voice, attain their own freedom, and make their own way.

The great objective of ending tyranny is the concentrated work of generations. The difficulty of the task is no excuse for avoiding it. America's influence is not unlimited, but fortunately for the oppressed, America's influence is considerable, and we will use it confidently in freedom's cause.

My most solemn duty is to protect this nation and its people from further attacks and emerging threats. Some have unwisely chosen to test America's resolve, and have found it firm.

We will persistently clarify the choice before every ruler and every nation: The moral choice between oppression, which is always wrong, and freedom, which is eternally right. America will not pretend that jailed dissidents prefer their chains, or that women welcome humiliation and servitude, or that any human being aspires to live at the mercy of bullies.

We will encourage reform in other governments by making clear that success in our relations will require the decent treatment of their own people. America's belief in human dignity will guide our policies, yet rights must be more than the grudging concessions of dictators; they are secured by free dissent and the participation of the governed. In the long run, there is no justice without freedom, and there can be no human rights without human liberty.

Some, I know, have questioned the global appeal of liberty—though this time in history, four decades defined by the swiftest advance of freedom ever seen, is an odd time for doubt. Americans, of all people, should never be surprised by the power of our ideals. Eventually, the call of freedom comes to every mind and every soul. We do not accept the existence of permanent tyranny because we do not accept the possibility of permanent slavery. Liberty will come to those who love it.

Today, America speaks anew to the peoples of the world: All who live in tyranny and hopelessness can know: the United States will not ignore your

oppression, or excuse your oppressors. When you stand for your liberty, we will stand with you.

Democratic reformers facing repression, prison, or exile can know: America sees you for who you are: the future leaders of your free country. The rulers of outlaw regimes can know that we still believe as Abraham Lincoln did: "Those who deny freedom to others deserve it not for themselves; and, under the rule of a just God, cannot long retain it" The leaders of governments with long habits of control need to know: To serve your people you must learn to trust them. Start on this journey of progress and justice, and America will walk at your side.

And all the allies of the United States can know: we honor your friendship, we rely on your counsel, and we depend on your help. Division among free nations is a primary goal of freedom's enemies. The concerted effort of free nations to promote democracy is a prelude to our enemies' defeat.

Today, I also speak anew to my fellow citizens: From all of you, I have asked patience in the hard task of securing America, which you have granted in good measure. Our country has accepted obligations that are difficult to fulfill, and would be dishonorable to abandon. Yet because we have acted in the great liberating tradition of this nation, tens of millions have achieved their freedom. And as hope kindles hope, millions more will find it. By our efforts, we have lit a fire as well—a fire in the minds of men. It warms those who feel its power, it burns those who fight its progress, and one day this untamed fire of freedom will reach the darkest corners of our world.

A few Americans have accepted the hardest duties in this cause—in the quiet work of intelligence and diplomacy ... the idealistic work of helping raise up free governments ... the dangerous and necessary work of fighting our enemies. Some have shown their devotion to our country in deaths that honored their whole lives—and we will always honor their names and their sacrifice.

All Americans have witnessed this idealism, and some for the first time. I ask our youngest citizens to believe the evidence of your eyes. You have seen duty and allegiance in the determined faces of our soldiers. You have seen that life is fragile, and evil is real, and courage triumphs. Make the choice to serve in a cause larger than your wants, larger than yourself—and in your days you will add not just to the wealth of our country, but to its character.

America has need of idealism and courage, because we have essential work at home—the unfinished work of American freedom. In a world moving toward liberty, we are determined to show the meaning and promise of liberty.

In America's ideal of freedom, citizens find the dignity and security of economic independence, instead of laboring on the edge of subsistence. This is the broader definition of liberty that motivated the *Homestead Act*, *the Social Security Act*, and *the G.I. Bill of Rights*. And now we will extend this vision by reforming great institutions to serve the needs of our time. To give every American a stake in the promise and future of our country, we will bring the highest standards to our schools, and build an ownership society. We will widen the ownership of homes and businesses, retirement savings and health insurance—preparing our people for the challenges of life in a free society. By making every citizen an agent of his or her own destiny, we will give our fellow Americans greater freedom from want and fear, and make our society more prosperous and just and equal.

In America's ideal of freedom, the public interest depends on private character—on integrity, and tolerance toward others, and the rule of conscience in our own lives. Self-government relies, in the end, on the governing of the self. That edifice of character is built in families, supported by communities with standards, and sustained in our national life by the truths of Sinai, the Sermon on the Mount, the words of the Koran, and the varied faiths of our people. Americans move forward in every generation by reaffirming all that is good

and true that came before—ideals of justice and conduct that are the same yesterday, today, and forever.

In America's ideal of freedom, the exercise of rights is ennobled by service, and mercy, and a heart for the weak. Liberty for all does not mean independence from one another. Our nation relies on men and women who look after a neighbor and surround the lost with love. Americans, at our best, value the life we see in one another, and must always remember that even the unwanted have worth. And our country must abandon all the habits of racism, because we cannot carry the message of freedom and the baggage of bigotry at the same time.

From the perspective of a single day, including this day of dedication, the issues and questions before our country are many. From the viewpoint of centuries, the questions that come to us are narrowed and few. Did our generation advance the cause of freedom? And did our character bring credit to that cause?

These questions that judge us also unite us, because Americans of every party and background, Americans by choice and by birth, are bound to one another in the cause of freedom. We have known divisions, which must be healed to move forward in great purposes—and I will strive in good faith to heal them. Yet those divisions do not define America. We felt the unity and fellowship of our nation when freedom came under attack, and our response came like a single hand over a single heart. And we can feel that same unity and pride whenever America acts for good, and the victims of disaster are given hope, and the unjust encounter justice, and the captives are set free.

We go forward with complete confidence in the eventual triumph of freedom. Not because history runs on the wheels of inevitability; it is human choices that move events. Not because we consider ourselves a chosen nation; God moves and chooses as He wills. We have confidence because freedom is the permanent hope of mankind, the hunger in dark places, the longing of the soul. When our Founders declared a new order of the ages; when soldiers died in wave upon wave for a union based on liberty; when citizens marched in peaceful outrage under the banner "Freedom Now" —they were acting on an ancient hope that is meant to be fulfilled. History has an ebb and flow of justice, but history also has a visible direction, set by liberty and the Author of Liberty.

When the Declaration of Independence was first read in public and the Liberty Bell was sounded in celebration, a witness said, "It rang as if it meant something." In our time it means something still. America, in this young century, proclaims liberty throughout all the world, and to all the inhabitants thereof. Renewed in our strength—tested, but not weary—we are ready for the greatest achievements in the history of freedom.

May God bless you, and may He watch over the United States of America.

切尼副主席、首席大法官、卡特总统、布什总统、克林顿总统、美国国会议员、尊敬的牧师、贵宾们、同胞们：

今天，按照宪法规定我们举行这个仪式。我们在此欢庆我国宪法常青的智慧，追寻我们团结全国的深切责任感。我感恩这个时刻带来的荣耀，意识到我们时代的期盼并期待着完成我的誓言，请你们做证。

这是我们第二次聚会，我们的责任并非由我的讲演来确定，它源于我们当前历史时期的要求。半个世纪以来，美国在遥远的边界上捍卫着我们的自由，极权专政破产后我们有相对平静、懒散的岁月，而后是火光四射的那一天。

我们已明了自身的弱点，我们也深知其根源。只要世界某些区域酝酿着不满，滋生着暴君，就会产生宣扬仇恨和为屠杀寻找借口的意识形态，就会聚集暴力和毁灭的能量，它们会越过严密把守的边界带来毁灭的威胁。这个世界只存在一种力量可以冲决仇恨、揭露暴君的虚伪、扶植容忍、培育尊严，

那就是人类的自由。

我们受常识的指引和历史的教诲得出如下结论：自由是否能在我们的土地上存在，正日益依赖于自由在别国的胜利。对和平的热切期望只能源于自由在世界上的扩展。

美国生死存亡的利益和我们基本的信念已合而为一。自立国始，我们就宣示：生于世间的每个人都拥有他们的权力、尊严和无可比拟的价值，因为他们拥有创造天地之神的形象。我们世代重申着民有政权的重要性，没有什么人应该是主人而另一些人应该做奴隶。实现这一理念的使命是我们的立国之本。我们的先父荣耀地完成了这一使命。进一步扩展这一理念是国家安全的要求，是我们的当务之急。

有鉴于此，美国的政策是寻求并支持世界各国和各种文化背景下成长的民主运动，寻求并支持民主的制度化。最终的目标是终结世间的任何极权制度。

这个目标最终不应由暴力达成，尽管在必要时我们将以武力自卫，并保卫我们的朋友。自由的性质要求公民去自觉地选择它，捍卫它，并通过立法加以维护，同时保障弱势者。当一个国家的魂魄最终选择自由时，它的制度将反映不同于我们的文化和传统。美国不会强迫任何国家接受我们的国家体制。我们的目的是帮助其他国家找到自己的声音，获得自身的自由，发现自己的自由之路。

终结专制统治的巨大使命是几代人努力的目标，其难度不是无所作为的借口。美国的影响是有限的，但值得庆幸的是，美国的影响也是有力的，我们将充满信心地在追求自由的道路上帮助你们。

我最庄严的责任是保护我的国家和它的人民不再受到任何袭击和威胁。有些人不明智地选择了试探美国的决心，他们发现了我们坚定的意志。

我们坚定地给每一位统治者和每一个国家提出这样的选择：请在压迫——这终究是错的，与自由——这永远是正确的，之间做出道义的选择。

美国不会装模作样地默许被关押的异议者自我选择了枷锁，也不会默许妇女成为可耻的代名词，看着她们变成奴仆，同样不会默许任何人类的一员仰人鼻息地生活。

我们将鼓励其他政府的改革，我们将明确表示若与美国建立良好的关系需要他们善待自己的公民。美国对人的尊严的信念将指导我们的政策，但是人民的权利并不是源于独裁者违心的让步，它们应该源于人民有反对的自由和被统治者的平等参与。从长远看，没有自由就没有正义，没有人民的自由就不存在人权。

我知道有些人质疑全球自由，尽管经过四十年自由迅猛的发展，这个怀疑似乎不合时宜。美国人民不应被我们理念的力量所震惊，最终自由的呼唤将发自每一个心灵。我们拒绝接受永恒的专制，因为我们拒绝接受永久的奴役。自由将来到热爱她的人们中间。

今天，美国再次向世界人民宣布：那些生活在专制下绝望的人民应该知道，美利坚合众国不会漠视你们被压迫，不会原谅你们的压迫者。当你们保卫自己的自由时，美国将站在你们的一边。

那些面对压制、监禁和流放的民主变革的参与者应该知道，美国知道你们的潜力，你们是自由国家未来的领袖。那些无法无天的统治者应该知道，我们仍然抱有林肯总统的信念："那些剥夺他人自由的人不配享有自由，而且在公正的上帝面前，他们也不会长久。"那些习惯于控制人民的统治者应该知道，为了服务你的人民你应该给予他们信任。开始踏上进步和正义之路，那样，美国将站在你这一边。

美国的所有盟友们应该知道，我们珍视我们的友谊，我们尊重你们的建议，我们依赖于你们的帮助。分裂自由国家的团结是自由敌人的目的。自由国家相互配合地推进民主是敌人失败的开始。

今天，我也要对我的同胞和公民们说：我要求得到你们所有人的耐心，保卫国家安全是艰巨的任务，这样的耐心你们已经给予我很多了。我们的国

家承担着一个困难重重的义务，中途放弃是可耻的。正是因为我们继续着我们国家解放者的传统，成千上万的人们获得了自由。希望催生新的希望，更多的人将获得自由。通过我们的努力，我们点燃了人们心中的火种，那火种温暖着感受到它力量的人们，并烧毁那些试图阻挠进步的人。终有一天，这不可熄灭的自由之火将照亮这个世界最阴暗的角落。

一些美国人已经接受这项事业中最困难的工作——那些默默无闻的情报和外交工作……那些帮助建立自由政府的理想主义的工作……那些打击我们的敌人危险而必要的工作。他们中的一些人献出了生命，他们的国家永远以他们为荣——我们也会永远记住他们的名字和他们的贡献。

所有的美国人都见证了这种理想主义，有些人是第一次看到。我要求我们的青年公民相信自己的亲眼所见。你们看到了我们的士兵充满责任和忠诚的坚毅面孔，你们也看到了生命的脆弱和魔鬼的真实，你们更看到了战胜邪恶的勇气。请选择参加这一进程，它比起个人需要重要得多，比个人自身伟大得多。一旦轮到你们，你们不但为我们的国家增加了财富，也将为她增添光彩。

美国需要理想主义和勇气，因为我们要完成国内的任务——美国自由的未竟之业。在一个走向自由的世界里，我们要展示自由的真义和自由的承诺。

在美国自由的信念里，公民享有尊严和经济上的独立，不是生活在潦倒的边缘。这是更广义自由的定义，它促生了《房屋法案》《社会安全法案》和《人权法案》。现在，我们将改革形成伟大的制度来服务于我们的时代，并扩展这一定义。每个美国人将分享国家的承诺和未来。我们将用最高的标准来要求我们的学校，建立一个有产者的社会。我们要让更多的人拥有自己的住房和事业，拥有自己的退休基金和医疗保险。让我们的人民对自由社会未来的挑战做好准备，让每个公民做自己命运的主人。我们将把美国人民从匮乏和担忧中解脱出来，并把我们的社会建成更为富强平等的社会。

在美国的自由信念中，公共利益依赖于个人品质，这包括完善的人格和宽容他人，以及有理性的生活。自我管理依赖于管理良好的自我。品格大厦的建立来自于家庭，以及社会对道德标准的支持，并在国家生活里贯彻始终。它依赖于西奈的真知、宝山临训、可兰经的教诲，与各种各样的信仰。它在每一代美国人民的推动下前进着，他们坚信源于历史的公益和真实——公正的理念和行为都是相同的，无论过去、现在，还是永远的未来。

在美国自由的信念中，个人权力的运用是由服务，宽容和对弱者的同情构成的。为全体的自由并不意味着人们的互相背离。我们国家依赖于那些互相守望的邻里和用爱围绕失落者的人们。美国人最良好的表现在于珍重我们每一个人的生活，而且永远记得那些所谓无用之辈也有他们的价值。我们的国家一定要丢弃一切种族主义的偏见，因为要知道我们不可能肩负自由的使命而又同时携带偏见的包袱。

从每一天看，就以今天为例，我们国家面临着诸多问题。从一个世纪看，我们面对的问题是集中而突出的。我们这一代有没有拓展自由的疆界？我们的所作所为有没有为这事业增添光彩？

这些问题是我们的裁判，并且团结了我们。因为无论是任何党派或背景的美国人，移民或出生于此的美国人，在自由的道路上都是不可分离的。我们知道分裂必须弥合我们才能向伟大的目标前进，我将做出最大的努力去弥合分裂，但是这种裂痕不能左右美国。当自由受到威胁时，我们深感相互的团结和关联，我们的反击也如出自同手一心。当美国仗义而行，当灾民们得到救助，当正义得到伸张，当人民获得自由，我们也同样自豪地感到我们是统一体。

我们所有人都满怀信心地踏着自由胜利之路前进。这并非因为这是不可避免的历史进程，而是因为人类的选择促成进步。我们并不认为我们的国家就是上帝的选民，上帝自有他的意志和选择。我们坚信这是因为自由是人类永恒的希望，是黑暗中的渴望，是灵魂的渴望。当我们的立国先贤宣布新时代的准则时，当一批批士兵为了保卫基于自由的联邦而牺牲时，当公民手举

"立即自由"的横幅和平抗议时——他们在实践着那古老的希望，这希望一定会成为现实。虽然公正在历史上潮起潮落，但是历史也有一条清晰的脉络，那是由自由和自由的实践者确定的。

当第一次对公众宣读独立宣言时，自由的钟声由此敲响。一个亲眼目睹的人这样说道："它在鸣响着，似乎意味深长。"在我们的时代，这钟声依然意味深长。美国在新的世纪向世界，向所有它的居民传播着自由。我们充满活力，我们经历过艰难的斗争，但并没有疲倦，—我们已做好准备去完成自由史上最伟大的功绩。

上帝保佑你们，愿他眷顾美国。

第三节 精彩语录

We have seen our vulnerability—and we have seen its deepest source. For as long as whole regions of the world simmer in resentment and tyranny—prone to ideologies that feed hatred and excuse murder—violence will gather, and multiply in destructive power, and cross the most defended borders, and raise a mortal threat.

我们已明了自身的弱点，我们也深知其根源。只要世界某些区域酝酿着不满，滋生着暴君，就会产生宣扬仇恨和为屠杀寻找借口的意识形态，就会聚集暴力和毁灭的能量，它们会越过严密把守的边界带来毁灭的威胁。

There is only one force of history that can break the reign of hatred and resentment, and expose the pretensions of tyrants, and reward the hopes of the decent and tolerant, and that is the force of human freedom.

这个世界只存在一种力量可以冲决仇恨、揭露暴君的虚伪、扶植容忍、培育尊严，那就是人类的自由。

We are led, by events and common sense, to one conclusion: The survival of liberty in our land increasingly depends on the success of liberty in other lands. The best hope for peace in our world is the expansion of freedom in all the world.

我们受常识的指引和历史的教诲得出如下结论：自由是否能在我们的土地上存在，正日益依赖于自由在别国的胜利。对和平的热切期望只能源于自由在世界上的扩展。

Every man and woman on this earth has rights, and dignity, and matchless value, because they bear the image of the Maker of Heaven and earth.

生于世间的每个人都拥有他们的权力、尊严和无可比拟的价值，因为他们拥有创造天地之神的形象。

Rights must be more than the grudging concessions of dictators; they are secured by free dissent and the participation of the governed. In the long run, there is no justice without freedom, and there can be no human rights without human liberty.

人民的权利并不是源于独裁者违心的让步，它们应该源于人民有反对的自由和被统治者的平等参与。从长远看，没有自由就没有正义，没有人民的自由就不存在人权。

Eventually, the call of freedom comes to every mind and every soul. We do not accept the existence of permanent tyranny because we do not accept the possibility of permanent slavery. Liberty will come to those who love it.

最终，自由的呼唤将发自每一个心灵。我们拒绝接受永恒的专制，因为我们拒绝接受永久的奴役。自由将来到热爱她的人们中间。

The rulers of outlaw regimes can know that we still believe as Abraham Lincoln did: "Those who deny freedom to others deserve it not for themselves; and, under the rule of a just God, cannot long retain it."

那些无法无天的统治者应该知道，我们仍然抱有林肯总统的信念："那些剥夺他人自由的人不配享有自由，而且在公正的上帝面前，他们也不会长久。"

And as hope kindles hope, millions more will find it. By our efforts, we have lit a fire as well—a fire in the minds of men. It warms those who feel its power, it burns those who fight its progress, and one day this untamed fire of freedom will reach the darkest corners of our world.

希望催生新的希望，更多的人将获得自由。通过我们的努力，我们点燃了人们心中的火种，那火种温暖着感受到它力量的人们，并烧毁那些试图阻挠进步的人。终有一天，这不可熄灭的自由之火将照亮这个世界最阴暗的角落。

When the Declaration of Independence was first read in public and the Liberty Bell was sounded in celebration, a witness said, "It rang as if it meant something." In our time it means something still.

当第一次对公众宣读独立宣言时，自由的钟声由此敲响。一个亲眼目睹的人这样说道："它在鸣响着，似乎意味深长。"在我们的时代，这钟声依然意味深长。

第十二章

打击恐怖主义，消除贸易壁垒

第一节 背景介绍

"9·11"恐怖袭击事件发生后，反恐成了国际社会妇孺皆知的主题词和关键词。的确，"9·11"事件以来，国际社会面临的最大威胁和挑战就是恐怖主义。2005年，进入了全球"向恐怖宣战"的第五个年头，恐怖主义从美洲蔓延到亚洲，又在欧洲"强势"登陆，恐怖袭击事件不仅有增无减而且愈演愈烈，全球反恐形势似乎陷入了越反越恐的尴尬局面。俗话说，时移事异。随着国际社会反恐的不断深入以及打击措施和手段的变幻，恐怖主义也开始凸显新的变化和特点。

恐怖袭击多缘于伊拉克战争的余波，不仅有大举回潮之势，而且矛头直指美英等国。继"9·11"之后，恐怖分子又成功延续了一年一次的标志性袭击，即英国伦敦的公交系统连环大爆炸，使在伊拉克战争中对美国亦步亦趋的英国也成为恐怖袭击的重点目标。埃及与约旦也没有幸免，同样遭到了来自伊拉克本土恐怖分子的袭击，因为在伊拉克战争和巴以问题上他们都给予美国支持与合作。

在反恐呼声日渐高涨，打击力度日渐加大的强大压力之下，恐怖势力开始重新分化演变。伊拉克形形色色的圣战组织和反美武装等与伊拉克的教派和民族矛盾结合在一起，与境外极端主义分子相整合，使伊拉克安全形势持续恶化。特别是扎卡维领导的伊拉克"基地"组织，在伊境内与美军对抗的同时，还不断在与伊接壤的阿拉伯国家发动恐怖袭击，大有超越本·拉登之势。扎卡维领导的伊拉克"基地"组织迅速"崛起"，表明在伊拉克战争的土壤上生长出新的恐怖主义势力。其组织实施的恐怖主义活动同伊拉克战争紧密联系，与"9·11"事件有很大的区别，已经发生了变异。在表象上更容易引起同情，容易与地区矛盾融为一体，使国际社会同恐怖主义的斗争更加复杂，更难将其消灭。有人说，恐怖主义就像弹簧，加大反恐力度，就会隐匿下去，一旦有机会，又会重新冒出来，这使反恐形势"越反越恐"。

整个2005年恐怖主义此起彼伏，几个回合下来，反恐进入了一个相持阶段。身陷伊拉克战场的美国和对国内安全局势高度紧张的英国，在经历了阿富汗、伊拉克等大规模"反恐战争"后，已暂时无力发动新的大规模"反恐"军事行动，其国民也渐渐对以单纯的军事行动进行"反恐"表示怀疑。于是，美国的反恐政策出现了新的动向和变化。美国国防部长拉姆斯菲尔德承认应该用"反恐怖斗争"代替"反恐战争"，各国依托联合国实施合作共同反恐前景堪忧。一方面，恐怖主义分子借助其活动的隐蔽性，出其不意、此起彼伏地实施袭击；另一方面，美英等国陷入战争和国内民众的诸多压力，又无法同其他大国真正地搞好合作，恐怖与反恐呈现出一种艰难的相持状态。此外，在打击恐怖主义的同时，美国既要面临自然灾害的侵害，重建家园，还要面对进出口贸易问题。

美国整体关税水平较低，但在一些部门仍然存在高关税和关税高峰。美国超过平均关税水平三倍以上的高关税税目约占总税目的7％，关税超过15％的税目约占总税目的4％。高关税和关税高峰主要体现在纺织品和服装、皮革、橡胶、陶瓷、鞋类和旅行产品等大类产品。

美国为控制进口数量，保护国内生产商利益，对部分农产品实行关税配额管理。配额内的平均关税水平为2.2％～5％，配额外的关税税率较高，各

产品不尽相同，如脱脂奶粉为 52.6%。美国从各国进口农产品的关税配额数量在《北美自由贸易协定》、《中美洲自由贸易协定》以及美国与澳大利亚、智利、摩洛哥、新加坡和泰国签订的《自由贸易协定》中做了具体规定。

美国海关在进口产品通关时要求出口商提供所有附加单证及相关信息，对某些进口产品，如纺织品、服装或鞋，要求提供的信息远远超出正常通关的需要。这些手续不仅繁琐而且费用高昂，对出口商特别是小出口商构成了壁垒。美国海关对纺织品、服装的进口在某些情况下还要求提供保密的加工程序信息。例如，对外表由一种以上材料构成的服装，必须提供相关重量、构成价值和每一部件的表面积等信息，此类做法客观上导致了成本增加。

另外，美国海关还将结税期最长延至 210 天。在某些情况下，发票上的小错误或小问题将导致结税期超过 210 天，美国海关不会给予具体的理由。在结税期内，美国海关可能要求额外的信息以便对产品进行分类并确定原产国。由于服装更新较快，必须马上售出，比如时装必须在二至三个月内售出。如果进口商无法在美国海关规定的结税期内保留进口服装，以便于美国海关确定最终的关税，美国海关将征收相当于进口货价值 100％的罚金。

美国国家安全事务顾问赖斯指出：此时此刻与 1945～1947 年那个时期相似，那是遏制政策形成的时期……今天国际政治的结构板块已经发生了巨变。"9·11"事件发生后，国家安全事务委员会要认真、严肃地思考如何利用和抓住这一机会从根本上改变美国的对外政策，重新安排世界，重新界定美国的利益和对国际机制的立场，所有这些均是从前难以实现的。

国际反恐形势依然不容乐观，要彻底根治恐怖主义国际社会还有很长的路要走。世界各国应该将眼前利益与长远利益相结合，加强协作与交流，彻底摒弃单边主义思维和"双重标准"，真正消除国际社会不公正现象，缩小发达国家与发展中国家的经济差距。通过政治对话、经济交往、文化交流等诸手段的综合运用，标本兼治地共同消除恐怖主义。

第二节 布什于 2005 年在联合国六十周年大会上的演讲

Mr. Secretary General, Mr. President, distinguished guests, ladies and gentlemen,

Thank you for the privilege of being here for the 60th anniversary of the United Nations. Thank you for your dedication to the vital work and great ideals of this institution.

We meet at a time of great challenge for America and the world. At this moment, men and women along my country's Gulf Coast are recovering from one of the worst natural disasters in American history. Many have lost homes, and loved ones, and all their earthly possessions. In Alabama and Mississippi and Louisiana, whole neighborhoods have been lifted from their foundations and sent crashing into the streets. A great American city is working to turn the flood waters and reclaim its future.

We have witnessed the awesome power of nature—and the greater power of human compassion. Americans have responded to their neighbors in need, and so have many of the nations represented in this chamber. All together, more than 115 countries and nearly a dozen international organizations have

stepped forward with offers of assistance. To every nation, every province, and every community across the world that is standing with the American people in this hour of need, I offer the thanks of my nation.

Your response, like the response to last year's tsunami, has shown once again that the world is more compassionate and hopeful when we act together. This truth was the inspiration for the United Nations. The U.N.'s founding members laid out great and honorable goals in the charter they drafted six decades ago. That document commits this organization to work to "save succeeding generations from the scourge of war," "reaffirm faith in fundamental human rights," and "promote social progress and better standards of life in larger freedom." We remain committed to those noble ideals. As we respond to great humanitarian needs, we must actively respond to the other great challenges of our time. We must continue to work to ease suffering, and to spread freedom, and to lay the foundations of lasting peace for our children and grandchildren.

In this young century, the far corners of the world are linked more closely than ever before—and no nation can remain isolated and indifferent to the struggles of others. When a country, or a region is filled with despair, and resentment and vulnerable to violent and aggressive ideologies, the threat passes easily across oceans and borders, and could threaten the security of any peaceful country.

Terrorism fed by anger and despair has come to Tunisia, to Indonesia, to Kenya, to Tanzania, to Morocco, to Israel, to Saudi Arabia, to the United States, to Turkey, to Spain, to Russia, to Egypt, to Iraq, and the United Kingdom. And those who have not seen attacks on their own soil have still shared in the sorrow—from Australians killed in Bali, to Italians killed in Egypt, to the citizens of dozens of nations who were killed on September the 11th, 2001, here in the city where we meet. The lesson is clear: There can be no safety in looking away, or seeking the quiet life by ignoring the hardship and oppression of others. Either hope will spread, or violence will spread—and we must take the side of hope.

Sometimes our security will require confronting threats directly, and so a great coalition of nations has come together to fight the terrorists across the world. We've worked together to help break up terrorist networks that cross borders, and rout out radical cells within our own borders. We've eliminated terrorist sanctuaries. We're using our diplomatic and financial tools to cut off their financing and drain them of support. And as we fight, the terrorists must know that the world stands united against them. We must complete the *Comprehensive Convention on International Terrorism* that will put every nation on record: The targeting and deliberate killing by terrorists of civilians and non-combatants cannot be justified or legitimized by any cause or grievance.

And the world's free nations are determined to stop the terrorists and their allies from acquiring the terrible weapons that would allow them to kill on a scale equal to their hatred. For that reason, more than 60 countries are supporting the Proliferation Security Initiative to intercept shipments of weapons of mass destruction on land, on sea, and in air. The terrorists must know that wherever they go, they cannot escape justice.

Later today, the Security Council has an opportunity to put the terrorists on notice when it votes on a resolution that condemns the incitement of terrorist acts—the resolution that calls upon all states to take appropriate steps to end such incitement. We also need to sign and implement the *International Convention for the Suppression of Acts of Nuclear Terrorism*, so that all those who seek radioactive materials or nuclear devices are prosecuted and extradited, wherever they are. We must send a clear message to the rulers of outlaw regimes that sponsor terror and pursue weapons of mass murder: You will not be allowed to threaten the peace and stability of the world.

Confronting our enemies is essential, and so civilized nations will continue to take the fight to the terrorists. Yet we know that this war will not be won by force of arms alone. We must defeat the terrorists on the battlefield, and we must also defeat them in the battle of ideas. We must change the conditions that allow terrorists to flourish and recruit, by spreading the hope of freedom to millions who've never known it. We must help raise up the failing states and stagnant societies that provide fertile ground for the terrorists. We must defend and extend a vision of human dignity, and opportunity, and prosperity—a vision far stronger than the dark appeal of resentment and murder.

To spread a vision of hope, the United States is determined to help nations that are struggling with poverty. We are committed to the Millennium Development Goals. This is an ambitious agenda that includes cutting poverty and hunger in half, ensuring that every boy and girl in the world has access to primary education, and halting the spread of AIDS—all by 2015.

We have a moral obligation to help others—and a moral duty to make sure our actions are effective. At Monterrey in 2002, we agreed to a new vision for the way we fight poverty, and curb corruption, and provide aid in this new millennium. Developing countries agreed to take responsibility for their own economic progress through good governance and sound policies and the rule of law. Developed countries agreed to support those efforts, including increased aid to nations that undertake necessary reforms. My own country has sought to implement the *Monterrey Consensus* by establishing the new Millennium Challenge Account. This account is increasing U.S. aid for countries that govern justly, invest in their people, and promote economic freedom.

More needs to be done. I call on all the world's nations to implement the *Monterrey Consensus*. Implementing the *Monterrey Consensus* means continuing on the long, hard road to reform. Implementing the *Monterrey Consensus* means creating a genuine partnership between developed and developing countries to replace the donor–client relationship of the past. And implementing the *Monterrey Consensus* means welcoming all developing countries as full participants to the global economy, with all the requisite benefits and responsibilities.

Tying aid to reform is essential to eliminating poverty, but our work doesn't end there. For many countries, AIDS, malaria, and other diseases are both humanitarian tragedies and significant obstacles to development. We must give poor countries access to the emergency lifesaving drugs they need to fight these infectious epidemics. Through our bilateral programs and the Global Fund, the United States will continue to lead the world in providing the resources to defeat the plague of HIV–AIDS.

Today America is working with local authorities and organizations in the largest initiative in history to combat a specific disease. Across Africa, we're helping local health officials expand AIDS testing facilities, train and support doctors and nurses and counselors, and upgrade clinics and hospitals. Working with our African partners, we have now delivered lifesaving treatment to more than 230,000 people in sub–Sahara Africa. We are ahead of schedule to meet an important objective: providing HIV–AIDS treatment for nearly two million adults and children in Africa. At the G–8 Summit at Gleneagles, Scotland, we set a clear goal: an AIDS–free generation in Africa. And I challenge every member of the United Nations to take concrete steps to achieve that goal.

We're also working to fight malaria. This preventable disease kills more than a million people around the world every year—and leaves poverty and grief in every land it touches. The United States has set a goal of cutting the malaria death rate in half in at least 15 highly endemic African countries. To achieve that goal, we've pledged to increase our funding for malaria treatment and prevention by more than $1.2 billion over the next five years. We invite other nations to join us in this effort by committing specific aid to the dozens

of other African nations in need of it. Together we can fight malaria and save hundreds of thousands of lives, and bring new hope to countries that have been devastated by this terrible disease.

As we strengthen our commitments to fighting malaria and AIDS, we must also remain on the offensive against new threats to public health such as the Avian Influenza. If left unchallenged, this virus could become the first pandemic of the 21st century. We must not allow that to happen. Today I am announcing a new International Partnership on Avian and Pandemic Influenza. The Partnership requires countries that face an outbreak to immediately share information and provide samples to the World Health Organization. By requiring transparency, we can respond more rapidly to dangerous outbreaks and stop them on time. Many nations have already joined this partnership; we invite all nations to participate. It's essential we work together, and as we do so, we will fulfill a moral duty to protect our citizens, and heal the sick, and comfort the afflicted.

Even with increased aid to fight disease and reform economies, many nations are held back by another heavy challenge: the burden of debt. So America and many nations have also acted to lift this burden that limits the growth of developing economies, and holds millions of people in poverty. Today poor countries with the heaviest debt burdens are receiving more than $30 billion in debt relief. And to prevent the build-up of future debt, my country and other nations have agreed that international financial institutions should increasingly provide new aid in the form of grants, rather than loans. The G-8 agreed at Gleneagles to go further. To break the lend-and-forgive cycle permanently, we agreed to cancel 100 percent of the debt for the world's most heavily indebted nations. I call upon the World Bank and the IMF to finalize this historic agreement as soon as possible.

We will fight to lift the burden of poverty from places of suffering—not just for the moment, but permanently. And the surest path to greater wealth is greater trade. In a letter he wrote to me in August, the Secretary General commended the G-8's work, but told me that aid and debt relief are not enough. The Secretary General said that we also need to reduce trade barriers and subsidies that are holding developing countries back. I agree with the Secretary General: The Doha Round is "the most promising way" to achieve this goal.

A successful Doha Round will reduce and eliminate tariffs and other barriers on farm and industrial goods. It will end unfair agricultural subsidies. It will open up global markets for services. Under Doha, every nation will gain, and the developing world stands to gain the most. Historically, developing nations that open themselves up to trade grow at several times the rate of other countries. The elimination of trade barriers could lift hundreds of millions of people out of poverty over the next 15 years. The stakes are high. The lives and futures of millions of the world's poorest citizens hang in the balance—and so we must bring the Doha trade talks to a successful conclusion.

Doha is an important step toward a larger goal: We must tear down the walls that separate the developed and developing worlds. We need to give the citizens of the poorest nations the same ability to access the world economy that the people of wealthy nations have, so they can offer their goods and talents on the world market alongside everyone else. We need to ensure that they have the same opportunities to pursue their dreams, provide for their families, and live lives of dignity and self-reliance.

And the greatest obstacles to achieving these goals are the tariffs and subsidies and barriers that isolate people of developing nations from the great opportunities of the 21st century. Today, I reiterate the challenge I have made before: We must work together in the Doha negotiations to eliminate agricultural subsidies that distort trade and stunt development, and to eliminate tariffs and

other barriers to open markets for farmers around the world. Today I broaden the challenge by making this pledge: The United States is ready to eliminate all tariffs, subsidies and other barriers to free flow of goods and services as other nations do the same. This is key to overcoming poverty in the world's poorest nations. It's essential we promote prosperity and opportunity for all nations.

By expanding trade, we spread hope and opportunity to the corners of the world, and we strike a blow against the terrorists who feed on anger and resentment. Our agenda for freer trade is part of our agenda for a freer world, where people can live and worship and raise their children as they choose. In the long run, the best way to protect the religious freedom, and the rights of women and minorities, is through institutions of self-rule, which allow people to assert and defend their own rights. All who stand for human rights must also stand for human freedom.

This is a moment of great opportunity in the cause of freedom. Across the world, hearts and minds are opening to the message of human liberty as never before. In the last two years alone, tens of millions have voted in free elections in Afghanistan and Iraq, in Lebanon and the Palestinian territories, in Kyrgyzstan, in Ukraine, and Georgia. And as they claim their freedom, they are inspiring millions more across the broader Middle East. We must encourage their aspirations. We must nurture freedom's progress. And the United Nations has a vital role to play.

Through the new U.N. Democracy Fund, the democratic members of the U.N. will work to help others who want to join the democratic world. It is fitting that the world's largest democracy, India, has taken a leadership role in this effort, pledging $10 million to get the fund started. Every free nation has an interest in the success of this fund—and every free nation has a responsibility in advancing the cause of liberty.

The work of democracy is larger than holding a fair election; it requires building the institutions that sustain freedom. Democracy takes different forms in different cultures, yet all free societies have certain things in common. Democratic nations uphold the rule of law, impose limits on the power of the state, treat women and minorities as full citizens. Democratic nations protect private property, free speech and religious expression. Democratic nations grow in strength because they reward and respect the creative gifts of their people. And democratic nations contribute to peace and stability because they seek national greatness in the achievements of their citizens, not the conquest of their neighbors.

For these reasons, the whole world has a vital interest in the success of a free Iraq—and no civilized nation has an interest in seeing a new terror state emerge in that country. So the free world is working together to help the Iraqi people to establish a new nation that can govern itself, sustain itself, and defend itself. It's an exciting opportunity for all of us in this chamber. And the United Nations has played a vital role in the success of the January elections, where eight and a half million Iraqis defied the terrorists and cast their ballots. And since then, the United Nations has supported Iraq's elected leaders as they drafted a new constitution.

The United Nations and its member states must continue to stand by the Iraqi people as they complete the journey to a fully constitutional government. And when Iraqis complete their journey, their success will inspire others to claim their freedom, the Middle East will grow in peace and hope and liberty, and all of us will live in a safer world.

The advance of freedom and security is the calling of our time. It is the mission of the United Nations. The United Nations was created to spread the hope of liberty, and to fight poverty and disease, and to help secure human rights and human dignity for all the world's people. To help make these promises real, the United Nations must be strong and efficient, free

of corruption, and accountable to the people it serves. The United Nations must stand for integrity, and live by the high standards it sets for others. And meaningful institutional reforms must include measures to improve internal oversight, identify cost savings, and ensure that precious resources are used for their intended purpose.

The United Nations has taken the first steps toward reform. The process will continue in the General Assembly this fall, and the United States will join with others to lead the effort. And the process of reform begins with members taking our responsibilities seriously. When this great institution's member states choose notorious abusers of human rights to sit on the U.N. Human Rights Commission, they discredit a noble effort, and undermine the credibility of the whole organization. If member countries want the United Nations to be respected—respected and effective, they should begin by making sure it is worthy of respect.

At the start of a new century, the world needs the United Nations to live up to its ideals and fulfill its mission. The founding members of this organization knew that the security of the world would increasingly depend on advancing the rights of mankind, and this would require the work of many hands. After committing America to the idea of the U.N. in 1945, President Franklin Roosevelt declared: "The structure of world peace cannot be the work of one man, or one party, or one nation." Peace is the responsibility of every nation and every generation.

In each era of history, the human spirit has been challenged by the forces of darkness and chaos. Some challenges are the acts of nature; others are the works of men. This organization was convened to meet these challenges by harnessing the best instincts of humankind, the strength of the world united in common purpose. With courage and conscience, we will meet our responsibilities to protect the lives and rights of others. And when we do, we will help fulfill the promise of the United Nations, and ensure that every human being enjoys the peace and the freedom and the dignity our Creator intended for all.

秘书长先生、主席先生、各位尊贵的来宾、女士们、先生们：

感谢你们让我有幸在联合国成立六十周年之际来到这里。感谢你们为这个机构的重要使命和伟大理想做出的奉献。

我们在美国和全世界面临重大挑战的时刻在这里聚会。此时此刻我国墨西哥湾沿岸地区的男女民众刚刚经历了美国有史以来最严重的自然灾害之一，正在恢复重建。很多人失去了家园、亲人和他们所有的财产。在亚拉巴马、密西西比和路易斯安那州，一个个街区被夷为平地，成为一片废墟。这座伟大的美国城市正在战胜洪灾，重建自己的未来。

我们目睹了大自然的惊人威力，但更有威力的是人类的关爱。美国人民向受灾同胞伸出援手，在座各位所代表的很多国家也提供了援助。总共有超过115个国家和十几个国际组织主动提出支援救灾。我谨代表我的国家，向在这个困难时刻援助美国人民的全世界每一个国家、每一个地区、每一个社区表示感谢。

你们的救援行动，与去年援助海啸灾区的行动一样，再次说明我们齐心协力能使全世界更富有关爱之情，也更有希望。这条真理正体现了联合国的精神所在。六十年前，联合国创始会员国在起草的宪章中阐明了伟大崇高的目标。宪章要求联合国决心"欲免后世再遭惨不堪言之战祸"，"重申基本人权之信念"，并"促成大自由中之社会进步及较善之民生"。我们一如既往决心实现上述崇高目标。我们在满足巨大的人道主义需求之时，必须积极应对我们这个时代其他的重大挑战。我们必须继续努力减轻苦难，积极传播自由，并为我们的子孙后代奠定持久和平的基础。

在这个新的世纪，全世界各个偏远的角落比以往任何时候都更加紧密地

联系在一起，没有任何国家能继续置身事外，对其他国家的艰苦奋斗无动于衷。当一个国家或一个地区充满绝望，充满怨恨，无力抵挡暴力和侵略意识之时，威胁就会穿越大洋和国界，有可能危及任何爱好和平国家的安全。

从仇恨和绝望中滋生的恐怖主义袭击了突尼斯、印度尼西亚、肯尼亚、坦桑尼亚、摩洛哥、以色列、沙特阿拉伯、美国、土耳其、西班牙、俄罗斯、埃及、伊拉克和英国等很多国家。在本国领土上未遇到袭击的人们也承受了恐怖袭击带来的悲伤——澳大利亚人在巴厘遇难，意大利人在埃及被害，2001 年 9 月 11 日，来自数十个国家的公民就在我们今天开会的这个城市被夺去了生命。教训是不言自明的：对此视若无睹，或为了寻求安宁生活对他人遭受的苦难和压迫不闻不问，绝对不可能带来安全。不是希望传遍人间，就是暴力四处蔓延。两者必居其一，而我们必须站在希望的一边。

有时我们为了安全而必须直接抗击威胁，许多国家因此而结成一个伟大的联盟，并肩打击世界各地的恐怖分子。我们共同努力，为瓦解跨国恐怖网络和摧毁本国境内的激进基层组织做出贡献。我们清除了恐怖分子的庇护所。我们正运用外交和财政手段切断他们的财源，断绝他们得到支援的渠道。恐怖分子必须明白，我们正在与他们进行斗争，全世界团结一致共同对敌。我们必须完成《全面制止国际恐怖主义公约》，使每个国家都明确：不论出于什么原因，也不论有什么怨恨，都不能成为恐怖分子蓄意袭击和杀害平民和非战斗人员的理由或使其行为合法化。

全世界的自由国家决心制止恐怖分子及其同盟者获得致命的大规模杀人武器发泄他们的仇恨。有鉴于此，有六十多个国家支持防扩散安全倡议，以阻截通过陆地、海上和空中运送的大规模毁灭性武器。恐怖分子必须明白，他们无论在何处藏身，都无法逃脱正义的惩罚。

今天晚些时候，安理会将表决谴责煽动恐怖行为的决议，向恐怖分子发出警告。这项决议要求所有的国家采取适当步骤终止这类煽动活动。我们还需要签署并实施《制止核恐怖行为国际公约》，使所有寻求放射性物质或核装置的人无论走到哪里都会受到起诉和引渡。我们必须向支持恐怖和寻求大规模毁灭性武器的非法政权统治者发出明确的信息：绝不允许你们威胁世界和平与稳定。

直接抗击我们的敌人是绝对必要的，因此文明国家必须继续主动向恐怖分子出击。然而，大家知道这场战争不能单靠武力获胜。我们必须在战场上击败恐怖分子，也必须在意识形态的战斗中战而胜之。我们必须向从不了解自由为何物的亿万人民传播自由的希望，铲除恐怖分子滋生和招兵买马的环境。我们必须帮助国力衰退的国家和停滞不前的社会，不使恐怖分子得到生长的土壤。我们必须保卫并扩大人类尊严、机会与繁荣的前景，这样的前景远比怨恨和屠杀的吸引力要强大。

为了传播希望的种子，美国决心帮助那些在贫穷中挣扎的国家。美国坚持要求实现千年发展目标。这是一个宏伟的目标，要求到 2015 年将贫穷挨饿的人口减少一半，保障全世界所有的儿童都能受到初级教育并制止艾滋病的蔓延等。

我们有帮助他人的道德义务，也有确保我们的行动切实有效的道德责任。2002 年，我们在蒙特雷一致同意有关在新千年消除贫困、制止腐败和提供援助的新设想。发展中国家同意通过良好的国家治理、健全的政策和法治承担本国经济发展的责任。发达国家同意支持这些努力，其中包括对采取必要改革措施的国家增加援助。我国设立了新的世纪挑战账户，以执行《蒙特雷共识》。这一账户逐渐增加美国对实行公正治理，为本国人民谋利益并促进经济自由的国家提供的援助。

还有更多的工作需要做。我呼吁世界所有的国家执行《蒙特雷共识》。执行《蒙特雷共识》意味着继续沿着改革这条艰巨和漫长的道路走下去。执行《蒙特雷共识》意味着在发达国家和发展中国家之间建立真诚的合作伙伴关系，取代过去援助与受援的关系。执行《蒙特雷共识》意味着欢迎所有发展中国家全面参与全球经济，享有所有必要的益处，同时承担所有的义务。

要求使援助与改革挂钩对消除贫困至关重要，但是我们的工作并不因此结束。对于许多国家而言，艾滋病、疟疾及其他疾病既是人道主义的悲剧，也是明显阻碍发展的绊脚石。我们必须为贫困国家提供他们所需的拯救生命的应急药物，帮助他们抗击这些传染病。通过我们的双边项目和全球基金，美国将继续发挥主导作用，为抗击艾滋病的危害提供资源。

今天，美国正与当地政府及组织合作，开展有史以来为抗击某一种疾病而采取的规模最大的行动计划。在非洲大陆，我们正帮助地方卫生官员扩大艾滋病测试设施，为医生、护士和辅导人员提供培训和支援，改善诊所和医院条件。我们与非洲合作伙伴共同努力，已向撒哈拉沙漠以南地区 23 万多人提供了拯救生命的治疗。我们提前完成一个重要目标，为非洲近 200 万成人和儿童提供艾滋病治疗。在苏格兰格伦伊格尔斯举行八国首脑会议期间，我们制定了明确的目标，为非洲这一代人根除艾滋病。我在此呼吁联合国各会员国采取具体措施实现这个目标。

我们还在努力防治疟疾。这个可以预防的疾病每年在全世界范围内造成100 多万人死亡。在这种疾病肆虐的每一个国家，人们都遭受了贫困和痛苦。美国已制定目标，要求至少使非洲十五个高发病国家的疟疾死亡率降低一半。为了实现这个目标，我们已承诺在今后五年内，为防治疟疾基金增拨 12 亿美元以上的资金。我们邀请其他国家与我们共同努力，承诺为需要基金帮助的其他几十个国家提供具体援助。通过共同努力我们就能防治疟疾，拯救成千上万人的生命，为受到这种可怕的疾病摧残的国家带来希望的曙光。

在承诺加强抗击疟疾和艾滋病的同时，我们还必须坚持积极防范禽流感等新的疾病，避免公众健康受到威胁。如果听之任之，禽流感病毒将引发21 世纪的第一场流行病。我们决不能坐视不顾。今天，我宣布新的"预防禽流感国际合作计划"。这个国际合作计划要求面临疾病爆发的国家迅速向世界卫生组织传递信息，提供病毒取样。通过增加透明度的要求，我们就能对危害健康的疫情做出迅速反应，及时防止病毒蔓延。许多国家已参加了这项计划，我们邀请所有国家参与。我们共同努力是十分必要的，我们在这么做的同时也在履行保护我国公民，救死扶伤和抚慰受害者的道义责任。

即使用于抗击疾病和改革经济的援助不断增加，许多国家仍然受困于另外一项严重挑战：债务负担。债务重担使发展中的经济增长受到限制，使千百万人民处于贫困状态。因此，美国及许多其他国家还采取行动减免债务重负。今天，债务负担最重的贫穷国家正在接受 300 多亿美元的债务救助。为了防止今后的债务累积，我国和其他国家已一致同意，国际金融机构应该逐步增加以赠款方式而不是以借贷的方式提供新的援助。八国集团在苏格兰的格伦伊格尔斯开会时同意采取进一步行动。为了永久打破"借贷—减免"的循环，我们同意百分之百取消全世界负债最重的一些国家的债务。我呼吁世界银行和国际货币基金组织尽快落实这项具有历史意义的协议。

我们将积极努力帮助遭受苦难的地区摆脱贫困的重荷——不只限于目前，而是持之以恒。为了实现更富裕的前景，最有保障的途径是扩大贸易。联合国秘书长在今年 8 月写给我的信中赞赏八国集团的工作，但他告诉我，援助与债务减免仍然不够。秘书长说，我们还需要取消阻碍发展中国家前进的贸易壁垒和补贴。我同意秘书长的看法：多哈回合谈判是实现这项目标的"最有希望的途径"。

多哈回合谈判取得成功将降低和取消阻碍农工产品贸易的关税及其他壁垒。不公平的农业补贴将不复存在。全球服务业市场将实现开放。根据多哈协议每个国家都会受益，而发展中国家会获得最大的收益。历史上凡是敞开贸易大门的发展中国家，经济增长率高于其他国家数倍之多。取消贸易壁垒有可能在今后十五年内使几亿人脱离贫困。此事关系重大。全世界千百万最贫穷人民的生活与未来何去何从——我们务必要促使多哈贸易谈判取得成功。

多哈谈判是朝一个更大目标迈出的重要一步：我们必须拆除阻隔发达国家和发展中国家的一道道围墙。我们必须使最贫穷国家的人民获得与富裕国

家人民同样的融入世界经济的能力，如此他们就能与其他人一样在世界市场上提供自己的商品，发挥自己的才能。我们需要保证他们拥有同样的机会实现他们的理想，供养他们的家庭，过上有尊严和自立的生活。

实现这些目标的最大障碍是关税壁垒、补贴以及把发展中国家人民与21世纪提供的重要机会隔离开来的种种障碍。今天，我重申我以前提出的艰巨任务：我们必须通过多哈谈判共同努力，取消扭曲贸易和阻碍发展的农业补贴，撤除关税壁垒及其他障碍，为全世界农民开放市场。今天，我通过提出下列保证扩大上述挑战的范围：美国准备与其他国家一起取消一切关税、补贴及其他阻碍商品和服务自由流通的各种障碍。这是全世界最贫穷国家战胜贫困的关键。我们必须为所有的国家促进繁荣，创造机会。

我们通过扩大贸易，让希望和机遇遍及全世界每个角落，并沉重打击在忿恨与不满中滋生的恐怖主义分子。我们扩大自由贸易的要求是我们增进世界自由的使命的一部分，使世界人民能够按照自己选择的方式生活、祈祷并养育子女。从长远来看，捍卫宗教自由和保护妇女和少数族裔权利的最佳途径是建立自我管理机制，从而使人们能够坚持并捍卫自己的权利。所有倡导人权的人也必须倡导人类自由。

当前自由的事业面临重大机遇。在世界各地人类自由的理念如此深入人心，堪称前所未有。仅在过去的两年中，千百万民众在阿富汗、伊拉克、黎巴嫩、巴勒斯坦领土、吉尔吉斯斯坦、乌克兰和格鲁吉亚的自由选举中参加了投票。他们行使自己的自由权利，同时也激励了大中东地区其他国家的千百万大众。我们必须鼓舞他们的士气。我们必须扶持民主进程。联合国应为此发挥关键作用。

通过新设立的联合国民主基金，联合国会员国中的民主国家将向希望加入民主共同体的国家提供帮助。世界上人口最多的民主国家印度承诺提供1000万美元启动民主基金，发挥了应有的主导作用。民主基金的成功关系到每一个自由国家的利益，每一个自由国家都有责任推进自由的事业。

实现民主不仅在于举行公平的选举，还必须建立长期维护自由的机制。民主在不同的文化中有不同的形式，但所有的自由社会都有一些共同的特点。民主国家维护法治，限制国家权力，并让妇女和少数族裔享有全部公民权利。民主国家保护私有财产、言论自由和宗教言论。民主国家奖励并尊重本国人民的聪明才智，从而使国力不断增强。民主国家依靠本国公民的努力实现国家强盛，从不对邻国强取豪夺，从而为和平与稳定做出贡献。

由于这些原因，自由伊拉克的成败关系到整个世界的重大利益，任何文明国家都不愿意看到一个新的恐怖政权在这个国家重新出现。因此，自由世界正共同努力，帮助伊拉克人民建立一个能够进行自治、自立和自卫的新国家。这为在座的所有人提供了一个令人振奋的机会。而联合国为今年 1 月伊拉克选举的成功发挥了极其重要的作用，850 万伊拉克选民不顾恐怖分子的威胁参加了投票。此后，联合国又支持伊拉克民选领导人起草新宪法。

为建立完全符合宪法原则的政府，伊拉克人民正走上这条征途，联合国及其会员国必须继续同他们站在一起。伊拉克人民一旦完成这项使命，他们的成功将鼓舞其他国家的人民争取自己的自由，中东将在和平、希望与自由的氛围中成长壮大，我们所有的人都将在一个更安全的世界上生活。

推进自由与安全是我们时代的呼唤，也是联合国承担的使命。联合国的创建就是为了传播自由的希望，为了抗击贫困和疾病，为了帮助全世界所有的人获得人的权利和人的尊严。为了实现这些许诺，联合国必须做到强大有效，必须拒绝受腐败侵蚀，必须向服务对象负责。联合国必须坚持廉正，必须以其为别人制订的高标准来要求自己。联合国有意义的机构改革必须包括采取措施改进内部监察机制，确定节省开支的方案，保证宝贵资源用于既定目的。

联合国已在改革道路上迈出了第一步。改革进程将在今秋的联合国大会期间继续进行，美国将与其他国家一起主导改革工作。而改革的进程应以会员国认真对待自己承担的责任为起点。这个重要机构的会员国曾推选臭名昭

著侵犯人权的国家为联合国人权委员会成员，使这项崇高的事业蒙羞，使整个联合国组织的信誉受到损害。会员国如果希望联合国受到尊重并发挥高效，就应该从保证联合国值得令人尊重开始。

新世纪伊始，全世界都需要联合国忠实于自己的理想并履行自己的使命。联合国的创始会员国笃信，全世界的安全日益取决于增进人类权利的努力，这需要多方面共同努力。富兰克林·罗斯福总统在 1945 年决定美国接受建立联合国的构想后表示："构筑世界和平绝非一人、一党、一国之功。"每一个国家和每一代人都肩负着维护和平的重任。

在每一个历史阶段，人类精神都不免因出现黑暗与混乱受到挑战。有一些挑战是天灾，也有一些挑战是人祸。联合国成立的宗旨是发挥人类的最高智慧，动员全世界团结一致迎接这些挑战。我们将以我们的胆识和良知履行保护人类生命和权利的职责。我们将努力实现联合国的承诺，保障我们大家都能按照造物主的意旨，人人享有平安、自由和尊严。

第三节 精彩语录

We have witnessed the awesome power of nature—and the greater power of human compassion.

我们目睹了大自然的惊人威力，但更有威力的是人类的关爱。

Your response, like the response to last year's tsunami, has shown once again that the world is more compassionate and hopeful when we act together. This truth was the inspiration for the United Nations.

你们的救援行动，与去年援助海啸灾区的行动一样，再次说明我们齐心协力能使全世界更富有关爱之情，也更有希望。这条真理正体现了联合国的精神所在。

In this young century, the far corners of the world are linked more closely than ever before—and no nation can remain isolated and indifferent to the struggles of others. When a country, or a region is filled with despair, and resentment and vulnerable to violent and aggressive ideologies, the threat

passes easily across oceans and borders, and could threaten the security of any peaceful country.

在这个新的世纪，全世界各个偏远的角落比以往任何时候都更加紧密地联系在一起，没有任何国家能继续置身事外，对其他国家的艰苦奋斗无动于衷。当一个国家或一个地区充满绝望，充满怨恨，无力抵挡暴力和侵略意识之时，威胁就会穿越大洋和国界，有可能危及任何爱好和平国家的安全。

Either hope will spread, or violence will spread—and we must take the side of hope.

不是希望传遍人间，就是暴力四处蔓延，两者必居其一，而我们必须站在希望的一边。

We must defend and extend a vision of human dignity, and opportunity, and prosperity—a vision far stronger than the dark appeal of resentment and murder.

我们必须保卫并扩大人类尊严、机会与繁荣的前景，这样的前景远比怨恨和屠杀的吸引力要强大。

By expanding trade, we spread hope and opportunity to the corners of the world, and we strike a blow against the terrorists who feed on anger and resentment. Our agenda for freer trade is part of our agenda for a freer world, where people can live and worship and raise their children as they choose.

我们通过扩大贸易，让希望和机遇遍及全世界每个角落，并沉重打击在忿恨与不满中滋生的恐怖主义分子。我们扩大自由贸易的要求是我们增进世界自由的使命的一部分，使世界人民能够按照自己选择的方式生活、祈祷并养育子女。

第十三章

振兴美国经济

第一节 背景介绍

美国在开国初期就有了国情咨文这种形式。国情咨文是美国统治阶级的施政纲领，主要阐明美国总统每年面临的国内外情况，也就是对于国家政治、经济、文化等方面基本情况的报告，以及政府将要采取的政策措施。按照美国惯例，每年年初现任总统都要在国会做年度报告，阐述政府的施政方针。

《美利坚合众国宪法》中写道："总统应随时向国会报告联邦情况。"也就是对于国家政治、经济、文化等方面基本情况的报告。这个"联邦情况"后来有了专用名"国情咨文"。乔治·华盛顿于 1790 年 1 月 8 日做了第一份关于"联邦情况"的报告，该报告当时被称为"年度咨文"。1801 年，托马斯·杰斐逊将他的"年度报告"以书面形式递交国会。此后，这一形式延续了 112 年。1913 年，伍德罗·威尔逊又回到国会大厦，亲自向国会做"年度报告"。1945 年，该报告开始被正式称为"国情咨文"，并且不再仅仅面对国会议员，而是通过广播电视面向广大民众传递总统的政策主张。1947 年，哈里·杜鲁门在电视上公开向全国做年度报告。自此以后，总统的年度报告被称为"国情咨文演说"。

国情咨文经过一百多年的演变，特别是电视直播的出现，已经从空洞的政策演说演变成一项重大的游说宣传。更是总统驾驭与国会关系的一个基本手段和发挥国家领导作用的有力方式。因此，美国历届总统都非常重视国情咨文的作用，历史上著名的"门罗主义"就是门罗总统通过国情咨文的形式传递出来的。

在此次国情咨文中，布什提到："美国经济正经历不确定阶段……长期来讲，美国人对经济增长持有信心。短期来看，我们发现经济增长正在放缓。"然而，正值全球经济正出现显著变化之时，由于担心美国经济陷入衰退，全球金融市场已经因为美国股市的剧烈震荡显示出"过山车"行情，令包括美国人在内的全球投资者神经高度紧张。布什也承认美国经济增速正在放缓，但他仍坚持长期基本面依然良好的判断。鉴于此，布什敦促国会参议院尽快通过总额为 1,500 亿美元的经济刺激计划，以支持消费开支和企业投资增长，确保经济健康和扩大就业。

布什呼吁国会能够永久实施他提出的减税措施，因为他确信这是确保美国经济持续健康发展的最重要一步，也是能促使美国经济增长的重要经济刺激计划，以保证美国人人有工作。他相信美国国会会尽快批复。此外，他还警告那些旨在提高税收的提案都将遭到他的否决。

由于美国的经济增长越来越依赖于其向全球出口美国商品和服务的能力。因此，布什敦促国会批准美国与哥伦比亚、巴拿马和韩国的自由贸易协定，想以此来缓解美国自身正遭遇的经济困难。

此次发表的国情咨文是布什总统在任期内的最后一次国情咨文演说，这也代表着他总统任期结束或结尾阶段的开始。

第二节 布什于 2008 年在国会大厦

最后一次发表国情咨文

Madam Speaker, Vice President Cheney, Members of Congress, distinguished guests, and fellow citizens,

Seven years have passed since I first stood before you at this rostrum. In that time, our country has been tested in ways none of us could have imagined. We have faced hard decisions about peace and war, rising competition in the world economy, and the health and welfare of our citizens. These issues call for vigorous debate, and I think it's fair to say we've answered that call. Yet history will record that amid our differences, we acted with purpose. And together, we showed the world the power and resilience of American self-government.

All of us were sent to Washington to carry out the people's business. That is the purpose of this body. It is the meaning of our oath. And it remains our charge to keep.

The actions of the 110th Congress will affect the security and prosperity of our Nation long after this session has ended. In this election year, let us show our fellow Americans that we recognize our responsibilities and are determined to meet them. And let us show them that Republicans and Democrats can compete for votes and cooperate for results at the same time.

From expanding opportunity to protecting our country, we have made good progress. Yet we have unfinished business before us, and the American people expect us to get it done.

In the work ahead, we must be guided by the philosophy that made our Nation great. As Americans, we believe in the power of individuals to determine their destiny and shape the course of history. We believe that the most reliable guide for our country is the collective wisdom of ordinary citizens. So in all we do, we must trust in the ability of free people to make wise decisions, and empower them to improve their lives and their futures.

To build a prosperous future, we must trust people with their own money and empower them to grow our economy. As we meet tonight, our economy is undergoing a period of uncertainty. America has added jobs for a record 52 straight months, but jobs are now growing at a slower pace. Wages are up, but so are prices for food and gas. Exports are rising, but the housing market has declined. And at kitchen tables across our country, there is concern about our economic future.

In the long run, Americans can be confident about our economic growth. But in the short run, we can all see that growth is slowing. So last week, my administration reached agreement with Speaker Pelosi and Republican Leader Boehner on a robust growth package that includes tax relief for individuals and families and incentives for business investment. The temptation will be to load up the bill. That would delay it or derail it, and neither option is acceptable. This is a good agreement that will keep our economy growing and our people working. And this Congress must pass it as soon as possible.

We have other work to do on taxes. Unless the Congress acts, most of the tax relief we have delivered over the past 7 years will be taken away. Some

in Washington argue that letting tax relief expire is not a tax increase. Try explaining that to 116 million American taxpayers who would see their taxes rise by an average of $1,800. Others have said they would personally be happy to pay higher taxes. I welcome their enthusiasm, and I am pleased to report that the IRS accepts both checks and money orders.

Most Americans think their taxes are high enough. With all the other pressures on their finances, American families should not have to worry about the Federal government taking a bigger bite out of their paychecks. There is only one way to eliminate this uncertainty: make the tax relief permanent. And members of Congress should know: If any bill raising taxes reaches my desk, I will veto it.

Just as we trust Americans with their own money, we need to earn their trust by spending their tax dollars wisely. Next week, I will send you a budget that terminates or substantially reduces 151 wasteful or bloated programs totaling more than $18 billion. And this budget will keep America on track for a surplus in 2012. American families have to balance their budgets, and so should their government.

The people's trust in their government is undermined by congressional earmarks—special interest projects that are often snuck in at the last minute, without discussion or debate. Last year, I asked you to voluntarily cut the number and cost of earmarks in half. I also asked you to stop slipping earmarks into committee reports that never even come to a vote. Unfortunately, neither goal was met. So this time, if you send me an appropriations bill that does not cut the number and cost of earmarks in half, I will send it back to you with my veto. And tomorrow, I will issue an Executive Order that directs Federal agencies to ignore any future earmark that is not voted on by the Congress. If these items are truly worth funding, the Congress should debate them in the open and hold a public vote.

Our shared responsibilities extend beyond matters of taxes and spending.

On housing, we must trust Americans with the responsibility of homeownership and empower them to weather turbulent times in the housing market. My administration brought together the HOPE NOW alliance, which is helping many struggling homeowners avoid foreclosure. The Congress can help even more. Tonight I ask you to pass legislation to reform Fannie Mae and Freddie Mac, modernize the Federal Housing Administration, and allow state housing agencies to issue tax–free bonds to help homeowners refinance their mortgages. These are difficult times for many American families, and by taking these steps, we can help more of them keep their homes.

To build a future of quality health care, we must trust patients and doctors to make medical decisions and empower them with better information and better options. We share a common goal: making health care more affordable and accessible for all Americans. The best way to achieve that goal is by expanding consumer choice, not government control. So I have proposed ending the bias in the tax code against those who do not get their health insurance through their employer. This one reform would put private coverage within reach for millions, and I call on the Congress to pass it this year. The Congress must also expand health savings accounts, create association health plans for small businesses, promote health information technology, and confront the epidemic of junk medical lawsuits. With all these steps, we will help ensure that decisions about your medical care are made in the privacy of your doctor's office—not in the halls of Congress.

On education, we must trust students to learn if given the chance and empower parents to demand results from our schools. In neighborhoods across our country, there are boys and girls with dreams—and a decent education is their only hope of achieving them. Six years ago, we came together to pass the *No Child Left Behind Act*, and today no one can deny its results. Last year,

fourth and eighth graders achieved the highest math scores on record. Reading scores are on the rise. And African-American and Hispanic students posted all-time highs. Now we must work together to increase accountability, add flexibility for states and districts, reduce the number of high school dropouts, and provide extra help for struggling schools. members of Congress: *The No Child Left Behind Act* is a bipartisan achievement. It is succeeding. And we owe it to America's children, their parents, and their teachers to strengthen this good law.

We must also do more to help children when their schools do not measure up. Thanks to the D.C. Opportunity Scholarships you approved, more than 2,600 of the poorest children in our nation's capital have found new hope at a faith-based or other non-public school. Sadly, these schools are disappearing at an alarming rate in many of America's inner cities. So I will convene a White House summit aimed at strengthening these lifelines of learning. And to open the doors of these schools to more children, I ask you to support a new $300 million program called Pell Grants for Kids. We have seen how Pell Grants help low-income college students realize their full potential. Together, we have expanded the size and reach of these grants. Now let's apply that same spirit to help liberate poor children trapped in failing public schools.

On trade, we must trust American workers to compete with anyone in the world and empower them by opening up new markets overseas. Today, our economic growth increasingly depends on our ability to sell American goods, crops, and services all over the world. So we are working to break down barriers to trade and investment wherever we can. We are working for a successful Doha round of trade talks, and we must complete a good agreement this year. At the same time, we are pursuing opportunities to open up new markets by passing free trade agreements.

I thank the Congress for approving a good agreement with Peru. Now I ask you to approve agreements with Colombia, Panama, and South Korea. Many products from these nations now enter America duty-free, yet many of our products face steep tariffs in their markets. These agreements will level the playing field. They will give us better access to nearly 100 million customers. And they will support good jobs for the finest workers in the world: those whose products say "Made in the USA".

These agreements also promote America's strategic interests. The first agreement that will come before you is with Colombia, a friend of America that is confronting violence and terror and fighting drug traffickers. If we fail to pass this agreement, we will embolden the purveyors of false populism in our hemisphere. So we must come together, pass this agreement, and show our neighbors in the region that democracy leads to a better life.

Trade brings better jobs, better choices, and better prices. Yet for some Americans, trade can mean losing a job, and the Federal government has a responsibility to help. I ask the Congress to reauthorize and reform trade adjustment assistance, so we can help these displaced workers learn new skills and find new jobs.

To build a future of energy security, we must trust in the creative genius of American researchers and entrepreneurs and empower them to pioneer a new generation of clean energy technology. Our security, our prosperity, and our environment all require reducing our dependence on oil. Last year, I asked you to pass legislation to reduce oil consumption over the next decade, and you responded. Together we should take the next steps: Let us fund new technologies that can generate coal power while capturing carbon emissions. Let us increase the use of renewable power and emissions-free nuclear power. Let us continue investing in advanced battery technology and renewable fuels to power the cars and trucks of the future. Let us create a new international clean technology fund, which will help developing nations like India and China

make greater use of clean energy sources. And let us complete an international agreement that has the potential to slow, stop, and eventually reverse the growth of greenhouse gases. This agreement will be effective only if it includes commitments by every major economy and gives none a free ride. The United States is committed to strengthening our energy security and confronting global climate change. And the best way to meet these goals is for America to continue leading the way toward the development of cleaner and more efficient technology.

To keep America competitive into the future, we must trust in the skill of our scientists and engineers and empower them to pursue the breakthroughs of tomorrow. Last year, the Congress passed legislation supporting the *American Competitiveness Initiative*, but never followed through with the funding. This funding is essential to keeping our scientific edge. So I ask the Congress to double Federal support for critical basic research in the physical sciences and ensure America remains the most dynamic nation on earth.

On matters of science and life, we must trust in the innovative spirit of medical researchers and empower them to discover new treatments while respecting moral boundaries. In November, we witnessed a landmark achievement when scientists discovered a way to reprogram adult skin cells to act like embryonic stem cells. This breakthrough has the potential to move us beyond the divisive debates of the past by extending the frontiers of medicine without the destruction of human life. So we are expanding funding for this type of ethical medical research. And as we explore promising avenues of research, we must also ensure that all life is treated with the dignity it deserves. So I call on the Congress to pass legislation that bans unethical practices such as the buying, selling, patenting, or cloning of human life.

On matters of justice, we must trust in the wisdom of our Founders and empower judges who understand that the Constitution means what it says. I have submitted judicial nominees who will rule by the letter of the law, not the whim of the gavel. Many of these nominees are being unfairly delayed. They are worthy of confirmation, and the Senate should give each of them a prompt up-or-down vote.

In communities across our land, we must trust in the good heart of the American people and empower them to serve their neighbors in need. Over the past seven years, more of our fellow citizens have discovered that the pursuit of happiness leads to the path of service. Americans have volunteered in record numbers. Charitable donations are higher than ever. Faith-based groups are bringing hope to pockets of despair, with newfound support from the Federal government. And to help guarantee equal treatment for faith-based organizations when they compete for Federal funds, I ask you to permanently extend Charitable Choice.

Tonight the armies of compassion continue the march to a new day in the Gulf Coast. America honors the strength and resilience of the people of this region. We reaffirm our pledge to help them build stronger and better than before. And tonight I am pleased to announce that in April we will host this year's North American Summit of Canada, Mexico, and the United States in the great city of New Orleans.

There are two other pressing challenges that I have raised repeatedly before this body, and that this body has failed to address: entitlement spending and immigration.

Every member in this chamber knows that spending on entitlement programs like Social Security, Medicare, and Medicaid is growing faster than we can afford. And we all know the painful choices ahead if America stays on this path: massive tax increases, sudden and drastic cuts in benefits, or crippling deficits. I have laid out proposals to reform these programs. Now I ask members of Congress to offer your proposals and come up with a bipartisan solution to

save these vital programs for our children and grandchildren.

The other pressing challenge is immigration. America needs to secure our borders—and with your help, my administration is taking steps to do so. We are increasing worksite enforcement, we are deploying fences and advanced technologies to stop illegal crossings, we have effectively ended the policy of "catch and release" at the border, and by the end of this year, we will have doubled the number of border patrol agents. Yet we also need to acknowledge that we will never fully secure our border until we create a lawful way for foreign workers to come here and support our economy. This will take pressure off the border and allow law enforcement to concentrate on those who mean us harm. We must also find a sensible and humane way to deal with people here illegally. Illegal immigration is complicated, but it can be resolved. And it must be resolved in a way that upholds both our laws and our highest ideals.

This is the business of our nation here at home. Yet building a prosperous future for our citizens also depends on confronting enemies abroad and advancing liberty in troubled regions of the world.

Our foreign policy is based on a clear premise: We trust that people, when given the chance, will choose a future of freedom and peace. In the last seven years, we have witnessed stirring moments in the history of liberty. We have seen citizens in Georgia and Ukraine stand up for their right to free and fair elections. We have seen people in Lebanon take to the streets to demand their independence. We have seen Afghans emerge from the tyranny of the Taliban to choose a new president and a new parliament. We have seen jubilant Iraqis holding up ink-stained fingers and celebrating their freedom. And these images of liberty have inspired us.

In the past seven years, we have also seen images that have sobered us. We have watched throngs of mourners in Lebanon and Pakistan carrying the caskets of beloved leaders taken by the assassin's hand. We have seen wedding guests in blood-soaked finery staggering from a hotel in Jordan, Afghans and Iraqis blown up in mosques and markets, and trains in London and Madrid ripped apart by bombs. And on a clear September day, we saw thousands of our fellow citizens taken from us in an instant. These horrific images serve as a grim reminder: The advance of liberty is opposed by terrorists and extremists—evil men who despise freedom, despise America, and aim to subject millions to their violent rule.

Since September 11, we have taken the fight to these terrorists and extremists. We will stay on the offense, we will keep up the pressure, and we will deliver justice to the enemies of America.

We are engaged in the defining ideological struggle of the 21st century. The terrorists oppose every principle of humanity and decency that we hold dear. Yet in this war on terror, there is one thing we and our enemies agree on: In the long run, men and women who are free to determine their own destinies will reject terror and refuse to live in tyranny. That is why the terrorists are fighting to deny this choice to people in Lebanon,Iraq, Afghanistan, Pakistan, and the Palestinian Territories. And that is why, for the security of America and the peace of the world, we are spreading the hope of freedom.

In Afghanistan, America, our 25 NATO allies, and 15 partner nations are helping the Afghan people defend their freedom and rebuild their country. Thanks to the courage of these military and civilian personnel, a nation that was once a safe haven for al-Qaeda is now a young democracy where boys and girls are going to school, new roads and hospitals are being built, and people are looking to the future with new hope. These successes must continue, so we are adding 3,200 Marines to our forces in Afghanistan, where they will fight the terrorists and train the Afghan Army and police. Defeating the Taliban and al-Qaeda is critical to our security, and I thank the Congress for supporting America's vital mission in Afghanistan.

In Iraq, the terrorists and extremists are fighting to deny a proud people their liberty and to establish safe havens for attacks across the world. One year ago, our enemies were succeeding in their efforts to plunge Iraq into chaos. So we reviewed our strategy and changed course. We launched a surge of American forces into Iraq. And we gave our troops a new mission: Work with Iraqi forces to protect the Iraqi people, pursue the enemy in its strongholds, and deny the terrorists sanctuary anywhere in the country.

The Iraqi people quickly realized that something dramatic had happened. Those who had worried that America was preparing to abandon them instead saw tens of thousands of American forces flowing into their country. They saw our forces moving into neighborhoods, clearing out the terrorists, and staying behind to ensure the enemy did not return. And they saw our troops, along with provincial reconstruction teams that include foreign service officers and other skilled public servants, coming in to ensure that improved security was followed by improvements in daily life. Our military and civilians in Iraq are performing with courage and distinction, and they have the gratitude of our whole nation.

The Iraqis launched a surge of their own. In the fall of 2006, Sunni tribal leaders grew tired of al Qaeda's brutality and started a popular uprising called "The Anbar Awakening." Over the past year, similar movements have spread across the country. And today, this grassroots surge includes more than 80,000 Iraqi citizens who are fighting the terrorists. The government in Baghdad has stepped forward as well—adding more than 100,000 new Iraqi soldiers and police during the past year.

While the enemy is still dangerous and more work remains, the American and Iraqi surges have achieved results few of us could have imagined just 1 year ago.

When we met last year, many said containing the violence was impossible. A year later, high profile terrorist attacks are down, civilian deaths are down, and sectarian killings are down.

When we met last year, militia extremists—some armed and trained by Iran—were wreaking havoc in large areas of Iraq. A year later, coalition and Iraqi forces have killed or captured hundreds of militia fighters. And Iraqis of all backgrounds increasingly realize that defeating these militia fighters is critical to the future of their country.

When we met last year, al–Qaeda had sanctuaries in many areas of Iraq, and their leaders had just offered American forces safe passage out of the country. Today, it is al–Qaeda that is searching for safe passage. They have been driven from many of the strongholds they once held, and over the past year, we have captured or killed thousands of extremists in Iraq, including hundreds of key al–Qaeda leaders and operatives. Last month, Osama bin Laden released a tape in which he railed against Iraqi tribal leaders who have turned on al–Qaeda and admitted that coalition forces are growing stronger in Iraq. Ladies and gentlemen, some may deny the surge is working, but among the terrorists there is no doubt. Al–Qaeda is on the run in Iraq, and this enemy will be defeated.

When we met last year, our troop levels in Iraq were on the rise. Today, because of the progress just described, we are implementing a policy of "return on success," and the surge forces we sent to Iraq are beginning to come home.

This progress is a credit to the valor of our troops and the brilliance of their commanders. This evening, I want to speak directly to our men and women on the frontlines. Soldiers, Sailors, Airmen, Marines, and Coast Guardsmen: In the past year, you have done everything we have asked of you, and more. Our nation is grateful for your courage. We are proud of your accomplishments. And tonight in this hallowed chamber, with the American people as our witness, we make you a solemn pledge: In the fight ahead, you will have all you need to protect our nation. And I ask the Congress to meet its responsibilities to these

brave men and women by fully funding our troops.

Our enemies in Iraq have been hit hard. They are not yet defeated, and we can still expect tough fighting ahead. Our objective in the coming year is to sustain and build on the gains we made in 2007, while transitioning to the next phase of our strategy. American troops are shifting from leading operations, to partnering with Iraqi forces, and, eventually, to a protective overwatch mission. As part of this transition, one Army brigade combat team and one Marine Expeditionary Unit have already come home and will not be replaced. In the coming months, four additional brigades and two Marine battalions will follow suit. Taken together, this means more than 20,000 of our troops are coming home.

Any further drawdown of U.S. troops will be based on conditions in Iraq and the recommendations of our commanders. General Petraeus has warned that too fast a drawdown could result in the "disintegration of the Iraqi security forces, al-Qaeda-Iraq regaining lost ground, and a marked increase in violence." Members of Congress: Having come so far and achieved so much, we must not allow this to happen.

In the coming year, we will work with Iraqi leaders as they build on the progress they are making toward political reconciliation. At the local level, Sunnis, Shia, and Kurds are beginning to come together to reclaim their communities and rebuild their lives. Progress in the provinces must be matched by progress in Baghdad. And we are seeing some encouraging signs. The national government is sharing oil revenues with the provinces. The parliament recently passed both a pension law and de-Ba'athification reform. Now they are debating a provincial powers law. The Iraqis still have a distance to travel. But after decades of dictatorship and the pain of sectarian violence, reconciliation is taking place—and the Iraqi people are taking control of their future.

The mission in Iraq has been difficult and trying for our nation. But it is in the vital interest of the United States that we succeed. A free Iraq will deny al-Qaeda a safe haven. A free Iraq will show millions across the Middle East that a future of liberty is possible. And a free Iraq will be a friend of America, a partner in fighting terror, and a source of stability in a dangerous part of the world.

By contrast, a failed Iraq would embolden extremists, strengthen Iran, and give terrorists a base from which to launch new attacks on our friends, our allies, and our homeland. The enemy has made its intentions clear. At a time when the momentum seemed to favor them, al-Qaeda's top commander in Iraq declared that they will not rest until they have attacked us here in Washington. My fellow Americans: We will not rest either. We will not rest until this enemy has been defeated. We must do the difficult work today, so that years from now people will look back and say that this generation rose to the moment, prevailed in a tough fight, and left behind a more hopeful region and a safer America.

We are also standing against the forces of extremism in the Holy Land, where we have new cause for hope. Palestinians have elected a president who recognizes that confronting terror is essential to achieving a state where his people can live in dignity and at peace with Israel. Israelis have leaders who recognize that a peaceful, democratic Palestinian state will be a source of lasting security. This month in Ramallah and Jerusalem, I assured leaders from both sides that America will do, and I will do, everything we can to help them achieve a peace agreement that defines a Palestinian state by the end of this year. The time has come for a Holy Land where a democratic Israel and a democratic Palestine live side-by-side in peace.

On the homefront, we will continue to take every lawful and effective measure to protect our country. This is our most solemn duty. We are grateful that there has not been another attack on our soil since September 11. This is not for a lack of desire or effort on the part of the enemy. In the past six years,

we have stopped numerous attacks, including a plot to fly a plane into the tallest building in Los Angeles and another to blow up passenger jets bound for America over the Atlantic. Dedicated men and women in our government toil day and night to stop the terrorists from carrying out their plans. These good citizens are saving American lives, and everyone in this chamber owes them our thanks. And we owe them something more: We owe them the tools they need to keep our people safe.

One of the most important tools we can give them is the ability to monitor terrorist communications. To protect America, we need to know who the terrorists are talking to, what they are saying, and what they are planning. Last year, the Congress passed legislation to help us do that. Unfortunately, the Congress set the legislation to expire on February 1. This means that if you do not act by Friday, our ability to track terrorist threats would be weakened and our citizens will be in greater danger. The Congress must ensure the flow of vital intelligence is not disrupted. The Congress must pass liability protection for companies believed to have assisted in the efforts to defend America. We have had ample time for debate. The time to act is now.

Protecting our nation from the dangers of a new century requires more than good intelligence and a strong military. It also requires changing the conditions that breed resentment and allow extremists to prey on despair. So America is using its influence to build a freer, more hopeful, and more compassionate world. This is a reflection of our national interest and the calling of our conscience.

America is opposing genocide in Sudan and supporting freedom in countries from Cuba and Zimbabwe to Belarus and Burma.

America is leading the fight against global poverty, with strong education initiatives and humanitarian assistance. We have also changed the way we deliver aid by launching the Millennium Challenge Account. This program strengthens democracy, transparency, and the rule of law in developing nations, and I ask you to fully fund this important initiative.

America is leading the fight against global hunger. Today, more than half the world's food aid comes from the United States. And tonight, I ask the Congress to support an innovative proposal to provide food assistance by purchasing crops directly from farmers in the developing world, so we can build up local agriculture and help break the cycle of famine.

America is leading the fight against disease. With your help, we are working to cut by half the number of malaria–related deaths in 15 African nations. And our Emergency Plan for AIDS Relief is treating 1.4 million people. We can bring healing and hope to many more. So I ask you to maintain the principles that have changed behavior and made this program a success. And I call on you to double our initial commitment to fighting HIV/AIDS by approving an additional $30 billion over the next five years.

America is a force for hope in the world because we are a compassionate people, and some of the most compassionate Americans are those who have stepped forward to protect us. We must keep faith with all who have risked life and limb so that we might live in freedom and peace. Over the past seven years, we have increased funding for veterans by more than 95 percent. As we increase funding, we must also reform our veterans system to meet the needs of a new war and a new generation. I call on the Congress to enact the reforms recommended by Senator Bob Dole and Secretary Donna Shalala, so we can improve the system of care for our wounded warriors and help them build lives of hope, promise, and dignity.

Our military families also sacrifice for America. They endure sleepless nights and the daily struggle of providing for children while a loved one is serving far from home. We have a responsibility to provide for them. So I ask you to join me in expanding their access to childcare, creating new hiring preferences

for military spouses across the Federal government, and allowing our troops to transfer their unused education benefits to their spouses or children. Our military families serve our nation, they inspire our Nation, and tonight our nation honors them.

The secret of our strength, the miracle of America, is that our greatness lies not in our government, but in the spirit and determination of our people. When the Federal Convention met in Philadelphia in 1787, our nation was bound by the *Articles of Confederation*, which began with the words, "We the undersigned delegates." When Gouverneur Morris was asked to draft the preamble to our new Constitution, he offered an important revision and opened with words that changed the course of our nation and the history of the world: "We the people."

By trusting the people, our Founders wagered that a great and noble nation could be built on the liberty that resides in the hearts of all men and women. By trusting the people, succeeding generations transformed our fragile young democracy into the most powerful nation on earth and a beacon of hope for millions. And so long as we continue to trust the people, our nation will prosper, our liberty will be secure, and the State of our Union will remain strong. So tonight, with confidence in freedom's power, and trust in the people, let us set forth to do their business.

议长女士、切尼副总统、各位国会议员、尊贵的来宾以及各位同胞：

我第一次站在这个讲坛上向各位发表国情咨文演说是在七年以前。当时，我国经受了我们大家都无法预见的考验。我们必须就和平与战争、世界经济中日益激烈的竞争以及我国公民的健康与福祉作出艰难的抉择。这些问题要求我们展开激烈的辩论，我认为可以公平地说，我们响应了这一召唤。而且历史将会见证，我们虽有分歧，但采取了果断行动。我们共同向世人展示了美国民治制度的力量和韧性。

我们在座的各位受命来到华盛顿都是要为民众服务。这是这个机构的使命，这是我们誓言的含义。这始终是我们应当履行的职责。

第110届国会采取的行动在其任期结束后仍将对我国的安全与繁荣产生深远影响。在这个大选年，让我们向美国同胞们表明我们深知自己的责任，并决心履行职责。让我们向他们表明共和党人和民主党人能在为赢得选票而竞争的同时为争取实效而合作。

从扩大机遇到保护国土，我们已取得长足进展。但我们还有很多工作要做，而美国人民要求我们完成这些工作。

在今后的工作中，我们必须奉行那些把我国造就成一个伟大国家的原则。作为美国人，我们相信个人能够掌握自己的命运并影响历史的进程。我们相信普通公民的集体智慧是我国最可靠的指南。因此，我们不论做什么都必须相信自由的人民有能力做出明智的决定，并让他们有力量改善自己的生活和前途。

为建设一个繁荣的未来，我们必须让人民支配自己的钱财，并让他们有能力推动我国经济增长。今晚我们在这里集会之时，我国经济正处于一个充满变数的时期。美国的就业机会连续五十二个月持续增加，打破了历史纪录，但目前的增速有所减缓。工资水平得到提高，但食品和汽油价格也不断上涨。出口正在增加，但房产市场却出现下滑。美国各地的家庭都在饭桌上谈论着对我国经济前景的担忧。

从长远来看，我们应当对我国的经济增长抱有信心。但在短期内，我们都看出增长速度正在减缓。因此，本届政府于上周同佩洛西议长和共和党领袖博纳就一套强有力的增长计划达成了协议，其中包括针对个人和家庭的退税计划以及鼓励企业投资的计划。人们难免希望增加议案的内容，但这样做会使议案拖延或脱轨，而这两种结果都是不可接受的。这是一项很好的协议，能保持我国经济增长，并保障人民就业。本届国会必须尽快

通过这项议案。

我们在税收方面还有其他工作有待完成。除非本届国会采取行动，否则我们七年来实施的大多数减税计划将由于到期而被废弃。华盛顿的某些人士声称让减税计划到期作废并不是提高税率。请这些人向 1.16 亿美国纳税人做出解释，他们要缴纳的税款为什么将平均增加 1,800 美元。还有一些人声称他们乐意付更高的税。我赞赏他们的热情，并乐意告诉他们国税局既收支票也收汇票。

大多数美国人都认为他们要付的税够高的了。美国家庭承受着种种经济压力，不应当再让他们担心联邦政府要从他们的收入中扣除更大的一部分。消除这种顾虑的唯一办法是将减税政策永久化。各位国会议员都应当知道：任何一项增税议案如果送到我这里都会被我否决。

就像我们相信美国人民会合理理财，我们也需要理智地使用他们缴纳的税金，以赢得他们的信任。下一周，我将向各位提交一份预算，终止和大幅削减 151 项浪费性或过分膨胀的项目，其总额超过 180 亿美元。按照我将提交的预算，美国可于 2012 年实现财政盈余。美国家庭必须平衡预算，他们的政府也应当这样做。

人民对自己政府的信任受到了国会专项拨款的损害，一些特殊利益项目常常在最后一刻被偷偷塞了进来，既不讨论也不辩论。去年，我请你们自动将专项拨款的数目和金额减少一半。我还请你们停止把从未经过表决的专项拨款偷偷塞进委员会的报告中。令人遗憾的是，两个目标都没有达到。因此，这一次如果你们送给我一份未能将专项拨款的数目和金额减少一半的拨款法案，我就会否决它，把它退还给你们。明天我将发布一个行政令，指示联邦机构将来不要理睬任何未经国会表决的专项拨款。如果这些项目确实值得花费资金，国会应该就其进行公开辩论，公开投票表决。

我们的共同责任不限于征税和开支。

在住房领域，我们必须让美国人能够担起房屋所有人的责任，让他们有能力渡过房产市场的动荡期。本届政府组成了"希望在眼前"联盟，帮助许多处境艰难的房主避免丧失房屋赎回权。国会可以提供更多的帮助。今晚，我吁请你们通过关于改革房利美公司和房贷美公司的法案，并对联邦住房管理局进行现代化改造，允许州住房机构发行免税债券，帮助房主重新贷款。美国很多家庭目前正经历难关，通过这些步骤，我们可以帮助更多的人保住房产。

为了建设一个有优质医疗保健的未来，我们必须把医疗决定权交到病人和医生手中，让他们获得更好的信息，拥有更好的选择。我们的一个共同目标是：让所有美国人都更能够负担和得到医疗服务。实现这一目标的最好办法是扩大消费者的选择，而不是政府的控制。因此我已提议，取消税法中对那些无法参加团体医疗保险计划的人不利的条款。此项改革可以使千百万人有能力自行购买保险，我吁请国会今年通过此项立法。国会还必须发展医疗储蓄帐户，为小企业制定联合医疗计划，推动医疗信息技术，并遏制虚假医疗诉讼的泛滥。通过采取这些措施，我们将帮助确保个人的医疗决定是在其医生的诊所，而不是在国会的大厅内做出。

关于教育我们必须相信，学生只要有机会就会学习，必须让父母有权利要求学校展示教学效果。全国各地社区都有满怀理想的学生——良好的教育是他们实现理想的唯一希望。六年前，我们共同通过了《不让任何一个孩子掉队法》。今天，它的成果无可否认。去年，四年级和八年级学生的数学分数达到最高纪录。阅读成绩正在提高。非洲裔和拉丁裔学生的成绩达到历史最高水平。现在我们必须共同努力，加强问责制，给予州和地区更大的灵活性，减少高中辍学率，为面临困难的学校提供更多帮助。各位议员：《不让任何一个孩子掉队法》是两党的共同成就，它正在取得成功。我们有责任为美国儿童、他们的父母和他们的老师加强这一良好的法律。

我们还必须付出更大努力帮助在落后学校中的孩子。你们批准的哥伦比亚特区机会奖学金使我国首都的 2,600 多名最贫困儿童从一个教会学校和其

他非公立学校获得了新的希望。可悲的是这类学校正在以令人不安的速度从许多美国城市的市区中大批消失。为巩固这些学习的生命线，我将召集一次白宫高峰会议。为了向更多的孩子敞开这些学校的大门，我请你们支持一项3亿美元的"佩尔儿童助学金"新项目。我们已经看到佩尔助学金如何使低收入家庭的大学生充分实现了他们的潜力。我们通过共同努力，扩大了这些赠款的规模和受益人数。现在，让我们以同样的精神来帮助贫困儿童从瘫痪的公立学校中解放出来。

在贸易问题上，我们必须相信美国劳工有与世界上任何人进行竞争的能力，并通过在国外开辟新市场加强他们的竞争力。今天，我国的经济增长越来越依赖于我们在世界各地出售美国商品、农产品和服务的能力。因此，我们正在一切可能的领域努力拆除贸易和投资壁垒。我们正在为多哈回合贸易谈判的成功而努力，我们必须在今年达成一项好的协议。同时，我们正在通过签定自由贸易协定的途径寻求打开新市场的机会。

我感谢国会批准了与秘鲁签定的好协定。现在，我请你们批准与哥伦比亚、巴拿马和韩国签定的协定。目前，这些国家的很多产品免关税进入美国，而我们的很多产品在这些国家的市场上却面临过高的关税。这些协定将创造平等的竞争条件。这些协定将为近一亿名顾客购买我国产品提供便利。这些协定将有助于世界上最优秀的工人保持良好的就业机会：在他们的产品上标有"美国制造"的字样。

这些协定还将推进美国的战略利益。最先请你们审议的将是与哥伦比亚签定的协定，美国的这一友邦正在勇敢地抗击暴力与恐怖，打击毒品贩子。如果我们不能批准这项协定，我们就将使本半球兜售虚假民粹主义的人更加肆无忌惮。因此，我们必须一致行动，通过这项协定，向本地区的邻国表明，民主会带来更美好的生活。

贸易创造更好的就业机会、更好的选择、更低廉的价格。但对有些美国人来说，贸易会导致失业，联邦政府有责任提供帮助。我请国会重新授权和改革贸易调整补助，以便帮助这些失业工人掌握新技能，找到新工作。

为了保障未来的能源，我们必须相信美国科研工作者和企业家的创造才智，使他们有能力开发新一代的清洁能源技术。我们的安全、我们的繁荣和我们的环境都要求我们减少对石油的依赖。去年，我促请你们通过未来十年减少油耗的法案，你们做出了响应。我们应该共同采取下列步骤：让我们为研发捕获碳排放的燃煤发电技术提供资金。让我们增加可再生动力和无排放核动力的使用。让我们继续对先进的电池燃料技术和可再生燃料进行投资，为未来的轿车和卡车提供动力。让我们设立新的国际清洁技术基金，帮助印度和中国等发展中国家更多地利用清洁能源。让我们达成一项有可能减缓和停止增加并最终减少温室气体排放的国际协议。要使这项协议产生效果，每个主要经济体都必须做出承诺，任何国家都不能坐享其成。美国致力于加强本国的能源安全，积极应对全球气候变化。实现这些目标的最佳途径就是美国继续带头开发更清洁、更高效的技术。

要保持美国的竞争力，我们就必须相信我国科技工作者和工程人员的技能，使他们有能力去实现明天的突破。去年，国会通过了支持《提高美国竞争力行动计划》的法案，但一直未能提供资金。提供资金对保持我国的科技优势是必不可少的。因此，我诚请国会将极为重要的对物理科学基础研究的资助加倍，确保美国继续是世界上最有活力的国家。

在生命与科学的问题上，我们必须相信医学科研工作者的创新精神，使他们有能力发现新的治疗方法，同时尊重伦理界限。11月，我们看到了一项具有里程碑意义的成就：科学工作者发现了将人体皮肤细胞改造成胚胎干细胞的方法。这一突破有可能使我们摆脱过去加深分歧的争论，扩展医学研究的领域，而无须毁灭人的生命。因此，我们正在扩大对这类符合伦理的医学研究的资助。在探索大有希望的研究途径时，我们还必须确保所有的生命都得到应有的尊重。因此，我吁请国会通过立法，禁止购买、出售克隆人的生命或就此颁发专利等违反道德的做法。

在司法问题上，我们必须相信我国建国先贤的智慧，使懂得宪法真谛的法官获得应有的职权。我已提交法官提名人，他们将依法作出裁决，而不是敲击木槌，心血来潮地做出裁决。其中很多法官提名人的审议被不公平地拖延。他们都应当获得批准，参议院应立即就每一位提名人进行表决。

在我国各地社区，我们必须相信美国人民是善良的人民，并要让他们能够为有需要的邻人提供服务。过去七年来，我们越来越多的同胞意识到，追求幸福意味着奉献。参与志愿服务的人数创下新高。慈善捐助超过以往任何时候。从联邦政府得到新的支持的信仰组织正为那些困境中的人带来希望。为确保信仰组织在竞争联邦资金时得到平等对待，我提请各位永久性地延长"慈善选择"条款。

今晚，关爱之军正在墨西哥湾沿岸朝向一个新的黎明继续挺进。美国敬佩这一地区人民的顽强力量。我们再次承诺帮助他们把家园建设得比过去更牢固、更美好。今晚我欣慰地宣布，4月份我们将在新奥尔良这个伟大城市举办今年的"加墨美北美洲峰会"。

我们还面临着另外两个我在国会多次提及，但国会未能做出反应的紧迫挑战：福利开支和移民问题。

在座各位都知道，社会保障、退休医疗和医疗补助等福利项目的开支增长速度大于我们的承受能力。我们都清楚，如果美国继续这一趋势，未来将面临痛苦的选择：税收大幅增加，福利急剧减少，或者赤字不堪重负。我已提出改革这些项目的方案。现在我请国会议员们提出你们的计划，并制定出跨党派解决方案，为我们的子孙后代保全这些重要项目。

另一紧迫挑战是移民问题。美国需要保护边界——在各位帮助下，本届政府正在采取相关措施。我们正在工作场所加强执法，我们正在设置屏障和采用先进技术阻止非法越境，我们实际上已经终止了边界的"随抓随放"政策，到今年年底我们将把边防巡逻人员增加一倍。然而，我们也需承认，除非建立一种途径使外籍工人能够合法前来为我国经济贡献力量，否则我们就不可能完全保护边界。这将缓解边界的压力，使执法工作集中于对付图谋危害我们的人。我们还必须找到一种合理和人道的方式处理非法居留者。非法移民问题虽然复杂但可以解决，我们必须以一种既捍卫我们的法律又维护我们的最高理念的方式予以解决。

这便是我国的国情。然而，为我国公民建设一个繁荣的未来还有赖于打击国外敌人和促进世界动荡地区的自由事业。

我国的外交政策基于一个明确的理念：我们相信，如果赋予机会人们将选择自由与和平的未来。在过去七年里，我们目睹了自由发展史上一些风云激荡的时刻。我们看到格鲁吉亚和乌克兰公民争取自由公正选举的斗争。我们看到黎巴嫩人民走上街头要求独立自主。我们看到阿富汗人民摆脱塔利班暴政并选举了新总统和新议会。我们看到喜气洋洋的伊拉克人民伸出浸有墨汁的手指，欢庆他们的自由。这些自由的画面激励人心。

在过去七年时间里，我们也看到令人警醒的画面。在黎巴嫩和巴基斯坦，我们看到抬着被刽子手杀害的敬爱领袖灵柩的哀悼人流。在约旦，我们看到参加婚礼的宾客礼服上浸透鲜血挣扎着走出宾馆。阿富汗人和伊拉克人在清真寺和街市被炸死。伦敦和马德里的地铁被炸弹炸毁。在9月的一个晴朗日子，我们目睹数千名美国同胞瞬间被夺走生命。这些可怕的画面无情地提醒我们：恐怖分子和极端分子反对自由进步，他们是蔑视自由、蔑视美国，妄图将亿万人置于其暴力统治之下的邪恶之徒。

自从"9·11"事件发生以来，我们向这些恐怖分子和极端分子主动出击。我们将保持攻势，保持压力，把我们的敌人绳之以法。

我们正在进行一场决定21世纪命运的思想斗争。恐怖分子反对我们珍惜的每一项人道与文明的原则。然而在这场反恐战争中，我们和我们的敌人在一件事情上具有相同的看法：长期而言，有权自由决定自己命运的人们最终会抵制恐怖行为，拒绝在暴政统治下生活。这就是恐怖分子为了不让黎巴嫩、伊拉克、阿富汗、巴基斯坦和巴勒斯坦领土的人民享有这种选择而发动

攻击的原因。这也是我们为了美国的安全和世界的和平正在传播自由的希望的原因。

在阿富汗，美国和美国的 25 个北约盟国以及 15 个伙伴国家正在帮助阿富汗人民捍卫他们的自由和重建他们的国家。由于这些军事和文职人员的勇气，一个曾是"基地"组织庇护所的国家，现在成了一个儿童上学读书、新的道路与医院正在建造、人民对未来怀着新希望的年轻民主国家。这些成果必须保持，因此我们向驻阿富汗部队增派了 3,200 名海军陆战队员，他们将在阿富汗与恐怖分子作战，并对阿富汗军队和警察进行培训。战胜塔利班与"基地"组织对我国的安全至关重要，我感谢国会对美国在阿富汗重要使命的支持。

在伊拉克，为了阻止自豪的伊拉克人民获得自由，为了建立一个能够在世界各地发动袭击的庇护所，恐怖分子与极端分子正在进行破坏活动。一年前，我们的敌人在使伊拉克陷入混乱方面一度得逞。因此我们回顾了我们的战略并改变了做法。我们向伊拉克增加了美国的兵力。我们向我们的军队布置了一项新的任务：与伊拉克部队合作保护伊拉克人民，追击躲在堡垒里的敌人，在伊拉克任何地方都不给恐怖分子以藏身之地。

伊拉克人民很快认识到局势发生了重大变化。那些曾经担心美国准备遗弃他们的人却看到数万名美国士兵前来增援他们的国家。他们看到我们的部队进入各个社区清剿恐怖分子，并留驻下来以确保敌人不再反扑。他们看到我们的部队同包括外交官和其他业务熟练的公职人员在内的省级重建队一起进驻，以确保在安全得到加强之后接踵而至的日常生活的改善。我们在伊拉克的军事和文职人员勇敢而杰出，我们全国人民感激他们。

伊拉克人自己的斗争也进入高潮。2006 年秋天，逊尼派部落领导人对"基地"组织的残暴行为忍无可忍，发动了一场名为"安巴尔觉醒"的群众运动。过去一年内，类似运动已遍及伊拉克各地。今天，这种基层力量已经壮大至包括正在与恐怖分子战斗的八万多名伊拉克公民。巴格达的伊拉克政府也迈出了前进的步伐，在过去一年里增加了十多万名伊拉克士兵与警察。

虽然敌人仍然十分危险，我们还有更多工作要做，但美国与伊拉克的增兵措施已取得了我们中很少有人在一年前能够想象的结果。

去年这个时候，许多人认为限制暴力行为是不可能做到的事情。一年后，重大恐怖主义袭击事件减少了，平民百姓的死亡减少了，教派之间的杀戮减少了。

去年这个时候，民兵极端分子——其中一些由伊朗武装和培训——正在伊拉克的广大地区造成严重的破坏。一年后，联盟部队和伊拉克部队已击毙和捕获了数百名民兵战斗人员。具有各种背景的伊拉克人日益认识到战胜这些民兵战斗人员对他们国家的前途至关重要。

去年这个时候，"基地"组织在伊拉克大有栖身之处，其头目当时还给美国军队指出离开伊拉克的安全出路。而今，是"基地"组织在寻找安全出路。他们被赶出了过去盘踞的很多据点，过去一年里，我们在伊拉克捕获和击毙了数千名极端分子，包括"基地"组织的数百名重要头目和成员。上个月，本·拉登在公开的一盘录像带中斥责与"基地"组织反目的伊拉克部落领袖，并承认联盟军队在伊拉克日益强大。女士们、先生们，也许有人否认增兵战略正取得成效，但恐怖主义分子对此确知无疑。"基地"组织正在伊拉克逃窜，我们的敌人将被击败。

去年这个时候，我们正在向伊拉克增加兵力。今天，由于取得了上述进展，我们正在实施"功成而归"的方针，被派到伊拉克的增援部队开始返回家园。

这一进展归功于我们英勇的战士和他们卓越的指挥官。今晚，我要直接对前线的将士讲话。陆海空三军战士们、海军陆战队员们、海岸警卫队员们：一年来，你们超量完成了我们交给你们的一切使命。祖国感谢你们的英勇气概，我们为你们的成就而骄傲。今晚，在这个神圣的会议厅，我们面对美国人民向你们庄严保证：在未来的战斗中，你们将得到保卫国家所需的一切。

我要求国会履行对这些勇士的职责，让我们的部队得到全部拨款。

伊拉克境内的敌人已受到沉重打击，但他们尚未溃败，未来还有艰苦的搏斗。我们在今后一年中的目标是，保持和扩大 2007 年的战果，同时向下一战略阶段过渡。美国军队正在从承担主要作战任务转向配合伊拉克部队的行动，最终将转为防护性监测。随着过渡的开始，一个陆军旅作战部队和一支海军陆战队远征队已经归国，并且不再派出换防部队。在未来几个月内，还将有另外四个旅和海军陆战队的两个营相继撤回。这意味着即将有两万多部队返回家园。

美国进一步的减兵计划将取决于伊拉克局势和我军指挥官的建议。彼得雷乌斯上将警告说，过于迅速地削减兵力有可能导致"伊拉克安全部队解体"，"基地"组织"卷土重来，暴力激增"。各位议员：时至今日，面对已经取得的进展与战果，我们绝不能让此种情况发生。

在未来一年中，我们将与伊拉克领导人合作，帮助他们在实现政治和解方面继续取得进展。在地方一级，逊尼派、什叶派和库尔德人开始团结起来，收复社区，重建生活。巴格达必须取得与外省同样的进展。我们已经看到一些令人鼓舞的迹象：中央政府与各省分享石油收入，议会最近通过了养老金法律和允许前复兴党支持者在政府任职的法律，并且正在讨论一部加强省政府权力的法案。伊拉克人仍然有一段很长的路要走。但是，经历了数十年的专制统治和族群冲突的痛苦之后，和解正在成为现实——伊拉克人民正在掌控自己的未来。

对我们的国家而言，在伊拉克承担的使命是困难而艰巨的，但取得成功对美国的利益至关重要。一个自由的伊拉克将不会为"基地"组织提供庇护所。一个自由的伊拉克将向中东地区千百万人民显示自由的未来是能够实现的。一个自由的伊拉克将是美国的朋友和反恐合作伙伴，并将在世界上一个危险的地区促进稳定。

相反，一个失败的伊拉克将使极端分子更加狂妄，将加强伊朗的力量，并将为恐怖分子提供一个向我们的朋友、盟国和我们的国土发动新攻击的基地。敌人的图谋已经昭然若揭。曾几何时，当形势看似对他们有利时，伊拉克"基地"组织的总指挥宣称他们在攻击华盛顿之前绝不罢手。同胞们：我们也不会罢手。我们在打败这个敌人之前绝不会罢手。我们必须现在完成这项困难的工作，这样，未来人们在回顾历史时会说，那一代人临危不惧，承担重任，在艰苦的斗争中取胜，为后代留下了一个更有希望的地区和更安全的美国。

我们还在"圣地"与极端主义势力斗争，我们有了新的理由对那里充满希望。一位巴勒斯坦人选出的总统认识到，与恐怖势力抗争对建立一个人民享有尊严，与以色列和平共处的巴勒斯坦国至关重要。以色列领导人认识到，一个和平、民主的巴勒斯坦国将促进持久的安全。这个月我在拉马拉和耶路撒冷向双方领导人保证，美国和我本人都将尽最大努力帮助他们在今年年底前达成一项确立巴勒斯坦国的和平协议。一个民主的以色列和一个民主的巴勒斯坦在"圣地"和平共处的日子已经到来。

在国内，我们将继续采取所有既合法又有效的手段来保卫国土。这是我们最庄严的职责。令我们感到欣慰的是，自"9·11"以来我国没有再遭受袭击。这并不是因为敌人没有这种企图或行为。六年来，我们挫败了无数起袭击，其中包括企图驾机撞毁洛杉矶最高建筑的阴谋，以及另一起妄图在大西洋上空炸毁飞往美国客机的阴谋。我国政府恪尽职守的工作人员为制止恐怖分子实施图谋而日夜操劳。这些优秀公民正在保护美国人民的生命，在座各位都应当向他们表示感谢。但这还不够，我们应给予他们保障我国人民安全所必需的工具。

我们能给予他们的最重要的工具之一是监控恐怖主义通讯的能力。为了保护美国的安全，我们需要知道恐怖分子在和谁通话，说些什么以及有何图谋。去年，国会通过了有助于我们采取上述行动的立法。但令人遗憾的是，国会限定这项立法于2月1日到期。这意味着如果你们不在星期五之前采取行动，

我们追踪恐怖主义威胁的能力就会被削弱，我国公民将处于更危险的境地。国会必须确保重要的情报渠道不被阻断。国会必须通过责任保护法，以保护那些据信在保卫美国的行动中提供了一臂之力的公司。我们已经花费大量的时间进行辩论，现在是采取行动的时候了。

要保卫国家并防范新世纪的种种威胁，单凭可靠的情报和强大的军队是不够的。还必须改变滋生怨恨、让极端分子乘机利用绝望情绪的环境。因此，美国正在利用其影响力来建设一个更加自由、更有希望、更富同情心的世界。这反映了我们的国家利益，也是我们良心的召唤。

美国反对苏丹的种族大屠杀。我们支持从古巴到津巴布韦，从白俄罗斯到缅甸的众多国家赢得自由。

美国正在以强有力的教育计划和人道援助领导并展开战胜全球贫困的斗争。我们还通过建立"世纪挑战账户"改变了提供援助的方式。这个项目的宗旨是在发展中国家加强民主，提高透明度并增强法治。我请你们为这项重要的计划提供足够的经费。

美国正在领导战胜全球饥饿的斗争。今天，全世界一半以上的食品援助来自美国。今晚，我请国会支持一项创新方案，通过直接从发展中国家的农民那里购买农产品来提供食品援助，使我们能够推动当地农业的发展，帮助终止连年饥荒。

美国正在领导战胜疾病的斗争。在各位的帮助下，我们正在做出努力，使十五个非洲国家与疟疾相关的死亡人数下降一半。我们的"防治艾滋病紧急救援计划"正在为140万人提供治疗服务。我们能够治疗更多的人，给他们带去希望。因此，我请你们维护使行为方式得到改变并使这一项目获得成功的原则。我吁请你们批准在今后五年追加拨款300亿美元，将我们承诺用于防治艾滋病的首期拨款翻一番。

美国在世界上是希望的力量，因为我国人民充满关爱之心，而那些挺身而出保卫我们的人是最有关爱之心的。我们必须守信于那些舍生忘死，使我们能够在自由与和平中生活的人。过去七年来，我们给退伍军人的拨款增加了 95% 以上。我们在增加拨款的同时还必须改革我们的退伍军人制度，以满足新型战争和新一代人的需要。我呼请国会实施多尔参议员和沙拉拉部长提议实行的改革，使我们能够改进护理我军伤兵的制度，帮助他们建设充满希望、憧憬和尊严的生活。

我国的军人家属也为美国做出了牺牲。当亲人在远方服役时，他们忍受了多少个不眠之夜，每天承担着养育子女的重担。我们有责任为他们提供帮助。因此，我请你们和我共同努力，让他们享受到更多子女入托服务，在整个联邦政府内制定优先照顾军属的新的人事政策，并允许军人将他们未使用的教育福利转让给他们的配偶或子女。我军家属为国效力，他们鼓舞着我们这个国家，因此，今晚全国民众向他们致敬。

我们的力量的秘密和美国的奇迹是：我们的伟大不在于我国政府，而在于我国人民的精神和意志。联邦制宪会议于 1787 年在费城召开时，我国就承诺遵循《邦联条例》，其开篇是"我们全体签名代表"。当有人请莫里斯起草我国新宪法导言时，他提出进行重要的修改，首句便是改变了我国的进程和世界历史的几个字"我们全体人民"。

我国的建国先贤通过托信于人民而表达了一种信念，即一个伟大而崇高的国家可以建立在常存于全体人民心中的自由之上。通过托信于人民，后来的一代又一代人将我们脆弱而年轻的民主制度打造成世界上最强大的国家和千百万人的希望灯塔。只要我们继续托信于人民，我国就会繁荣富强，我们的自由就会得到保障，我们的国家就会保持强盛。因此，今晚，让我们怀着对自由力量的信心和对人民的信任，为成其大业而奋斗。

第三节 精彩语录

We believe that the most reliable guide for our country is the collective wisdom of ordinary citizens. So in all we do, we must trust in the ability of free people to make wise decisions, and empower them to improve their lives and their futures.

我们相信普通公民的集体智慧是我国最可靠的指南。因此，我们不论做什么都必须相信自由的人民有能力做出明智的决定，并让他们有力量改善自己的生活和前途。

Let us complete an international agreement that has the potential to slow, stop, and eventually reverse the growth of greenhouse gases. This agreement will be effective only if it includes commitments by every major economy and gives none a free ride.

让我们达成一项有可能减缓和停止增加并最终减少温室气体排放的国际协议。要使这项协议产生效果，每个主要经济体都必须做出承诺，任何国家都不能坐享其成。

We trust that people, when given the chance, will choose a future of freedom and peace.

我们相信，如果赋予机会人们将选择自由与和平的未来。

My fellow Americans: We will not rest either. We will not rest until this enemy has been defeated. We must do the difficult work today, so that years from now people will look back and say that this generation rose to the moment, prevailed in a tough fight, and left behind a more hopeful region and a safer America.

同胞们：我们也不会罢手。我们在打败这个敌人之前绝不会罢手。我们必须现在完成这项困难的工作，这样，未来人们在回顾历史时会说，那一代人临危不惧，承担重任，在艰苦的斗争中取胜，为后代留下了一个更有希望的地区和更安全的美国。

We must keep faith with all who have risked life and limb so that we might live in freedom and peace.

我们必须守信于那些舍生忘死使我们能够在自由与和平中生活的人。

By trusting the people, our Founders wagered that a great and noble nation could be built on the liberty that resides in the hearts of all men and women. By trusting the people, succeeding generations transformed our fragile young democracy into the most powerful nation on earth and a beacon of hope for millions. And so long as we continue to trust the people, our nation will prosper, our liberty will be secure, and the State of our Union will remain strong.

我国的建国先贤通过托信于人民而表达了一种信念，即一个伟大而崇高的国家可以建立在常存于全体人民心中的自由之上。通过托信于人民，后来

的一代又一代人将我们脆弱而年轻的民主制度打造成世界上最强大的国家和千百万人的希望灯塔。只要我们继续托信于人民，我国就会繁荣富强，我们的自由就会得到保障，我们的国家就会保持强盛。

第十四章

雷曼倒了，危机来了

第一节 背景介绍

　　2008 年注定是不平凡的一年，雷曼兄弟控股公司于 2008 年 9 月 15 日申请破产，由此揭开了后来蔓延世界的金融危机的序幕。时任美国总统的小布什，自然是众多亲历者中最宏观和最全面的见证人。

　　任何事情的发生都是有一定缘由的，美国此次的金融危机也毫不例外。美国在 2007 年爆发的次级抵押贷款危机（简称次贷危机），政府的许多救援措施并没能遏制危机的蔓延，从而逐渐转变为世界范围内的金融危机，并且影响到世界各国的实体经济。主要发达国家的经济普遍受到此次金融危机的冲击而出现增长放缓的局面。

　　根据借款人的信用条件高低，美国的抵押贷款市场主要分三类：优惠级抵押贷款、中间级抵押贷款和次级抵押贷款。所谓次级抵押贷款，指的就是贷款机构向信用程度较差和收入不高的借款人提供的贷款。由于这些借款人申请不到优惠贷款，只能在次级市场寻求贷款，但其贷款利率通常比优惠级抵押贷款高 2% ~ 3%，并要求遵守更严格的还款方式。

　　因为次级抵押贷款人的信用状况比较差，所以，极易发生违约现象，而且这类现象在某些情况下会日益严重，便会带来严重后果。放贷机构即使由

于贷款人违约无法收回贷款，也可以通过再融资，或者出售抵押的房产收回
贷款并获得收益，当然，这要在信贷环境宽松或房价上涨的情况下才能做到。
如果是在信贷环境改变，特别是房价下降的情况下，再融资或者出售抵押的
房产不仅难以实现，而且即使出售价格下跌的抵押房产也难以收回全部贷款。
当较大规模地集中发生这类事件时，次贷危机就会发生。

"9・11"恐怖袭击后，美国经济便出现了较大程度的滑坡，美国国内
股票市场狂跌，大批网络公司纷纷倒闭。美国政府为扭转经济的不景气，刺
激经济发展，采取了低利率的货币政策，大力发展信贷业务，使房地产业进
入了一个良好的发展周期。从 2001 年初至 2003 年 6 月，美联储先后 13 次
降低利率，使联邦基金利率从 6% 降到 1%，成为四十六年中的最低点。宽松
的货币政策环境，使住房贷款利率持续下降，人们的购房热情不断提高。而
一些银行和金融机构纷纷降低贷款信用门槛，住房贷款首付率出现了逐年下
降的趋势，从历史上标准的 20% 一度降到了零，甚至出现了负首付，大大减
轻了购房者的压力，导致连续多年的房贷市场繁荣。

但是，为了抑制通货膨胀，美联储的低利率政策从 2004 年 6 月起开始
逆转，开始了一个连续 17 次的加息周期。导致联邦基金利率从 2003 年 6 月
的 1% 提高到 2006 年 8 月的 5.25%。连续升息的过程在提高了房屋借贷成本
的同时，也促发了房价的迅速下跌，以及抵押违约风险的大量增加，成为次
贷危机的一根导火线。

在经济全球化的趋势下，全球范围内利率下降、美元贬值、资产价格上
升等因素，也使得次贷产品在投资回报方面有了更高的增长空间，吸引了美
国之外的大量来自欧洲、亚洲等其他国家和地区的投资者，将在美国经济掩
盖下的"次贷风险"，隐埋在世界金融体系中。因此，由"次贷危机"所引
发的金融危机席卷了全球各个金融市场，并对世界各主要经济体产生巨大的
影响。

此次危机对许多新兴金融市场的快速发展产生了消极的影响。面对这样

一场起始于发达国家的金融危机时，将给借鉴和参考发达国家金融市场发展经验发展起来的新兴市场带来巨大的联动效应，使其金融体系显得更加脆弱。同时，一些欧美等金融业发达的国家和地区的很多银行、投资基金直接或者间接购买了大量由次级抵押贷款衍生出来的证券投资产品，当危机来临时，不可避免地遭受巨额损失，大量的投资银行、投资基金、金融公司先后倒闭或者被收购。当这些金融机构要么倒闭要么陷入财务危机时，必将加大金融市场的系统型风险，抑制其在经济发展中所应发挥的融通资金、资源配置的基本功能。

第二节 布什关于金融危机的演讲

Good morning. I thank Treasury Secretary Hank Paulson, Federal eserve Chairman Ben Bernanke, and SEC Chairman Chris Cox for joining me today.

This is a pivotal moment for America's economy. Problems that originated in the credit markets—and first showed up in the area of subprime mortgages—have spread throughout our financial system. This has led to an erosion of confidence that has frozen many financial transactions, including loans to consumers and to businesses seeking to expand and create jobs. As a result, we must act now to protect our nation's economic health from serious risk.

There will be ample opportunity to debate the origins of this problem. Now is the time to solve it. In our nation's history, there have been moments that require us to come together across party lines to address major challenges. This is such a moment. Last night, Secretary Paulson and Chairman Bernanke and Chairman Cox met with congressional leaders of both parties—and they had a very good meeting. I appreciate the willingness of congressional leaders to confront this situation head on.

Our system of free enterprise rests on the conviction that the federal government should interfere in the marketplace only when necessary. Given the precarious state of today's financial markets—and their vital importance to the daily lives of the American people—government intervention is not only warranted, it is essential.

In recent weeks, the federal government has taken a series of measures to help promote stability in the overall economy. To avoid severe disruptions in the financial markets and to support home financing, we took action to address the situation at Fannie Mae and Freddie Mac. The Federal Reserve also acted to prevent the disorderly liquidation of the insurance company AIG. And in coordination with central banks around the world, the Fed has injected much-needed liquidity into our financial system.

These were targeted measures designed primarily to stop the problems of individual firms from spreading even more broadly. But more action is needed. We must address the root cause behind much of the instability in our markets—the mortgage assets that have lost value during the housing decline and are now restricting the flow of credit. America's economy is facing unprecedented challenges, and we are responding with unprecedented action.

Secretary Paulson, Chairman Bernanke, and Chairman Cox have briefed leaders on Capitol Hill on the urgent need for Congress to pass legislation approving the federal government's purchase of illiquid assets, such as troubled mortgages, from banks and other financial institutions. This is a decisive step that will address underlying problems in our financial system. It will help take pressure off the balance sheets of banks and other financial institutions. It will allow them to resume lending and get our financial system moving again.

Additionally, the federal government is taking several other steps to address the trouble of our financial markets.

The Department of the Treasury is acting to restore confidence in a key element of America's financial system—money market mutual funds. In the past, government insurance was not available for these funds, and the recent stresses on the markets have caused some to question whether these investments are safe and accessible. The Treasury Department's actions address that concern by offering government insurance for money market mutual funds. For every dollar invested in an insured fund, you will be able to take a dollar out.

The Federal Reserve is also taking steps to provide additional liquidity to money market mutual funds, which will help ease pressure on our financial markets. These measures will act as grease for the gears of our financial system, which were at risk of grinding to a halt. They will support the flow of credit to households and businesses.

The Securities and Exchange Commission has issued new rules temporarily suspending the practice of short selling on the stocks of financial institutions. This is intended to prevent investors from intentionally driving down particular stocks for their own personal gain. The SEC is also requiring certain investors to disclose their short selling, and has launched rigorous enforcement actions to detect fraud and manipulation in the market. Anyone engaging in illegal financial transactions will be caught and persecuted.

Finally, when we get past the immediate challenges, my administration looks forward to working with Congress on measures to bring greater long-term transparency and reliability to the financial system—including those in the regulatory blueprint submitted by Secretary Paulson earlier this year. Many of the regulations governing the functioning of America's markets were written in a different era. It is vital that we update them to meet the realities of today's global financial system.

The actions I just outlined reflect the considered judgment of Secretary

Paulson, Chairman Bernanke, and Chairman Cox. We believe that this decisive government action is needed to preserve America's financial system and sustain America's overall economy. These measures will require us to put a significant amount of taxpayer dollars on the line. This action does entail risk. But we expect that this money will eventually be paid back. The vast majority of assets the government is planning to purchase have good value over time, because the vast majority of homeowners continue to pay their mortgages. And the risk of not acting would be far higher. Further stress on our financial markets would cause massive job losses, devastate retirement accounts, and further erode housing values, as well as dry up loans for new homes and cars and college tuitions. These are risks that America cannot afford to take.

In this difficult time, I know many Americans are wondering about the security of their finances. Every American should know that the federal government continues to enforce laws and regulations protecting your money. Through the FDIC, every savings account, checking account, and certificate of deposit is insured by the federal government for up to $100,000. The FDIC has been in existence for 75 years, and no one has ever lost a penny on an insured deposit—and this will not change.

America's financial system is intricate and complex. But behind all the technical terminology and statistics is a critical human factor—confidence. Confidence in our financial system and in its institutions is essential to the smooth operation of our economy, and recently that confidence has been shaken. Investors should know that the United States government is taking action to restore confidence in America's financial markets so they can thrive again.

In the long run, Americans have good reason to be confident in our economic strength. America has the most talented, productive, and entrepreneurial workers in the world. This country is the best place in the world to invest and do business. Consumers around the world continue to seek out American products, as evidenced by record-high exports. We have a flexible and resilient system that absorbs challenges and makes corrections and bounces back.

We've seen that resilience over the past eight years. Since 2001, our economy has faced a recession, the bursting of the dot-com bubble, major corporate scandals, an unprecedented attack on our homeland, a global war on terror, a series of devastating natural disasters. Our economy has weathered every one of these challenges, and still managed to grow.

We will weather this challenge too, and we must do so together. This is no time for partisanship. We must join to move urgently needed legislation as quickly as possible, without adding controversial provisions that could delay action. I will work with Democrats and Republicans alike to steer our economy through these difficult times and get back to the path of long-term growth. Thank you very much.

早上好。我要感谢财政部长汉克·鲍尔森、联邦储备委员会主席本·伯南克和美国证券交易委员会主席查尔斯·考克斯今天的到来。

如今对于美国的经济来说，已经到了一个关键时期。此次经济问题源自信贷市场——次级贷款首次出现的地方，现在已经蔓延到我们的整个金融体系。这导致了信任度的丧失，从而使许多金融贷款遭遇冻结，其中包括对消费者、对试图扩大规模并创造就业机会的企业贷款。因此，我们现在必须行动起来，以确保我们国家的经济安全，使其免遭严重风险的威胁。

我们将有足够多的时间来讨论这次问题的起因，然而，现在当务之急是解决问题。回溯我们国家的历史，曾经有过需要我们跨越党派界限共同努力，解决我们所面临的挑战的时刻。现在，我们再次面临这样的时刻。昨天晚上，鲍尔森部长连同伯南克和考克斯两位主席共同会见了两党的最高领导人，进

行了一次成功的会议商讨。我很赞赏国会领导人在这种情况下能够直面困难的行为。

我们的自由企业体系依赖于一个信念，即联邦政府仅在必要的时候才对市场进行干预。然而，考虑到与美国人民日常生活息息相关的金融市场目前所处状态，政府的介入不仅是合理的而且是必要的。

近几周内，联邦政府已采取了一系列措施维护总体经济的稳定。为避免金融市场受到严重破坏并支撑起家庭经济，我们采取措施解决房利美和房地美所发生的情况。美国联邦储备委员会也同样采取行动防止美国国际集团保险公司破产。通过和世界各国的中央银行相协调，美联储已经向我们的金融体系注入了其急需的流动资金。

这些都是有针对性的措施，首要的目的是阻止发生在个别企业中的问题向更广的范围扩散，但是我们还需要采取更多的行动。我们必须解决隐藏在市场不稳定表象后面的根本问题——抵押资产在房地产市场衰退期内已经失去了价值，转而限制了信贷的流通。美国的经济正面临着前所未有的挑战，而我们正在以前所未有的行动予以回应。

鲍尔森部长、伯南克主席和考克斯主席已经向国会领导们简要介绍了通过立法，批准联邦政府从银行和其他金融机构购置流动性资产的迫切性，这种流动性资产中就包括出现问题的抵押贷款。这个决定性的措施将致力于解决我们金融体系中的潜在问题。它将有助于减轻银行和其他金融机构间资产负债失衡的压力，使它们能够恢复信贷机制，让我们的金融体系重新运转起来。

此外，联邦政府正在采取一些其他措施来应对我们金融市场上的困难。

财政部正在努力恢复人们对美国金融体系中一个关键因素的信心——货币市场共同基金。在过去货币共同基金无法得到政府的保险，可是近来市场上的压力已经引起了一些质疑：这些投资是否是安全的、开放的？对此财政部已经通过向货币共同基金提供政府援助做出了回答，顺利化解了人们的担忧。你们投入保险基金中的每 1 美元，都能够分文不差地提取出来。

联邦储备委员会也在采取措施，为货币市场储备金的流动性提供更好的环境或平台，这将有助于缓解我们在金融市场上的压力。这些措施将像润滑剂那样，使我们被这次风险压制得几近停滞的金融体系齿轮转动起来，它们将会支撑着贷款流向家庭和企业。

证券管理委员会已经出台新的规定，暂时禁止卖空金融机构股票，这是为了防止投机商故意压低特定股票的价格为自己谋取私利。证券交易委员会还要求某些投资者披露他们的卖空行为，并开始采取严格的强制手段，用来查明市场上的欺诈和操纵行为。所有从事违法金融交易的人都将受到最严厉的制裁。

最终，在我们顺利地通过这次挑战之后，我的管理团队期待与国会合作，为给我们的金融体系带来更加长久的透明度与稳固性而共同努力——包括鲍尔森部长在今年早期提出的管理蓝图中的那些项目。在历史中，许多支配着美国市场运作的法规被固定下来，重要的是我们要及时地更新它们，以便适应当今全球金融体系的现状。

刚才我所略述的行动和措施如实地反映了鲍尔森部长、伯南克主席和考克斯主席的想法。我们相信这一决定性的政府措施，对于保护美国的金融体系和维持美国的整体经济是必要的。这些措施需要我们冒着失败的风险投入大笔税收，实施这些行动也需要承担风险，但是我们认为这些资金最终能够收到回报。政府计划购买的巨额资产不久将会带来良好的收益，因为大多数的房主依然在继续偿还他们的贷款。反之，如果不采取行动，危险会更大——金融市场上的压力会导致大规模的失业、退休金账目的侵蚀、房屋价值的进一步降低，并且造成新建住房、汽车和大学学费贷款的枯竭。这些都是美国无法承担的风险。

在这个困难的时期，我知道很多美国人都在担心他们的财产安全。所有的美国公民都应当知道，政府依然在执行法律法规保护你们的财产。通过联

邦存款保险公司，每一个储蓄账户、支票账户和存款凭证都得到了联邦政府高达10万美元的保险。联邦存款保险公司已经存在了七十五年，没有人曾在这种保险的储蓄下失去过1分钱——这一点今后也不会改变。

美国的金融体系虽然是错综复杂的，但是在所有的技术术语和统计数据的背后，存在着一个关键的人性因素——信心。在我们的金融体系和金融制度中，信心对于我们经济的平稳运作是必不可少的，但是近来这种信心却发生了动摇。投资者们应该知道，美国政府正在努力恢复人们对美国金融市场的信心，使它能够重振雄风。

从长远来看，美国人民应该有理由相信我们的经济实力。美国拥有全世界最具才能、最高产、最善于创业的工人。这个国家是世界上最有利于投资和做生意的地方。全世界的消费者还在继续寻找着美国的产品，创纪录的出口额就是有力的证据。我们拥有一个灵活、弹性的体系，直面各种挑战，做出积极改进并能迅速恢复功能。

在过去的八年中，我们已经看到了美国经济的这种恢复能力。自2001年以来，我们就面临着经济衰退、互联网泡沫的破裂、大量的企业丑闻、针对我国的前所未有的恐怖袭击、全球性的反恐战争，以及一系列破坏性的自然灾害。然而，我们的经济承受住了所有的这些考验，并且依然在前进。

这一次，我们也同样会安全地度过难关，为此我们必须要团结一致。这是一个需要摒弃党派偏见的时期。我们必须联合起来，尽快建立迫切需要的法律法规，不要加入那些会延缓我们行动的争议性的条款。我会无差别地同民主党和共和党一起合作，驾驭我们的经济安全地度过这个困难的时期，并使它回到长期增长的轨道上来。谢谢大家。

第三节 精彩语录

These measures will act as grease for the gears of our financial system, which were at risk of grinding to a halt. They will support the flow of credit to households and businesses.

这些措施将像润滑剂那样，使我们被这次风险压制得几近停滞的金融体系齿轮转动起来，它们将会支撑着贷款流向家庭和企业。

Confidence in our financial system and in its institutions is essential to the smooth operation of our economy, and recently that confidence has been shaken.

在我们的金融体系和金融制度中，信心对于我们经济的平稳运作是必不可少的，但是近来这种信心却发生了动摇。

We will weather this challenge too, and we must do so together. This is no time for partisanship. We must join to move urgently needed legislation as

quickly as possible, without adding controversial provisions that could delay action.

这一次，我们也同样会安全地度过难关，为此我们必须要团结一致。这是一个需要摒弃党派偏见的时期。我们必须联合起来，尽快建立迫切需要的法律法规，不要加入那些会延缓我们行动的争议性的条款。

第十五章

经济形势十分严峻

第一节 背景介绍

　　2007年3月，美国出现大批次级抵押贷款的借款人不能按期偿还贷款，进而引发次贷危机。次年，情况更加糟糕，多家规模巨大的金融机构陷入困境，这实际上就是美国金融危机激化的过程。美国此次金融危机直接导致了美国大量金融机构的破产或重组，造成了货币供给的紧缩，美国经济增长的势头由此逆转。

　　金融危机主要划分为三大类：银行危机、货币危机、债务危机。银行危机是指实际或潜在的银行运行障碍或违约导致银行中止其负债的内部转换，储户对银行丧失信心从而发生挤提，银行最终破产倒闭或需要政府提供大量援助；货币危机是本国货币汇率大幅度贬值所导致的金融危机；债务危机是本国不能偿还规模较大的外国债务所导致的金融危机。此次的美国金融危机属于银行危机，是从大量出现不能偿还次级抵押贷款开始的，但因为抵押贷款被证券化，许多金融机构都投资了这种以抵押贷款为基础发行的证券，所以银行业的危机迅速波及到投资银行业和保险业，演变为整个金融业的危机。

　　金融危机所导致的经济衰退是通过一定传导机制来实现的。美国的金融危机主要通过以下三个方面对美国经济产生影响。

首先是银行破产。美国金融危机发生以后，除了房利美公司、房地美公司、华盛顿互惠银行、花旗集团等规模巨大的银行陷入困境以外，美国的中小银行出现了倒闭的浪潮。

由于企业的闲置资金存放在银行，在银行破产的时候企业只能得到部分赔偿。再加上社会需求收缩，企业产品难以销售，部分企业将随之破产，从而对美国的生产和就业造成不利影响。

其次是资金融通。在发生金融危机的情况下，银行的不良资产增加，银行对发放贷款采取更加保守的态度，整个经济的信贷将会收缩，企业获得资金将变得更加困难。一般来说，企业除了从商业银行融通资金以外，还可以从货币市场融通资金。在发生金融危机的情况下，金融资产贬值，投资者不愿意购买金融资产，企业同样难以在货币市场筹集资金。这样，企业生产受到不利影响。

最后是社会需求。在发生金融危机的情况下，一方面融通资金的困难导致消费需求和投资需求减少，另一方面投资环境恶化导致企业不愿意增加投资。另外，在发生金融危机的情况下，股票价格在经济增长前景暗淡的情况下趋向下跌，造成个人和企业的金融财富减少，并在财富效应的影响下导致个人减少消费支出和企业减少投资支出，国内生产总值将下降。美国私人国内总投资支出反应更为强烈。

在金融危机的影响下，美国经济进入衰退期。美国政府和美国联邦储备系统迅速做出反应。布什政府通过向出现问题并对经济具有重要影响的金融机构融通资金的方式防止大金融机构的倒闭，同时提出了 7,000 亿美元的金融救援计划来抑制金融危机的扩散。

第二节 布什就金融危机后美国经济形势发表演讲

Good morning.

This week, Congress passed a bipartisan rescue package to address the instability in America's financial system. This was a difficult vote for many members of the House and Senate, but voting for it was the right choice for America's economy and for taxpayers like you. I appreciate their efforts to help stop the crisis in our financial markets from spreading to our entire economy. And I appreciate their willingness to work across party lines in the midst of an election season.

The legislation Congress passed provides the necessary tools to address the underlying problem in our financial system. The root of this problem is that, as assets that banks hold have lost value, their ability to provide credit has been restricted, making it more difficult for businesses and consumers to obtain affordable loans.

Without decisive action, this credit crunch threatens to harm our entire economy. With this legislation, the Federal government can help banks and other financial institutions resume lending. This will allow them to continue providing the capital that is essential to creating jobs, financing college educations, and helping American families meet their daily needs.

Though the $700 billion dedicated to this plan is a large amount, the final cost to taxpayers will actually be much lower. Many of the assets that the government will be purchasing still have significant underlying value. As time passes, they will likely go up in price. And this means that the government should eventually be able to recoup much, if not all, of the original expenditure.

This package will also increase the safety of Americans' personal finances. For 75 years, the FDIC has provided insurance for savings accounts, checking accounts, and certificates of deposit. A similar insurance program is in effect for deposits in credit unions. And since these programs were instituted, no one has ever lost a penny on an insured deposit. The rescue package expands this protection by temporarily increasing the amount insured by the Federal government in banks and credit unions from $100,000 to $250,000. These steps should reassure Americans, especially small business owners, that their money is safe—and it should restore confidence in the health of our banking system.

In addition to addressing the immediate needs of our financial system, this package will also help to spur America's long–term economic growth. This week, we learned that our Nation lost more jobs in September. Under these circumstances, it is essential for the government to reduce the burdens on workers and business owners. And that is why the rescue package includes relief from the Alternative Minimum Tax, which would otherwise increase taxes for 26 million taxpayers by an average of $2,200. And that is why it includes tax relief for businesses, which can use these savings to hire new employees and finance new investment.

By taking all these steps, we can begin to put our economy on the road to recovery. While these efforts will be effective, they will also take time to

implement. My Administration will move as quickly as possible, but the benefits of this package will not all be felt immediately. The Federal government will undertake this rescue plan at a careful and deliberate pace to ensure that your tax dollars are spent wisely.

I know many of you listening this morning are anxious about the state of our economy and what it means for your personal finances. I am confident that the implementation of this relief package can begin to address those concerns. I'm confident by getting our markets moving, we will help unleash the key to our continued economic success: the entrepreneurial spirit of the American people.

Thank you for listening.

早上好！

本周国会批准了民主、共和两党共同参与修改的经济援助法案，这一法案的实施解决了阻碍美国经济良性发展的不稳定因素。尽管对于大部分参众两院的议员来说，这是一次相当困难的投票，但是这次投票无论对美国宏观的整体经济形势，还是对任何一位像你们一样的纳税人来说都是一次无比正确的选择。我非常感谢议员们投票通过了这一法案，并对阻止金融市场的危机扩散到美国经济的每一个角落所做出的不懈努力。我更钦佩两党的议员们在美国大选之际能够排除党派的干扰诚恳地坐在一起并为全体美国人的利益而同心协力。

国会刚刚批准的法案为解决我们的金融体系存在的问题提供了诸多必要的解决方法。我们此次所要面对的金融问题的根源在于，由于银行所持有的资产大幅度缩水，使银行提供信贷的能力大大降低，进而导致消费者和他们所从事的行业贷款越来越难，贷款利率也越来越高。

如果不采取紧急措施，这一信贷危机就将危害到美国宏观经济。随着这一法案的批准，联邦政府可以帮助银行和其他金融机构重新以低利率发放贷款。这一援助法案将会使它们继续向美国纳税人提供扩大就业、子女教育等所必需的资金，并满足美国家庭的日常需要。

尽管实施这一法案需要联邦政府支出高达 7,000 亿美元，然而对美国全体纳税人来说，他们的付出将远远低于预期。政府出资收购的大部分银行资产仍潜在着巨大价值。随着时间的推移，这些资产很可能将再次升值。这就意味着政府最终将会收回即使不是全部也是绝大部分的前期支出。

这一援助法案同样会提高美国人个人理财的安全系数。在过去的七十五年里，美国银行业监管者联邦存款保险公司一直为美国公民的储蓄账户、支票账户和定期存单提供保险。一个在信贷机构中类似的保险项目正在实施当中。这次的援助法案正是拓展了这一保险项目，使联邦政府把每一个银行储户的存款理赔额上限从 10 万美元提高到 25 万美元。这些措施能够保障美国人，尤其是小企业的经营者们手中现金的安全性。这些措施同样能够恢复银行系统的良性循环。

除了解决金融系统的短期需求，这一法案还将有助于刺激美国长期稳定的经济增长。就在本周，我们深刻地感受到 9 月份越来越多的美国人失去了他们的工作。在这种情况下，政府出面减轻劳动者和小企业经营者的负担就显得尤其重要。该法案中附加的减税法案包含一套颇受企业欢迎的企业税务优惠，也附加了让 2,600 多万中产阶级纳税人免缴另计最低税的条款，预计共耗费 1,100 亿美元。同时也为企业减轻了负担，使它们能够用这部分资金雇佣新员工和投资新项目。

随着这一法案的实施，我们将使美国能够回到经济恢复的轨道上来。尽管这些努力将会是卓有成效的，但实施起来还会加以时日。我领导的政府将会竭尽所能迅速做出反应，但是这一法案所带来的好处可能不会立即显现。联邦政府以小心谨慎的态度来实施这一法案以确保纳税人的钱不会付诸东流。

我深刻地体会到今天早上坐在收音机前的很多美国人既对我们国家的经

济形势充满了焦虑，又很想知道这一法案对你们个人的财政到底意味着什么。我非常自信地认为这一援助法案的实施将会解开人们心中所有的疑团。我个人坚信随着市场的逐渐好转，我们终将找到美利坚合众国经济持续稳定发展的秘密，那就是美国人民的拼搏精神。

感谢大家的倾听。

第三节 精彩语录

This was a difficult vote for many members of the House and Senate, but voting for it was the right choice for America's economy and for taxpayers like you. I appreciate their efforts to help stop the crisis in our financial markets from spreading to our entire economy.

尽管对于大部分参众两院的议员来说，这是一次相当困难的投票，但是这次投票无论对美国宏观的经济形势，还是对任何一位像你们一样的纳税人来说都是一次无比正确的选择。我非常感谢议员们投票通过了这一法案，并对阻止金融市场的危机扩散到美国经济的每一个角落所做出的不懈努力。

I'm confident by getting our markets moving, we will help unleash the key to our continued economic success: the entrepreneurial spirit of the American people.

我个人坚信随着市场的逐渐好转，我们终将找到美利坚合众国经济持续稳定发展的秘密，那就是美国人民的拼搏精神。

第十六章

昂首离开白宫

第一节 背景介绍

　　小布什在 2009 年 1 月 20 日，结束了八年的总统任期。当日，在美国首都华盛顿小布什与妻子向民众挥手告别，最后一次乘总统专机离开华盛顿，返回家乡得克萨斯州。

　　八年，足以让一个人变得风华正茂；八年，也足以让一位总统变成"最不受欢迎的人"。然而，小布什自己却不这么认为，回首这八年执政历程，布什总统依然一如既往地对其八年执政进行了一番辩护。自"9·11"恐怖袭击事件发生后，美国接连发动反恐战争，美国国土再未受到恐怖袭击。此外，在过去八年里，美国在教育、医疗、环保、税收、退伍军人、社会福利等方面的政策取得了较好效果。对于金融危机，美国政府采取了一系列决定性措施。布什呼吁只要美国人民团结一致，充满信心，努力工作，美国经济就会重现活力，恢复增长。

　　布什在白宫一待就是八年，在这八年间，留在人们记忆深处的是两次反恐战争和蔓延全球的金融危机。美国在 2001 年 10 月 7 日打响了阿富汗战争，在阿富汗战争还没有结束时又发动了伊拉克战争。两场战争让美国深陷泥潭，难以自拔，这让美国民众和士兵都很疲惫。美国境内的反战声音也越来越高。开始于 2007 年 8 月的次贷危机，也称次级房贷危机，造成次级抵押贷款机构破产、投资公司关闭、股市剧烈震荡。此次危机迅速席卷了美国、欧洲和日本，引发了全球性的金融危机。

美国的国际名声因为反恐战争受到极大损伤，布什也被认为是美国历史上最差的总统。布什一贯执拗的个性和乐观的态度使他高估了反恐战争的成果。尽管美国本土没有再遭受恐怖袭击，但是全世界的恐怖活动有增无减。金融危机所带来的后果也越来越明显，企业破产、失业增加都让民众苦不堪言。《华盛顿邮报》的专栏作家查尔斯·克劳斯莫尔毫不客气地说："除了尼克松，没有一任总统会比布什更不受待见！"但《华尔街日报》为布什"抱不平"。该报刊登的评论文章称，美国人会记得布什曾让一个受到精神创伤、深陷哀痛的国家重新恢复信心，人们会记得他是一位"9·11"总统。

布什执政期间，其顶点无疑是"9·11"时期，他当时的施政满意度曾高达 88%。但好景不长，随后他的施政满意度便跌至 25%，创下美国近现代史上总统满意度最低纪录。

小布什走了，留给美国人的记忆更多的是从关塔那摩到伊拉克阿布格里卜监狱，从"卡特里娜"飓风到华尔街的金融风暴。布什留给后任的是两个战争泥潭、一个经济难题，以及超过 1.2 万亿美元的财政赤字。不过，一向不肯妥协的布什仍高昂着头。但在离任告别演说中，布什也无奈地说："如果老天再给我一次机会重新开始，许多事情上我的选择会有所不同。"

不管人们如何评价，父亲老布什一直认为小布什是一个强有力的领导者，虽然新闻界不喜欢他，但老布什依然认为自己是一个非常自豪的父亲。即使小布什的民调在下降，但中美关系比以往任何时候都好，而这与他的贡献有很大关系。老布什坦率地说："我很高兴他回家，作为儿子和前总统他回来了，历史将对他做出评价。"

小布什在华府举行迄今为止最为坦诚的告别记者会。布什总统结束了他八年的执政，回到德州享受退休总统的悠闲生活，成为全球的头条新闻。八

年的岁月是白宫权力的时间极限。而对布什总统的历史评价，也会随着布什时代的落幕而纷至沓来。两极化的意见，恐怕会成为美国总统历史评价中罕见的现象。

小布什对自己退休后的轻松生活充满了期待。他说，每天早晨他都要为妻子煮咖啡并送上餐桌，然后浏览报纸，与朋友聚会，读书，养狗，钓鱼，散步。但是布什同时强调，他将继续保持活跃，他说："我已经退休了，但不意味着我已经完全退出。"布什还谈到了自己准备写的书，他说："我希望人们能够了解当我做一些艰难决定时，白宫所发生的一切。历史总是使人记住发生过什么，然后对发生的一切做一个评论。当然，我希望成为书写这段历史的一部分。"

第二节 布什于 2009 年在白宫发表告别演说

Fellow citizens，

For eight years, it has been my honor to serve as your president. The first decade of this new century has been a period of consequence—a time set apart. Tonight, with a thankful heart, I have asked for a final opportunity to share some thoughts on the journey that we have traveled together, and the future of our nation.

Five days from now, the world will witness the vitality of American democracy. In a tradition dating back to our founding, the presidency will pass to a successor chosen by you, the American people. Standing on the steps of the Capitol will be a man whose history reflects the enduring promise of our land. This is a moment of hope and pride for our whole nation. And I join all Americans in offering best wishes to President-elect Obama, his wife Michelle, and their two beautiful girls.

Tonight I am filled with gratitude—to Vice President Cheney and members of my administration; to Laura, who brought joy to this house and love to my life; to our wonderful daughters, Barbara and Jenna; to my parents, whose examples

have provided strength for a lifetime. And above all, I thank the American people for the trust you have given me. I thank you for the prayers that have lifted my spirits. And I thank you for the countless acts of courage, generosity and grace that I have witnessed these past eight years.

This evening, my thoughts return to the first night I addressed you from this house—September the 11th, 2001. That morning, terrorists took nearly 3,000 lives in the worst attack on America since Pearl Harbor. I remember standing in the rubble of the World Trade Center three days later, surrounded by rescuers who had been working around the clock. I remember talking to brave souls who charged through smoke-filled corridors at the Pentagon, and to husbands and wives whose loved ones became heroes aboard Flight 93. I remember Arlene Howard, who gave me her fallen son's police shield as a reminder of all that was lost. And I still carry his badge.

As the years passed, most Americans were able to return to life much as it had been before 9/11. But I never did. Every morning, I received a briefing on the threats to our nation. I vowed to do everything in my power to keep us safe.

Over the past seven years, a new Department of Homeland Security has been created. The military, the intelligence community and the FBI have been transformed. Our nation is equipped with new tools to monitor the terrorists' movements, freeze their finances and break up their plots. And with strong allies at our side, we have taken the fight to the terrorists and those who support them. Afghanistan has gone from a nation where the Taliban harbored al-Qaeda and stoned women in the streets to a young democracy that is fighting terror and encouraging girls to go to school. Iraq has gone from a brutal dictatorship and a sworn enemy of America to an Arab democracy at the heart of the Middle East and a friend of the United States.

There is legitimate debate about many of these decisions. But there can be little debate about the results. America has gone more than seven years without another terrorist attack on our soil. This is a tribute to those who toil night and day to keep us safe—law enforcement officers, intelligence analysts, homeland security and diplomatic personnel, and the men and women of the United States Armed Forces.

Our nation is blessed to have citizens who volunteer to defend us in this time of danger. I have cherished meeting these selfless patriots and their families. And America owes you a debt of gratitude. And to all our men and women in uniform listening tonight: There has been no higher honor than serving as your commander in chief.

The battles waged by our troops are part of a broader struggle between two dramatically different systems. Under one, a small band of fanatics demands total obedience to an oppressive ideology, condemns women to subservience and marks unbelievers for murder. The other system is based on the conviction that freedom is the universal gift of Almighty God, and that liberty and justice light the path to peace.

This is the belief that gave birth to our nation. And in the long run, advancing this belief is the only practical way to protect our citizens. When people live in freedom, they do not willingly choose leaders who pursue campaigns of terror. When people have hope in the future, they will not cede their lives to violence and extremism. So around the world, America is promoting human liberty, human rights and human dignity. We're standing with dissidents and young democracies, providing AIDS medicine to dying patients—to bring dying patients back to life, and sparing mothers and babies from malaria. And this great republic born alone in liberty is leading the world toward a new age when freedom belongs to all nations.

For eight years, we've also strived to expand opportunity and hope here at home. Across our country, students are rising to meet higher standards in public schools. A new Medicare prescription drug benefit is bringing peace of

mind to seniors and the disabled. Every taxpayer pays lower income taxes. The addicted and suffering are finding new hope through faith–based programs. Vulnerable human life is better protected. Funding for our veterans has nearly doubled. America's air and water and lands are measurably cleaner. And the federal bench includes wise new members like Justice Sam Alito and Chief Justice John Roberts.

When challenges to our prosperity emerged, we rose to meet them. Facing the prospect of a financial collapse, we took decisive measures to safeguard our economy. These are very tough times for hardworking families, but the toll would be far worse if we had not acted. All Americans are in this together. And together, with determination and hard work, we will restore our economy to the path of growth. We will show the world once again the resilience of America's free enterprise system.

Like all who have held this office before me, I have experienced setbacks. There are things I would do differently if given the chance. Yet I've always acted with the best interests of our country in mind. I have followed my conscience and done what I thought was right. You may not agree with some of the tough decisions I have made. But I hope you can agree that I was willing to make the tough decisions.

The decades ahead will bring more hard choices for our country, and there are some guiding principles that should shape our course.

While our nation is safer than it was seven years ago, the gravest threat to our people remains another terrorist attack. Our enemies are patient, and determined to strike again. America did nothing to seek or deserve this conflict. But we have been given solemn responsibilities, and we must meet them. We must resist complacency. We must keep our resolve. And we must never let down our guard.

At the same time, we must continue to engage the world with confidence and clear purpose. In the face of threats from abroad, it can be tempting to seek comfort by turning inward. But we must reject isolationism and its companion, protectionism. Retreating behind our borders would only invite danger. In the 21st century, security and prosperity at home depend on the expansion of liberty abroad. If America does not lead the cause of freedom, that cause will not be led.

As we address these challenges—and others we cannot foresee tonight—America must maintain our moral clarity. I've often spoken to you about good and evil, and this has made some uncomfortable. But good and evil are present in this world, and between the two of them there can be no compromise. Murdering the innocent to advance an ideology is wrong every time, everywhere. Freeing people from oppression and despair is eternally right. This nation must continue to speak out for justice and truth. We must always be willing to act in their defense—and to advance the cause of peace.

President Thomas Jefferson once wrote, "I like the dreams of the future better than the history of the past." As I leave the house he occupied two centuries ago, I share that optimism. America is a young country, full of vitality, constantly growing and renewing itself. And even in the toughest times, we lift our eyes to the broad horizon ahead.

I have confidence in the promise of America because I know the character of our people. This is a nation that inspires immigrants to risk everything for the dream of freedom. This is a nation where citizens show calm in times of danger and compassion in the face of suffering. We see examples of America's character all around us. And Laura and I have invited some of them to join us in the White House this evening.

We see America's character in Dr. Tony Rehcasner, a principal who opened a new charter school from the ruins of Hurricane Katrina. We see it

in Julio Medina, a former inmate who leads a faith-based program to help prisoners returning to society. We've seen it in Staff Sgt. Aubrey McDade, who charged into an ambush in Iraq and rescued three of his fellow Marines.

We see America's character in Bill Krissoff—a surgeon from California. His son, Nathan—a Marine—gave his life in Iraq. When I met Dr. Krissoff and his family, he delivered some surprising news: He told me he wanted to join the Navy Medical Corps in honor of his son. This good man was 60 years old— 18 years above the age limit. But his petition for a waiver was granted, and for the past year he has trained in battlefield medicine. Lieutenant Commander Krissoff could not be here tonight, because he will soon deploy to Iraq, where he will help save America's wounded warriors—and uphold the legacy of his fallen son.

In citizens like these, we see the best of our country—resilient and hopeful, caring and strong. These virtues give me an unshakable faith in America. We have faced danger and trial, and there's more ahead. But with the courage of our people and confidence in our ideals, this great nation will never tire, never falter, and never fail.

It has been the privilege of a lifetime to serve as your president. There have been good days and tough days. But every day I have been inspired by the greatness of our country, and uplifted by the goodness of our people. I have been blessed to represent this nation we love. And I will always be honored to carry a title that means more to me than any other—citizen of the United States of America.

And so, my fellow Americans, for the final time: Good night. May God bless this house and our next president. And may God bless you and our wonderful country. Thank you.

各位同胞：

过去的八年，我很荣幸地成为你们的总统。这个世纪的头十年是一个非常重要的时期。今晚，带着一颗感恩的心，我将利用这最后的机会和你们一起分享我的一些看法，对过去一起走过的时光以及我们国家未来的看法。

再过五天，世界将见证充满活力的美国民主政治。根据我们建国时创立的传统，总统职位将交给你们——美国人民选举出来的继任者。届时站在国会台阶上的那个人，他的经历将折射出我们这个国家长久以来的承诺。对于我们整个国家来说，这是一个充满希望和自豪的时刻。我将和其他所有美国人民一起，向当选总统奥巴马、他的妻子米歇尔以及他们两位美丽的女儿表达最美好的祝愿。

今晚，我的内心充满感激。我要感谢副总统切尼以及白宫的每一位工作人员；我要感谢劳拉，是她带给了这个家庭无比的快乐，带给我爱；我要感谢两名优秀的女儿——巴巴拉和杰纳；我要感谢我的父母，他们树立的榜样为我的一生提供了动力。除此之外，还我要感谢所有美国人民给予我的信任。谢谢你们的祈祷让我斗志昂扬。在过去的八年时间里，你们给了我无穷的勇气和宽厚，我对此表示深深地感谢。

今晚，我的思绪重新回到 2001 年 9 月 11 日，当时我第一次在这里发表晚间演说。那天上午，恐怖分子对美国发动了自珍珠港事件以来最为严重的恐怖袭击，造成约 3,000 人死亡。我清楚地记得，我三天后站在世贸大楼的残骸前，周围是夜以继日不停工作的救援人员。我记得我同那些穿过五角大楼浓烟密布的走廊进行救援的勇士们交谈，同那些 93 号航班英雄们的妻子和爱人们对话。我还记得阿勒内·霍华德，她将自己已经牺牲的儿子的警徽送给我，提示我们所失去的一切。直到现在，我都一直保存着他的徽章。

随着时光流逝，绝大多数美国人重新回到了"9·11"以前的生活状态。但我却从来没有。每天早上，我都会听取国家面临威胁的一个简报。那时我会发誓要尽我最大的努力来保证我们的安全。

在七年前，一个全新的机构——国土安全部正式成立了。美国的军队、情报机构以及联邦调查局都进行了改造，我们的国家使用最新的装备来监控恐怖分子的动向，冻结他们的财产并且粉碎他们的阴谋。和我们强有力的盟友一起，我们对恐怖分子以及他们的支持者宣战。阿富汗原来是一个塔利班政权包庇"基地"组织，妇女走在街头会遭到石头袭击的国家，但现在却成为了一个新兴的民主国家，它在与恐怖势力做斗争并且鼓励女孩们上学。伊拉克也从一个残暴的独裁政权，一个发誓与美国不共戴天的国家，变成为中东心脏地带的民主国家，变成为美国的朋友。

关于这些决策存在着一些合理的争论，但对于这些结果却没有任何争议。美国在过去的七年多时间里没有再在本土遭到过恐怖袭击，这要感谢那些日夜辛勤工作保卫我们安全的人，包括执法人员、情报分析人员、国土安全和外交官员，以及美国军队的士兵们。

我们的国家非常幸运地拥有这样的国民，当我们的国家处在危险之中时，他们自愿起来保卫我们的国家。我非常珍视与这些无私的爱国者以及他们家人进行的会面，美国应该感谢你们。对于那些今晚正在聆听这次演讲的军人们，我想说的是：这个世界上再也没有比成为你们的总司令更让人感到荣幸了。

我们的军队目前正在进行的战争，广义上来看其实是两种不同体系之间的战争。一种是一小撮狂热分子要求人们完全臣服于压迫的意识形态，他们迫害妇女并且杀害那些和他不一样信仰的人。另外一种体系则建立在普世的民主基础上，自由和正义照亮了和平之路。

我们的国家正是在这种信念下诞生的。长期来看，倡导这种信念是保卫我们国民的唯一切实有效的方法。当人们生活在民主政治中，他们就不会选举出那些追随恐怖势力的领导人。当人们对未来充满希望，他们就不会选择放弃生命来发动暴力袭击。因此，美国一直在全世界倡导自由、人权和尊严。我们向那些新兴的民主政体提供支持，向艾滋病人提供药物让垂死的病人起死回生，让母亲和婴儿们免受疟疾的困扰。这个在自由基础上诞生的伟大国家，正带领全世界走向一个新时代，这个时代民主将属于所有的国家。

过去八年里，我们也努力地在国内扩张机会和希望。在全国，学生们现在可以在公立学校接受条件更好的教育；新的医疗福利政府让老人和残疾人更加安心；每一位纳税人的个人所得税降低；通过信心重建计划，那些吸毒者也找到了新的希望；人们脆弱的生命得到更好的保护；为老兵提供的资金保障几乎增加了一倍；美国的空气、水源以及土地比以前更加清洁。

当繁荣遇到挑战时，我们采取了行动。在面临金融崩溃时，我们采取了决定性的措施来保卫经济。对于那些辛苦工作的家庭来说，这是一个非常艰难的时期，但是如果我们不采取行动后果会更严重，所有的美国人都受到了影响。团结一心的美国人将通过坚定信心和辛勤的工作来使我们的经济再次走上成长之路。我们将向世界再次展示，美国自由企业制度的坚韧性。

和所有前任一样，我也经历过挫折，我也有一些失误。不过，我的行动总是以我们国家的最佳利益为出发点。我对的起自己的良心，采取了我认为是正确的措施。你们可能不同意我所作出的一些艰难决定，但是我希望，你们能认为，我是一位愿意作出艰难决定的总统。

我们的国家在未来将面临更多的艰难选择，必须用一些指导性原则来指引我们的路线。

虽然我们的国家现在比七年前更为安全，但我们所面临的最严重威胁仍然是恐怖袭击。我们的敌人很有耐心，他们决心再次对我们发动袭击。美国没有试图挑起冲突或者作过任何导致冲突的错事。但我们有庄严的责任，必须负起责任。我们必须克服自满，必须保持决心，不能放松警惕。

与此同时，我们必须抱有信心和明确目的与世界进行接触。在面临海外威胁的情况下，人们很容易受到孤立主义的诱惑，但是我们必须抵制孤立主义和保护主义，撤退至我们的国境线内只会招来危险。在 21 世纪，国内的

安全和繁荣取决于自由事业在海外的扩展。如果美国不领导自由事业，那么自由事业将没有领导者。

在我们应对这些挑战时，我们今晚还无法预测其他的挑战，美国必须保持道德上的纯洁。人们经常对你们谈起正义和邪恶，这可能使一些人感到不舒服，但是这个世界存在着正义和邪恶，两者之间不可能有妥协。无论何时何地，杀害无辜者来推动一种意识形态都是错误的，把人们从压迫和绝望中解放出来永远是正确的。美国必须为正义和真相说话。我们必须保卫它们，推进和平事业。

托马斯·杰斐逊总统曾写道："我不缅怀过去的历史，而致力于未来的梦想。"在我即将离开他两个世纪前所居住的白宫时，我也持这种乐观的态度。美国是一个年轻的国家，富有活力，在不断成长和更新自己。即使是在最困难的时刻，我们也可以展望未来的前景。

我对美国的未来充满信心，因为我知道美国人民的性格。这是一个激发移民冒着失去所有东西的风险来追求自由梦想的国家，这是公民们在危险时刻表现平静，在遭受苦难时表现出同情心的国家。我们在身边可以看到这样的例子，我和劳拉今晚邀请了一些这样的人到白宫。

我们可以在托尼·里卡斯尼尔的身上看到美国的性格。这位校长在卡特里娜飓风的废墟上重建了他的学校。我们可以在胡利奥·梅迪纳看到这种性格，这位前犯人领导着一个基于信仰的项目来帮助犯人们重返社会。我们也可以在奥布里·麦克达德参谋军士身上看到这种性格，他冲入包围圈，营救出了三名海军陆战队战友。

我们在加州医生比尔·克里索夫身上看到了美国的这种性格，他的儿子纳塔恩作为一名海军陆战队队员在伊拉克献出了自己的生命。当我遇到克里索夫和他的家人时，他告诉我一些令我意想不到的消息：他告诉我为了纪念自己的儿子，他想加入海军医疗部门。这位好人已六十岁，超过规定年龄的上限十八年，但他所提出的例外申请获得了批准，他在过去一年一直在接受战场救治的训练。克里索夫中校今晚不能来到这里，因为他即将被部署至伊拉克，他将在那里帮助救护美军伤员，维护他为国牺牲的儿子所留下的遗产。

我们在这些公民身上看到我们国家最优良的品质：坚韧和抱有希望、有爱心和坚强。这些品质使我对美国有不可动摇的信心。我们曾面临危险和考验，未来还会有更多的危险和考验。但是借助于我们人民的勇气和我们对理想的信心，这个伟大的国家将永远不会疲倦，不会松懈，不会失败。

作为你们的总统为你们服务是我一生的荣耀，任期内有过好日子和艰难的日子，但我每天都被我们国家的伟大所鼓舞，为我们人民的善良所振奋。我对自己有机会代表我们所热爱的国家感到幸福，我将永远对自己是美国公民而感到荣耀，对我来说，这一身份比任何其他身份都有份量。

所以，亲爱的美国同胞，让我最后一次对你们说：晚安。愿上帝保佑白宫和我们的下一位总统。愿上帝保佑你和我们这个美好的国家。谢谢。

第三节 精彩语录

When people live in freedom, they do not willingly choose leaders who pursue campaigns of terror. When people have hope in the future, they will not cede their lives to violence and extremism.

当人们生活在民主政治中，他们就不会选举出那些追随恐怖势力的领导人。当人们对未来充满希望，他们就不会选择放弃生命来发动暴力袭击。

President Thomas Jefferson once wrote, "I like the dreams of the future better than the history of the past."

托马斯·杰斐逊总统曾写道："我不缅怀过去的历史，而致力于未来的梦想。"

We have faced danger and trial, and there's more ahead. But with the courage of our people and confidence in our ideals, this great nation will never tire, never falter, and never fail.

我们曾面临危险和考验，未来还会有更多的危险和考验。但是借助于我

们人民的勇气和我们对理想的信心，这个伟大的国家将永远不会疲倦，不会
松懈，不会失败。